The Ages of the X-M

ALSO OF INTEREST AND
EDITED BY JOSEPH J. DAROWSKI

The Ages of Wonder Woman:
Essays on the Amazon Princess in Changing Times (2014)

The Ages of Superman:
Essays on the Man of Steel in Changing Times (2012)

The Ages of the X-Men

Essays on the
Children of the Atom
in Changing Times

Edited by
JOSEPH J. DAROWSKI

McFarland & Company, Inc., Publishers
Jefferson, North Carolina

Library of Congress Cataloguing-in-Publication Data

The Ages of the X-Men : Essays on the Children of the Atom in
   Changing Times / edited by Joseph J. Darowski.
      p.   cm.
   Includes bibliographical references and index.

   ISBN 978-0-7864-7219-2 (softcover : acid free paper) ∞
   ISBN 978-1-4766-1634-6 (ebook)

   1. X-men (Comic strip)   2. X-Men (Fictitious characters)
3. Comic books, strips, etc.—United States.   I. Darowski,
Joseph J., editor of compilation.
PN6728.X2A38 2014
741.5'973—dc23   2014015599

British Library cataloguing data are available

Cover illustration © 2014 DigitalVision

Printed in the United States of America

*McFarland & Company, Inc., Publishers
   Box 611, Jefferson, North Carolina 28640
   www.mcfarlandpub.com*

To Joseph F. Darowski

Table of Contents

Introduction

The X-Men is undeniably one of the most successful franchises in comic book history, though its success was far from a sure thing when the series launched in 1963. After initially failing and being canceled, the franchise has endured several twists and turns in its 50 year history, several of which will be considered in this collection. From a failed series in the 1960s that was relaunched to acclaim and a corresponding growth in popularity in the 1970s, the X-Men have branched out with additional comic book series as well as popular adaptations in several forms of media. While the adaptations of the X-Men would be insightful to study academically, the essays in this collection will focus solely on the comic books that have been produced as part of the franchise.

The X-Men seem especially suitable for deeper consideration because the concept of "mutants" has been used as a metaphor for a wide range of issues, including race, gender, ideology, religion, and sexuality. Dependent upon both the creative process and reader reception, the metaphor can be and has been applied in myriad ways, as evidenced in the wide array of topics addressed in these essays. The essays in this collection are arranged chronologically according to the X-Men storylines on which each contributor focuses. Beginning with the earliest issues of X-Men comic books through the "Mutant Messiah" storyline, almost 50 years of X-Men history is addressed by scholars. Each essay will take a specific period of X-Men history and consider the impact contemporary societal issues may have had on the creation and interpretation of the comic books. It goes without saying that additional or alternative readings of the stories are valid, but each essay in this collection successfully adds insight to X-Men comic books, complex and multi-faceted artifacts of American popular culture.

Brad J. Ricca, John Darowski, and Jean-Philippe Zanco each explore the earliest era of X-Men comics. In "Origin of the Species: Popular Science, Dr. Hermann Muller and the X-Men," Ricca considers the influence popular science of the 1950s and 1960s had on the language, themes, and characterizations of the early 1960s X-Men comic books. In Darowski's essay, "'Evil Mutants Will Stop at Nothing to Gain Control of Mankind!' X-Men, Communists and Cold War Containment Culture," the interpretive lens of global politics, particularly the Red Scare and Communism is aimed at early issues of *The X-Men*. Zanco uses theories of community identity to explore the group dynamics established among the X-Men in "Call for Community: Charles Xavier's School for Gifted Youngsters as Hippie Community Experience."

Joseph J. Darowski's "When Business Improved Art: The 1975 Relaunch of Marvel's Mutant Heroes" looks at some of the behind the scenes aspects of the publishing of *Giant-Size X-Men* #1. *The X-Men* had been canceled in 1970, and the successful revival of the team and subsequent issues written by Chris Claremont resulted in an extreme growth in popularity for the franchise. The following essays by Margaret Galvan, Clancy Smith, Jacob Rennaker and Nicholaus Pumphrey all analyze stories penned by Claremont.

"From Kitty to Cat: Kitty Pryde and the Phases of Feminism," written by Galvan, links feminist issues with the evolution of a character codenamed Shadowcat. Feminist scholars, contemporary issues and the narrative evolution of a new character are connected in a thought-provoking analysis of one of the superhero comic books' most popular and enduring female characters.

Smith and Rennaker both explore issues of prejudice in X-Men comic books, one of the most oft-recurring themes in the series. Smith addresses issues of government enforced prejudice in "Days of Future Past: Segregation, Oppression and Technology in X-Men and America." Rennaker explores prejudice from a religious point of view in "'Mutant Hellspawn' or 'More Human Than You'? The X-Men Respond to Televangelism."

Nicholaus Pumphrey examines the transformation of Magneto, one of the most interesting characters in the X-Men series, in "From Terrorist to Tzadik: Reading Comic Books as Post-Shoah Literature in Light of Magneto's Jewish Backstory." The character had a rather extreme reinterpretation between his appearances in the 1960s as a maniacal terrorist and his more sympathetic portrayals in the 1980s.

Timothy Elliott and Robert Dennis Watkins look at the highest selling comic book of all time in "Sexy Art, Speculative Commerce: *The X-Men* #1 Launch Extravaganza." They connect issues of commerce, collectability and the portrayal of women with *X-Men* #1. Looking instead at the portrayal of men, Gerri Mahn's "Fatal Attractions: Wolverine, the Hegemonic Male and the Crisis of Masculinity in the 1990s" analyzes one of the iconic "tough guys" of the superhero genre. Mahn uses Wolverine's brutal injuries at the hands of Magneto to gain insights into the role of men in society and popular culture in the 1990s.

Generation X was a series chronicling the adventures of teenaged mutants learning to use their powers. David Allan Duncan's "*Generation X*: Mutants Made to Order" makes connections between these comic book superheroes and the identifiable traits of the real world's Generation X, an age group that would have been among the target audience for this series.

Jeff Geers explores an alternative timeline story called the Age of Apocalypse in light of looming millennial concerns in American society. "What Happens 'After Xavier'? Millennial Fears and the Age of Apocalypse" interprets the storyline as a part of apocalyptic literature that addressed societal fears and concerns that were being voiced with the approaching year 2000.

Adam Capitanio's "Race and Violence from the 'Clear Line School': Bodies and the Celebrity Satire of *X-Statix*" analyzes Paul Milligan and Mike Allred's run on *X-Force/X-Statix*. Capitanio positions these series as satires and critiques of racial representations in comic books, the celebrity obsessed culture in America at that time and the excessive violence prevalent in superhero comic books of the 1990s.

In "Mutating Metaphors: Addressing the Limits of Biological Narratives of Sexuality," Christian Norman uses storylines involving the Legacy Virus and "the cure" for mutations and addresses attempts to reposition the X-Men as a metaphor for issues of sexuality. Norman identifies the problematic limitations of shifting the longstanding "mutant metaphor" of X-Men comic books towards sexuality rather than race.

Eric Garneau and Maura Foley's "Grant Morrison's Mutants and the Post–9/11 Culture of Fear" and Nicolas Labarre's "From Columbine to Xavier's: Restaging the Media Narrative as Superhero Fiction" look at different aspects of Grant Morrison's run writing *New X-Men*. Garneau and Foley examine the storylines in light of post 9/11 fears. Labarre considers the cultural narrative that developed around school shootings following the tragedy at Columbine and what elements were reflected in the "Riot at Xavier's" storyline. Also addressing the educational aspect of the X-Men series, Rich Shivener's "No Mutant Left Behind: Lessons from *New X-Men: Academy X*" explores debates surrounding the American educational system as reflected in X-Men comic books.

Todd Kimball Mack's "Autism and the Astonishing X-Men" is a more personal essay than most in this collection, employing the concept of a cure for mutants and the varied reactions in the comic books to the similarly complex reactions to the idea of a cure for autism. As a parent of autistic children, Mack uses his own experiences to deepen the insights and connections he sees within these topics.

The final essay comes from Morgan B. O'Rourke and Daniel J. O'Rourke. "A Prophet of Hope and Change: The Mutant Minority in the Age of Obama" compares the character of Hope in the X-Men comic books to the rhetoric that surrounded the Barack Obama presidential campaign.

With more than 40 years of material to potentially explore, there are certainly many other stories worthy of academic consideration in the X-Men comic books. There are also many other theoretical methodologies that could be successfully applied to these comic books. But the essays in this collection provide a wonderful launching point for a deeper consideration of one of the most important American popular culture products of the last half century.

—Joseph J. Darowski

Origin of the Species: Popular Science, Dr. Hermann Muller and the X-Men

Brad J. Ricca

Stan Lee's explanation of how he came up with the idea for the X-Men in the early sixties is infamous for its practicality:

> But by now I had run out of ways for characters to get super powers because I'm not very good at that. I mean I take the simplest, easiest way, the coward's way out. I had Spider-Man—Peter Parker was bitten by a radioactive spider: That's easy. You can say that in one sentence. He became Spider-Man. He was bitten by a radioactive spider. The Hulk, Bruce Banner, was subjected to gamma rays. There was a gamma ray explosion. He got caught in it. I have no idea what a gamma ray is but it sounds pretty scientific, logical. Well, now I had already done radioactivity. I had already done a gamma ray. What am I gonna do next? They're mutants. They were born that way [Lee].

This was a simple solution for a creator running out of ideas. But the notion of Marvel authorship, particularly of the early work under Lee, Jack Kirby, and Steve Ditko is both messy and ambiguous. As Charles Hatfield notes in his study of Jack Kirby, *Hand of Fire*: "authorship slips beyond our grasp" when it comes to the early days of the "improvisational" Marvel (96). The genesis of the X-Men concept is particularly problematic, mostly because of the loss of Lee's original synopsis, leaving few objective sources available for scholars and readers. Still, Lee's high rate of scientific terms in his above explanation— "radioactive," "gamma," "rays,"—may belie the author's own protestations against their importance in superhero narrative. In fact, Lee's admission that superhero origins should be "pretty scientific, logical" through the use of terms that even he admits to "have no idea" what they mean, proposes the possibility of an exterior scientific source for the X-Men as well.

When Lee finally turned in his pitch, he described the process as follows:

> So when I finally wrote the thing and I brought it to Martin [Goodman], my publisher, I wanted to call the book The Mutants. He said, "Stan" because he still didn't have much respect for the readers in those days. He said, "Nobody is gonna know what a mutant is. You can't call them the Mutants" [Lee].

Though Goodman won the argument, the word "mutant" actually was in fairly widespread use at that time, appearing not only in popular science magazines, but in the *New York Times*, largely in articles concerning atomic age radiation fears. In this essay, I wish to investigate the popular scientific subtext of the X-Men through these and other available terms in order to unveil a new context for how *The X-Men* was, perhaps, initially understood across a spectrum of mutation, eugenics, and education, ultimately leading to a new way of framing the book's unique cultural position.

Terms and Fears

By 1960, the word "mutant" had already made its way into the everyday lexicon of popular news media. A 1956 article titled "Atomic Mutants Unseen in Japan" in the *New York Times* provides an accurate summary of the general attitudes towards radiation in the period just before the dawn of the sixties. Eleven years after the bombs decimated Hiroshima and Nagasaki, Americans were perhaps more concerned with the results of radiation, both practically for their own safety and, for many, the symbolic safeties of their souls. A 1951 New York educational documentary with the intimate title "You and the Atomic Bomb" assured viewers that "there's nothing mysterious about radiation, and that the atomic bomb will not create a race of monsters" (Macdonald 43).

Individually, the apocalyptic fear of "nuclear fallout, the silent killer" of the early fifties had been replaced with fears over long-term mutation; this transformation was not only quite prevalent in popular science (my focus here), but also in films such as *Godzilla* in 1954 and *Rodan* ("Rodan") in 1956 (Ellwood 127). The article concerned with "Atomic Mutants" thus straddles those particular realms by evoking at least the hint of the monstrous in a tragic, real-life context. The article reassures the public that radiation is perhaps not as harmful as once feared; that the bombs dropped on Japan "had no measurable effect on subsequent births to parents exposed to radiation" ("Foster"). The reassurance that "a small dose might cause a slight shortening of lifespan, a disposition toward illness, or some other subtle change" is disturbing, but is hardly the realization of the scary, misleading use of "Atomic Mutants" in the article's title ("Foster"). The article title grabs readers, but the contents make them feel better—all is well in Japan.

But these fears do not go away as more and more articles about genetic mutation and radiation appeared in news articles from the *Times* to *Popular Mechanics* with greater frequency in the years leading up to the publication of Lee and Kirby's *X-Men* in 1963. Though these news articles were not science fiction stories, they shared similar, pulpy headlines, just as the "Atomic Mutants" article does.

In a May 27, 1955 article titled "Menace to Humanity in a Prolonged Series of Explosions of Atomic Bombs," Waldemar Kaempffert tells readers that atomic mutations are perhaps the "Progenitors of monstrosities," even stating outright that soon mutation would be "as common as blue eyes or long heads" (Kaempffert). He backs off this worn image by again admitting that though most human mutation will probably be detrimental rather than uncanny, such mutations will probably consist of vague, general symptoms, including "a loss of vigor, a reduction in health, an increase in hereditary disease, [and] a decline in physical ability" (Kaempffert).

In addition to addressing general fears over the effects of radioactive fallout, these articles about the possibility of human mutation were jumpstarted by a major event in the scientific community: the First International Congress of Human Genetics held in Copenhagen in the first week of August in 1956. This historic meeting was "sponsored by committees of fourteen different nations outside the Iron Curtain [and] drew delegates from more than thirty countries" (Blyth 133).

The *Times* covered the Conference in a multi-page feature complete with the portraits of nearly a dozen grim-faced scientists presiding under a simple block byline: "Text of Genetics Committee Report Concerning Effects of Radioactivity" ("Text" 18). Like the "Atomic Mutants" article, the accepted conclusion of the Congress ran counter to its imposing images. The Committee concludes that "Geneticists Find No Atomic Harm" but that "X-ray radiation [is] harmful" enough to be examined further ("Hillaby"). The official transcripts of the event have ominous tones towards the idea of a transforming human genome: "The genetics of normal human variation is as yet unexplored country" (Blyth 133). Since the bombs, the "spontaneous and well justified fear" over nuclear devastation had swept over the country's collective mind and manifested itself in news articles that dug into these real fears. But this fear was being replaced with the threat of genetic mutation, which was being reported with only slightly less scary news tactics than the postwar "what if" stories in which Manhattan was reduced to radioactive mist. As time passed, the American fear of radiation became one of long-term result rather than immediate action.

Dr. X

The most popular geneticist of the late fifties and early sixties was Dr. Hermann J. Muller of the University of Indiana, who won the 1946 Nobel Prize in "Physiology or Medicine" for discovering "that high energy radiations such as x-rays will produce mutations in the genes of animals and plants, and thereby placed in the hands of man a really formidable power to alter the agents of heredity" (Glass 7). Muller took all of the nation's radioactive fears since World War II and finally proved them true, resulting in a long period of media exposure that would shape the public's imagination over genetic mutation for decades. The ominous tenor to his research—that radiation indeed *did* produce mutation—was probably why he appeared in the press and magazines so regularly. In his Nobel Prize lecture on December 12, 1946 entitled "The Production of Mutations," Muller makes the claim that "there are sudden jumps, going all the way from one 'elementary species' to another, and involving radical changes in numerous characters at once" (Muller). These "jumps" were point mutations, which Muller claims to have proven in experiments on *Drosophila*, the fruit fly, the best of subjects for genetic experimentation because of their quick breeding and short lifespans. Muller argues that in order "to appreciate the qualitative and quantitative multiplicity of mutations," the application of radiation, specifically "X-radiation," which he says result in "individual mutations" that "result from individual 'hits'" (Muller). In accompanying photographs, Muller is slim in his suits and is almost completely bald; in press photos he is often shown seated over lab equipment.

Though Muller's discoveries were in the late forties, the mutation articles of the late fifties rediscovered his work for a willing popular audience. The press generally agreed with Muller and thus began to range away from the assurances of the earlier articles about a thriving Japan. These articles, the ones that quote Muller's work, instead focus on the dangers of radiation. In the 1956 article "Fall-out Data Cited in Dispute," the *Times* notes that "The report emphasized that all radiation was potentially harmful to human beings" due to "an unavoidable quantity of so-called spontanteous mutations" ("56 Fallout").

The conversation shifts again when Muller's most radical views take center stage in *Popular Science* in March, 1960 in a piece provocatively titled "How to Breed Supermen." The article notes that "Indiana University's blunt-spoken Hermann J. Muller ... wants to upgrade the tired old human race into a worldwide family of paragons—upright, loyal, tolerant, kindly, and very, very smart" ("How to" 23). Muller adds that "Physical improvement is needed, too [including] a 'third eye' [that] would display thoughts as pictures" ("How to" 23). These proposed radical physiological changes—from a Nobel winner, of all people—concerning a group of mutants with strange powers who would be good citizens, were persuasively strange and real.

In the June 1960 *Popular Science*, two angry letter-writers to the magazine argue that "Hermann J. Muller is no better than Adolf Hitler" in his idea of a "super race" (Fanning 13). Harvey Steinfeld of New York City writes: "His ideas are fine for chickens and rabbits, but completely unsuited to human application ... let him stick to his test tubes and leave human problems to humane minds" (Steinfeld 13). The editor responds in italics, reminding the readers that Muller only wants a race of "paragons," not oppressors.

What Muller does is move the popular genetics dialogue from one evocative of monstrosity to a nearly straight conversation on eugenics that is echoed in other early sixties articles. In "Heredity Control: Dream or Nightmare," readers are told that "According to the Nobel prize-winning chemist Dr. Wendell M. Stanley, the next century will find mankind able to control to a remarkable degree the hereditary traits of plants, animals and humans" (Lasagna). But there is always a price: "The notion that man may be able to manipulate his genetic endowment is at once exciting and troublesome: how accurate are such predictions likely to be, and how desirable is the prospect of their fulfillment?" (Lasagna). Eugenics, the integration of biological life with the social world, would raise new questions for thinking about the implications of genetic mutation.

Education

Muller's detailed scientific observations on the fruit fly had the tendency to translate easily into the long-range philosophical and social issues associated with eugenics, especially in the popular media. Some of these issues took a more public shape at a 1959 conference at the University of Chicago celebrating the hundred year anniversary of Darwin's *Origin of Species*. An account of the conference in the *Times* notes that "One of the most provocative presentations was made by Prof. Hermann J. Muller, Nobel Prize-winning geneticist of the University of Indiana, who outlined a program for the "guidance of human evolution" (Laurence). Though Muller is adamant (and correct) that human change would only occur "through billions of years of blind mutations," the press seized more on impossible, but interesting, near-future scenarios (Laurence). Muller projects of these mutants that "the increasing recognition by individuals of their responsibility not only for the education and living conditions but also for the genetic endowment of the generations succeeding" (Laurence). In one sentence, Muller admits that mutation will take "billions of years," but in the next, he debates the education of these mutant children as if it were starting in September:

> The chief aims in the bringing up and education of children—more robust health; keener, deeper and more creative intelligence; genuine warmth of fellow feeling and cooperative disposition.... All these faculties require the proper environment and education for their development, but it is the genetic endowment of an individual that forms the basis of their realization [Laurence].

Unsurprisingly, "special educational facilities for the so-called 'the gifted'" were also being debated in the media at the time (Diamond). Schools such as Hunter Elementary in New York City that limited "its enrollment to children with I.Q.'s of at least 130, [were] revolutionizing its entire approach to the teaching of the intellectually gifted child" even as other groups wanted them closed (Terte).

By bringing in education to a conversation about human genetics, the general tone of the media coverage begins to suggest that these fictional ("billions of years" away) alterations to human genetics might—might—be positive more than not. Even the 1956 Genetics Committee Report notes that "Mutations within this sort would not necessarily be harmful" ("Text of Genetics"). In the same article, the dominant example used is more safe than monstrous: that of red hair, a "recessive character" that is still a "mutant gene" ("Text of Genetics").

For all the science-fiction possibilities—from monstrous to uncanny—that the media and focused on, every article does make clear that human mutation of any import would, most likely, cause "its bearer severe pain, unhappiness, or illness throughout his life" ("Text of Genetics"). Still, "mutations are a necessary part of evolution" and even though these genes are recessive and not as dramatic as Muller's third eye, "We all carry a supply of these spontaneous mutant genes" ("Text of Genetics"). This spectrum of ideas about human genetics as seen in the popular scientific press—as the possibility of "spontaneous" change coupled with personal "unhappiness"—had Marvel Comics written all over it.

X-rays

Thanks to Muller, much of this ongoing discussion over the mechanism of so-called "spontaneous mutation" had to do with X-rays. Even the news stories get technical quickly; the general scare was that the populace was absorbing too much "X-radiation." The National Academy of Sciences concludes that the only solution is to impose limits. For though "all-out nuclear war conceivably could make the earth uninhabitable," the simpler action to "reduce use of X-rays to the lowest limit consistent with medical necessity" would help a great deal to reduce mutation (Leviero). This article, "special to" the *Times,* again brings up that "Overshadowing all others because of its implication for mankind was the report of the genetics panel.... Even if the mutation is in one gene, there is some harmful effect [that] sometimes but not often produces deformed or freakish children" (Leviero).

A common source of X-ray radiation to the public were the fluoroscope machines found at shoe stores. At these tall, wooden cabinets, children would place their eyes into a hard plastic visor molded around their head and "stare with awe and sometimes without regard to time at the shadows of their foot bones" (Congressional 17801). News stories argued that these machines were harmless, actually containing about one-tenth radiation of "luminous watches and clocks" (Carter 28), though it is impossible to tell for sure what their effects truly were.

The ongoing, fearful discussion in the popular scientific press was not only about X-rays, but very often just involved the letter "X" itself. The Committee reports that "to the best of our present knowledge, if we increase the radiation by X%, the gene mutations caused by radiations will also be increased by X%" ("Text of Genetics"). In "Steps Towards Breaking the Genetic Code," diagrams of crossing over chromosome pairs results in an "X" symbol called the "double mutant strand" that is diagrammed on the page as a small black "X" (Anfinsen 325).

Results

All of these various contexts for the word "mutant" made their way, on purpose or not, into *The X-Men* #1 (Sep. 1963). The idea of a school for the gifted is on page one as Professor Xavier tells his students (and readers) that "Class is now in session!" (Lee and Kirby 1). By page nine, the correlation between mutant and gifted education is explained as Professor X talks to Jean Grey, his newest, red-haired (a recessive mutation) student and only female charge:

> You, Miss Grey, like the other four students at this most exclusive school, are a mutant! You possess an extra power..one which ordinary humans do not!! That is why I call my students...X-Men, for Ex-tra power! [Lee and Kirby 9].

Just as he does with the Hulk, Iron Man, and Spider-Man, Lee defines this "extra power" in terms of the scientific popular discourse of the time. Xavier explains to his students that

> I was born of parents who had worked on the first A-bomb project! Like yourselves, I am a mutant ... possibly the first such mutant! I have the power to read minds, and to project my own thoughts into the brains of others.... Normal

people feared me, distrusted me! I realized the human race is not ready to accept those with extra powers! So I decided to build a haven ... a school for X-Men!" [Lee and Kirby 11].

Professor X warns Jean that "there are many mutants walking the earth....and more are born" (Lee and Kirby 11), which echoes much of the popular science literature that "There is no minimum amount of radiation which must be exceeded before mutations occur" ("56 Fall-out").

By page twelve however, the old fears of atomic monsters return, as Magneto appears: "The Day of the mutants is upon us! The first phase of my plan shall be to show my power ... to make Homo Sapiens bow to Homo Superior!" (Lee and Kirby 12). Magneto looks human, but has monstrous morals—he is the eugenics oppressor feared by the *Popular Science* letter writers. Magneto's use of the term "Homo Superior," according to many, reflects Lee's likely knowledge of "a popular theme of science fiction" that dealt with mutants dealing with their new powers (Trushell 154). But even pulp fiction mutant supermen made their way into the everyday newspaper: in a *Times* book review of a science fiction anthology, Basil Davenport notes that

> Of the better entries, "But Without Horns," by Norvell W. Page, is the story of the struggle against homo superior, the suddenly mutated superman who is born with hypnotic powers and no conscience. The story, though an old one, is told with real suspense: but may one suggest that the final defeat of homo sapiens is becoming as much of a convention as the happy ending used to be.

Magneto, wearing red and with tiny horns on his helmet, represents the far range of the eugenics argument that, though present in popular science, was more easily evoked in science fiction.

Conclusions

In *The X-Men* #1 (Sep. 1963), Lee sets the stage for an ongoing narrative with roots in the popular scientific topic of genetic mutation. By moving deftly from issues of radioactive fears to more complex ones of eugenics and education—all played out in colorful melodrama meant to both contain and express these very ideas—Lee presents his readers with a science fiction story that is very much in line with the ongoing scientific discussion of the times. In many ways, *The X-Men* is the most scientifically-minded of all the early Marvel titles, though Lee himself insists otherwise.

The X-Men have most often been read as a trope for difference. In fact, most scholars and readers agree that "Professor Xavier and his X-Men, who sought accommodation with homo sapiens, recalled moderate elements of the

civil rights movement of the 1960s as exemplified by Martin Luther King, Jr."
(Trushell 154). Does a reading of the initial X-Men idea as beholden to scientific ideas preclude the popular reading of the "X-Men's connection to the civil rights struggle" (Howe 48)? Of course not, but it is worth thinking about their connections rather than their differences.

The fears of the atomic bomb were symbolic, scientific, but still full of unanswerable questions, as much of "the atomic age naturally began in ignorance" (Miller, Nowak 46). For Marvel Comics—the Fantastic Four, the Hulk, Spider-Man, and Daredevil—all radioactive successes, these characters acted out the fantasy that

> In America, those who do not succumb to radiation are transformed into super-heroes, in much the same way that America became a superpower after the bombing. Perhaps this is a reverse "guilt of the survivor"—or proof that there is no "guilt of the survivor" at all, or at least not yet. This Darwinian attitude assures the perpetrator that they become bigger, better, and stronger by undermining others' survival [Packer 124].

Just as Lee's X-Men may be read as a kind of guilty survivalism for the atomic age, it functions not only on a purely scientific plane, but on a cultural one as well.

In 2011, Edward Calbrese of the University of Massachusetts publicly questioned Hermann Muller's methodology, claiming that "he has uncovered evidence that [Muller] knowingly lied when he claimed in 1946 that there is no safe level of radiation" (University). Calabrese argues that Muller was more interested in ideology than science, though his "impact on the world of today is almost incalculable. He couldn't have imagined it" (University).

That there is an ideology to Muller's work, on purpose or not, perhaps helps to understand how *The X-Men* too crossed over into an ideological narrative. The August 3, 1961 issue of *New Scientist* warns that "Far too little heed is being paid to Hermann J. Muller," especially his "warning against an overload of mutations induced by survival and reproduction of increasing numbers of physically handicapped individual" (Lear, "Organized" 282). This idea of preserving "genetic heritage" as seen in eugenics articles and in discussion of schools for the gifted brings a racial tone to the discussion. In fact, the November 12, 1959 issue of *Jet* reports that Muller says that his plan to freeze the genes of prominent men is "raceless."

> After declaring the genes of superior Negro men, when artificially inseminated after their deaths "would act just as those genes of other great men," Muller refused to state whether the mixing of genes of superior whites and Negroes would make for a superior breed of human beings. "I would rather not make a statement on a subject of such a controversial nature because it may be misinterpreted," he said, then added: "Maybe I will later on" ["Prof Says" 21].

Muller's hesitation here reveals the question of race that the discussion of human genetics inherently reveals: all discussions of changing race (here, the human race) bring with them questions and fears of social equality and inclusion.

The language of human genetics is sometimes incendiary and can sound like Lee's prose, which would always use superlatives to make his colorful stories seem important to everybody:

> The problems of the Atomic Age affect every man, woman and child—in fact, every living thing—in our country, and of course, in the whole world as well. Although many of these problems are technical in nature, it is nevertheless of importance to our democracy that these matters be as widely understood as possible ["Text of Genetics"].

In this short passage, the Committee equates "atomic," "technical," and "democracy" as cross-linked ideas. Lee, the barker and storyteller, seems to agree in the finish to his recollection of pitching the original idea:

> But I had a name. I had won my battle. I didn't want to have any problems and you know, on and on. Then I did a lot of others and we were lucky and they sold and now I'm talking into a microphone for the whole world to listen [Lee].

Using the figure of a future human mutant, who popular science often remarked would "survive the vicissitudes of life but still be a social misfit," Lee found a perfect Marvel character who was of another race, but still human (Kaempffert). Words like "afflicted," "harmful," and "social misfit," were not scary to Stan Lee and his various partners: they were the DNA of the Marvel Age of Comics.

This idea of mutation offering a sound analogy to cultural issues is called "cultural genetics," and echoes the deep radioactive and political tension felt in the "Atomic Mutants" articles. In the June 30, 1960 issue of *New Scientist*, John Lear reports on the work of Yeshiva University's Dr. Max Hamburgh, who argues that cultural genetics exposes groups of people in history, specifically "strange collection of misfits, cranks, visionaries, impracticable idealists and dreamers" (Lear, "A Genetic" 1654). Using Christ as his example, Lear argues that it was the "Roman road system" and "communal living" of the early A.D. that made Christ a "cultural mutant" (because he had to adapt to new differences) and whose teachings made people "open to the unexpected" (Lear, "A Genetic" 1654). In the same way, using the "intellectual tools of the study of genetics," *The X-Men* can be read as an analogy for racial difference, "most likely to maximize change through multiple representation" (Lear, "A Genetic" 1654).

In an art show review of Stefan Martin and Fiorenco Giorgi in 1961, Brain O'Doherty notes in the *Times* that

Putting a man into space has been a hazardous adventure. It is less well known that artists have also, for some time, been trying to put a man into a space where his survival is doubtful—a space filled by the cosmic energies of abstract expressionism. Like the sequel to a movie, this project is usually called "Return of the Image" [O'Doherty 33].

Lee and Kirby's solution to putting man into a place "where his survival is doubtful" because of "cosmic energies" was the *Fantastic Four*, who satisfied American scientific fears while at the same time embracing a (fictional) space victory over the Soviets. The popular story of human mutation was the same: it involved danger, fear, and hope for reconciliation with the guilt of the past horrors of war. The solution, for Lee and Marvel Comics, was a new kind of similar abstract expressionism; that is, an illustrative style whereby monsters could shoulder the guilt of fallout in the form of despair and segregation, but at the same time overcome these difficulties as a heroic cultural mutant. Martin's show was located at the Rook Gallery, at 867 Madison Avenue, several blocks from Marvel's offices. O'Doherty continues:

Although the mutant school of horrors has provided Mr. Martin with some of his subjects (including fetus and bird-man), he uses them with the anguished earnestness of youth ...attempt a search for human dignity in the midst of human degradation [O'Doherty 33].

What readers first saw in *The X-Men* was perhaps not the racial narrative that contemporary readers first see, but perhaps a discussion of human genetics that ultimately staged the argument we understand—and absorb—so readily.

WORKS CITED

Anfinsen, Christian B. "Steps Towards Breaking the Genetic Code." *New Scientist* 247 (August 1961): 324–327.

Blyth, Helen. "Proceedings of the First International Congress of Human Genetics." *Eugenics Review* 50, 2 (1958): 133–134.

Carter, T.C. "Man-Made Radiations and the Reproductive Cells." *New Scientist* (May 22, 1958): 28.

"Chromosomal genes." From *Nobel Lectures, Physiology or Medicine 1942–1962*. Amsterdam: Elsevier, 1964.

Congressional Record. Vol. 109:13 (1963). U.S. Government Printing Office, 1963.

Davenport, Basil. "Spacemen's Realm." *New York Times* (1923-Current file): 1. May 11, 1952. *ProQuest*. Web. 28 May 2013.

Diamond, Morris. "School for Gifted Recalled." *New York Times* (1923-Current file): 36. Nov. 6, 1961. *ProQuest*. Web. 28 May 2013.

Fanning, R.H. Letter to Editor. *Popular Science* June 1960: 13.

"56 Fall-Out Data Cited in Dispute." *New York Times* (1923-Current file): 12. 10, 1957. *ProQuest*. Web. 28 May 2013.

Glass, Bentley. "Information Crisis in Biology." *Bulletin of the Atomic Scientists* (October 1962): 6–12.

Hailey, Foster. "Atomic Mutants Unseen in Japan." *New York Times* (1923–Current file): 4. Sep. 8, 1956. ProQuest. Web. 28 May 2013.

Hatfield, Charles. *Hand of Fire: The Comics Art of Jack Kirby.* Jackson: University of Mississippi Press, 2012.

Hillaby, John. "Geneticists Find no Atomic Harm." *New York Times* (1923–Current file): 17. Aug. 2, 1956. *ProQuest.* Web. 28 May 2013.

"How to Breed Superman." *Popular Science* (March 1960): 23–24.

Howe, Sean. *Marvel Comics: The Untold Story.* New York: HarperCollins, 2012.

Kaempffert, Waldemar. "Menace to Humanity in a Prolonged Series of Explosions of Atomic Bombs." *New York Times* (1923–Current file): 1. Mar. 27, 1955. ProQuest. Web. 28 May 2013.

Lasagna, Lous. "Heredity Control: Dream or Nightmare?" *New York Times* (1923–Current file): 162. Aug. 5, 1962. *ProQuest.* Web. 28 May 2013.

Laurence, William. "Science in Review." *New York Times* (1923-Current file): 1. Nov. 29, 1959. *ProQuest.* Web. 28 May 2013.

Lear, John. "A Genetic Theory of History," *New Scientist* (June 30, 1960): 1654.

_____. "Organized Charity Raises Some Problems." *New Scientist* Aug. 3, 1961: 246.

Lee, Stan. Interview with Jo Reed.for National Medal of Arts.http://www.arts.gov/av/avCMS/Lee-long-transcript.html 2008.

Lee, Stan (w) and Jack Kirby (a). "X-Men," *The X-Men* #1 (Sep. 1963). New York: Marvel Comics.

Leviero, Anthony. "Scientists Term Radiation a Peril to Future of Man." *New York Times* (1923–Current file): 1. June 13, 1956. *ProQuest.* Web. 28 May 2013.

Macdonald, J. Fred. *Television and the Red Menace: The Video Road to Vietnam.* New York: Prager, 1985.

Miller, Douglas, and Marion Nowak. *The Fifties: The Way We Were.* Garden City, NY: Double Day, 1975.

Muller, Hermann J. Muller. "The Production of Mutations." Nobelprize.org. 23 May 2013 http://www.nobelprize.org/nobel_prizes/medicine/laureates/1946/muller-lecture.html

O'Doherty, Brian. "Art: A Man into Space." *New York Times* (1923–Current file): 33. May 17, 1961. *ProQuest.* Web. 28 May 2013.

Packer, Sharon. *Superheroes and Superegos: Analyzing the Minds Behind the Masks.* Santa Barbara, CA: Praeger/ABC-CLIO, 2010.

Poniewozik, James. "TV Makes a Too-Close Call." *Time* (20 Nov. 2000): 70–71.

"Prof Says 'Frozen Gene' Theory Is Raceless." *Jet* (12 Nov. 1959): 21.

Steinfeld, Harvey. Letter to Editor. *Popular Science* (June 1960): 13.

Terte, Roberth H. "School for Gifted to Alter Program." *New York Times* (1923–Current file): 32. Apr. 13, 1961. *ProQuest.* Web. 28 May 2013.

"Text of Genetics Committee Report Concerning Effects of Radioactivity on Heredity." *New York Times* (1923-Current file): 18. June 13, 1956. *ProQuest.* Web. 28 May 2013.

Trushell, John M. "American Dreams of Mutants: The X-Men—'Pulp' Fiction, Science Fiction, and Superheroes." *Journal Of Popular Culture* 38.1 (2004): 149–168. *Academic Search Complete.* Web. 28 May 2013.

University of Massachusetts at Amherst. "No Safe Level of Radiation Exposure? Researcher Points to Suppression of Evidence on Radiation Effects by Nobel Laureate." *ScienceDaily* (20 Sep. 2011). Web. 28 May 2013.

"Evil mutants will stop at nothing to gain control of mankind!" X-Men, Communists and Cold War Containment Culture

JOHN DAROWSKI

In *The X-Men* #4 (Mar. 1964), Magneto and his Brotherhood of Evil Mutants conquer the South American country of Santo Marco as the first step in a plan for global domination. It is only through the intervention of the American teenage mutants, the X-Men, that the tiny nation is freed and the villains prevented from unleashing a nuclear bomb. Despite the X-Men's regularly cited informing metaphor of mutants as minority, this story, seemingly inspired by the Cuban Missile Crisis, is indicative of a Cold War narrative that underlies the X-Men's earliest adventures. This should not be surprising as the Marvel Age of superhero comics came directly out of the Cold War culture. But the first years of these merry mutants were also a time of transition from the external threat of Communism to the internal dissent of the countercultural movement; a transition chronicled as the super-powered teenagers negotiated the trends and anxieties of the time before embracing their inherent minority metaphor and the contemporary Civil Rights movement. As such, the first two years of the X-Men's bi-monthly adventures,[1] published from *The X-Men* #1 (Sep. 1963)–*#13* (Sep. 1965), serve as a text that reflects an American society mediating between the hegemonic consensus of the Cold War and the countercultural spirit that would define the Sixties.

The X-Men, created by writer Stan Lee and artist Jack Kirby, was the first original team to appear in the Marvel Universe following the pioneering *Fantastic Four*.[2] Of creating the team of mutants, Lee has recounted in his inimitable prose:

Before 1963 had ended, we decided it was time for us to magnanimously bestow another team of superheroes upon the eagerly waiting world. Once again I had to figure out a "scientific" way for the new group of characters to attain their superpowers. But this time I took the cowardly way out.

[...] Why couldn't I create a group of teenagers who had simply mutated and therefore gained their varied and extraordinary powers? No further explanation was needed and I could introduce as many as I wanted because nature never set a limit of such things.

The title was simplicity itself. I'd call our new group "The Mutants."

[Publisher] Martin [Goodman] liked the concept but hated the title. He said our readers wouldn't know a mutant was. [...] I tried to dream up another name, and then it hit me. They were heroes with extra powers. I had even named their adult mentor Professor Xavier. So why not call them *The X-Men*?

This time Martin okayed the title although I never really understood his logic. If our readers wouldn't know what a mutant was, how would they know what an X-Man is? [Lee, *Excelsior* 165].

The story in *The X-Men* #1 (Sep. 1963),[3] simply titled "X-Men," introduced the world to "the strangest superheroes of all" (1): Cyclops (Scott Summers), with powerful beams that shoot from his eyes; Angel (Warren Worthington III), who has feathered wings growing from his back for flight; Iceman (Bobby Drake), with the ability to create and shape ice; the ape-like Beast (Hank McCoy); and the newest member, the telekinetic Marvel Girl (Jean Grey). They are all students at an exclusive private school where they are taught and trained by the wheel-chair bound Professor X (Charles Xavier) "to help those who would distrust us if they knew of our existence!" (11).

The creation of a team of teenage superheroes came at a fortuitous time. After readers accepted a teenager as an independent hero and not merely relegated to the role of sidekicks with Spider-Man, the market was ready for an expansion of the concept to a whole team. As teenagers made up the main reading audience, they were thrilled to see characters going through problems similar to what they were experiencing. Additionally, teenagers were at the forefront of many of the changes that would define the 1960's counterculture.

The very idea of "teenager" as a distinct period of adolescences was still relatively new in the 1960s, resulting from the economic prosperity and changing educational structures and familial priorities of the post–World World II era (Getner 970). With both free time and disposable income, teenagers became independent consumers and therefore a desirable market for advertisers (Wright 200). The result was consumers seeking authentic self-identity and a market geared towards self-expression. Surrounding this was a confluence of events (social injustice, political assassination, war, race, sex, drugs and rock and roll) that would all come together in a social, cultural, and ideological rebellion of the younger generation against the consensus culture of the previous decade; a counterculture that would become a defining feature of the '60s (Johnson 94; Gabilliet 63).

The countercultural movement and this time period have become so interrelated that the two are synonymous. Because of this, when one discusses "the '60s," one may not be referring to the calendar decade. Instead, it infers a cultural calendar marked by events of social importance. In *Super-History*, Jeffery K. Johnson compiled a list of events that various historians have used to delineate the time period, including: John F. Kennedy sworn in as president in Jan. 1961; The Cuban Missile Crisis in Oct. 1962; the assassination of JFK in Nov. 1963; the first appearance of the Beatles on the Ed Sullivan Show in Feb. 1964; or the Gulf of Tonkin Resolution that expanded the Vietnam War in Aug. 1964. Possible endpoints could be: Woodstock in 1969; the break-up of the Beatles in Apr. 1970; the removal of U.S. troops from Vietnam in 1973; the fall of Saigon in Apr. 1975; or the Watergate scandal in 1975 (87–88). Clearly this was a turbulent period and the transformation of *The X-Men* from a Cold War to a Civil Rights narrative between 1963 and 1965 reflects the evolving cultural climate.

The counterculture can only be understood in the context of what they were rebelling against: the consensus culture of the 1950s. Following WWII, the United State assumed for the first time a leading role in international affairs, helping to rebuild nations and to export democracy and capitalism. In this endeavor the U.S. was countered by its former ally, the communist USSR. As both sides possessed nuclear weapons, a heated war would have resulted in mutually assured destruction. So instead the two superpowers engaged in a cold war of containment, a zero-sum game wherein a gain for one side was a loss for the other. Security came to be defined as preventing the USSR and its allies from expanding their sphere of influence (Costello 34).

In a bi-polar conflict such as this, society both justified its course of action and sublimated its concerns and anxieties by projecting any negative values onto the external Other. As the Soviet Union was portrayed as oppressive and totalitarian, the United States became enshrined in democracy and freedom (York and York 6). The use of absolutes to define the conflict resulted in a consensus ideology that codified what it meant to be American.

A side effect of this negation was the fear that the external enemy could infiltrate and become an internal threat. Any behavior that deviated from the norm was thus considered to be un–American (Costello 39). Citizens were warned to carefully observe their neighbors in case any of them were a communist agent attempting to destroy the American way of life (Johnson 78). This fear was personified by the communist witch hunts of Senator Joseph McCarthy and the investigations of the House Un-American Activities Committee. Containment became not just a foreign policy but also a domestic one, focusing on the family and, by extension, teenagers.

Comic books were an effective tool to tap into all the ambient discourses. Cold War propaganda portrayed the U.S. combating a villain with nuclear capabilities in a struggle over the fate of the planet (Johnson 63). The moral certainties of superheroes stories, with their stark contrasts between good and evil, easily aligned themselves with the Cold War narratives being expounded by experts and leaders (Costello 63). Superheroes of the '50s and early '60s, including the X-Men, became parables for the hegemonic identity by embodying American virtue and battling threats from abroad. In doing so, they reflected the policies of foreign and domestic containment.

The beginnings of the United States' containment policy towards the USSR is attributed to George Kennan, who in a 1946 telegram outlined Russian policy and an appropriate response (Johnson 63). But what began as a concept of limiting Russia's political influence evolved into geographic containment, especially after Communism reached the Western Hemisphere in the Cuban Revolution in 1959 (Costello 58). This naturally became a military issue and the policy was utilized in the creation of NATO as well as justification for the police actions in Korea and Vietnam.

Key to the military containment strategy was the arms race, the endeavor to stockpile more nuclear weapons in strategic locations than the enemy. This strategy resulted in the harrowing episode of the Cuban Missile Crisis. In Sept. 1962, the Soviet Union began positioning nuclear missiles in their ally, Cuba, less than a hundred miles off the United States. The Soviets claimed this was to prevent a U.S. invasion, while the American government viewed it as an act of aggression and threatened to blockade Cuba. The result was the closest the world has come to nuclear war, only resolved through tense days of negotiation (Johnson 58).

The containment policy was not limited to geopolitical confrontations but extended to other spheres including culture, athletics, science and even to the stars through what became the space race. When Sputnik orbited the world in 1957, citizens feared that the Russians were spying on them. That paranoia escalated to the threat of being attacked by weapons from space, making the space race an extension of the arms race (Payne and Spaeth 196). Whoever could control the outer reaches of the planet would have a significant advantage in any conflict and whoever could reach the moon first could declare at least a moral victory.

All these concerns informed the Cold War culture and were great fodder for comic book superheroes, where weapons became super-weapons and any villain could be a Communist agent. And none were better at turning reality into hyperbolic fisticuffs than Stan Lee and the artists of the Marvel Comics bullpen. The Fantastic Four's origin was explicitly linked to the space race, as four intrepid astronauts launched an experimental shuttle in an attempt to beat the Russians, only to be bombarded by cosmic rays. Iron Man and the Hulk resulted from the military industrial complex. Spider-Man and Daredevil received their superpowers from accidents involving radioactivity. Even Thor, the mythical Norse god, battled communist villains early on.

But the X-Men were different. In addition to being born with powers instead of gaining them through some accident, they did not fight Soviet agents directly but through the proxy of evil mutants. The villainous aim of world domination aligned such antagonists with the totalitarian goals attributed to the Soviet Union (Costello 70). Their first enemy from issue #1 was Magneto, the master of magnetism. With a costume of predominately red and a helmet whose emblem in some panels looks like devil horns, he was the definition of a red menace. Magneto's first goal was militaristic, interfering with the tests of a new missile and then taking over a military base, only to be thwarted by the X-Men. The X-Men acted like citizen soldiers, showing that it was every citizen's duty to prevent evil mutants (communists) from gaining more power.

Magneto became the X-Men's first recurring foe, returning in *The X-Men* #4, "The Brotherhood of Evil Mutants!," alongside his own team of mutants, consisting of the acrobatic leaper Toad; Mastermind, with the ability to project illusions; and the speedster Quicksilver and his sister Scarlett Witch, who could cast hexes that caused bad luck. Magneto and the Brotherhood returned again in *The X-Men* #5, "Trapped: One X-Man!," where they first attempt to infiltrate the X-Men to discover their secret base and then kidnap Angel to Magneto's base, the orbiting satellite called Asteroid M; thus addressing concerns over both spying and the space race. Magneto would continue to antagonize the mutant teens throughout their second year (#6, #7, #8, and #11), though these issues would take on the theme of containment more directly by having the X-Men prevent Magneto from recruiting new mutants, such as Namor the Sub-Mariner, the Blob and Unus the Untouchable, to his cause. The fact that Magneto constantly returns to plague the heroes is suggestive of the ongoing nature of the Cold War (Costello 63).

The Cold War was thematically consistent throughout the first year of *X-Men*'s publication. *The X-Men* #2, "No One Can Stop the Vanisher!," witnessed the teleporting mutant Vanisher stealing the United States' new continental defense plans with the threat of handing them over to the Communists. *The X-Men* #3, "Beware of the Blob!," doesn't fit the them as clearly, as the Blob only has a vague notion of world conquest once he discovers he is homo superior. It does, however, continue a theme of physical deformity among villains. Drawing the villains as physically repulsive (in the Blob's case, morbidly obese) marks them as the Other and gives them license to embody a lack of virtue if not outright moral bankruptcy (Costello 65). This theme is evident in other early X-Men villains, such as the Brotherhood of Evil Mutants' Toad and Mastermind; the Vanisher merely wore a hideous costume.

If physical deformity is equated with a lack of morals, it must inversely be implied that attractiveness enhances a characters virtue. All the X-Men are shown as attractive, perhaps best illustrated by the scene in issue #2 where Angel is mobbed by a group of teenage girls shouting: "'Look! It's the Angel!' 'Hold him! I want his autograph!' 'Autograph, nothing! I want a kiss! Mmmmm!'" (27). Little fear of mutants evidenced in that sequence, or almost anywhere in the early issues. Instead, the X-Men are more like a military unit, with their matching uniforms and constantly shown practicing their powers in an obstacle at school rather than at lessons. They even have the tacit approval of the government; in issue #2, Professor X is shown having a direct telepathic line to the FBI while in issue #5, Jean Grey's mother comments: "When [Professor Xavier] first asked us if Jean could attend your school, we were a bit hesitant! But then, when we were contacted by Washington, D.C., recommending your course so highly, we knew it was the best thing for our daughter!" (38, 101). The X-Men are clearly not viewed as a mutant threat but as citizen soldiers working to contain external threats.

The bulk of the X-Men's early adventures take place within the United States, marking the importance of internal as well as external containment.[4] With the development of a powerful consensus in the 50s, the citizenry was cautioned against any abnormal behavior that could indicate foreign conspirators. The stability of traditional roles became a matter of political security. The epitome of this tradition and normalcy became enshrined in the nuclear family, consisting of a father, a mother, and children acting within their assigned spheres (Genter 957).

The nuclear family came to be viewed as the fulfillment of the American way. The X-Men formed an ersatz family with Professor X as the father, the boys as siblings and Marvel Girl filling al the female roles of mother/sister/girlfriend, depending on the needs of the moment. The instability inherent in this pseudo-familial arrangement reflects the fact that even though popular discourse of the 50s emphasized the importance of families, leaders were unable to normalize the family image (Genter 937). However, the success of the X-Men in negotiating the roles stood in contrast to the Brotherhood of Evil Mutants, where Magneto controlled Mastermind and the Toad through fear and intimidation while constantly reminding Quicksilver and the Scarlett Witch that he had saved their lives. That the Brotherhood was constantly defeated by the X-Men turns the series into a morality tale about the power of the nuclear family to defeat intruders (Genter 959).

Key to the success of the family in this era was the idea that each member fulfill their assigned role. "The most fundamental job of the American woman," as defined by Secretary of Labor James P. Mitchell in 1957, was "being a good housewife, a homemaker, a mother" (Gardner 94). This placed a special burden on Marvel Girl as the only teenage girl on the team. Jean Grey had to fulfill both the domestic duties of a mother and the romantic ideal of the girlfriend.

These dual roles are not mutually exclusive. Jean's homemaking skills, such as filling in for the cook (issue #6), serving as a nurse (issues #4 and 13), and even using her powers in a sewing exercise (issue #8), reveal her to be an ideal potential spouse, which overlaps into the sphere of a love interest. All the men on the team do express romantic interest in Jean in one form or another, from numerous comments on her attractive appearance to Beast stealing a kiss (issue #1) or Angel sweeping her away for a "date" when they have to investigate a carnival (issue #3) (11, 53). Not even Professor X is immune. In a troubling panel from issue #3, Xavier mental declares: "'Don't worry!' As though I could help worrying about the one I love! But I can never tell her! I have no right! Not while I'm leader of the X-Men, and confined to this wheelchair!" (52). Fortunately, that plot line was immediately dropped in favor of panels of Jean and Scott Summers expressing their silent longing through thought balloons, a trope familiar from the romance comics of the time.

This influence of the romance comics also reinforces the implied idea of '50s femininity that a woman can only find meaning as part of a heterosexual pair (Darowski 105). Jean Grey is regularly shown being in need of rescue or protection from the men, making her role on the team that of damsel in distress. Much of this stems from the strain of using her powers. Though the exact limit of her abilities seem to change sporadically from issue to issue, when she exerts them too much she will faint. Worse, she has to be instructed in the most basic use of her powers. In issue #3, the X-Men are captured but the Blob's fellow carnies and Professor X must instruct Jean to telekinetically remove her blindfold and summon a throwing knife to release her bonds (70). While Jean's strength and confidence grow in subsequent stories, her role in the initial issues were proscribed by the limiting boundaries of domestic containment.

Women's roles were not the only ones limited in society by the unwritten policies of domestic containment. Teenagers were also affected. The rise of adolescent independence, so unlike the lifestyle of the previous generation, was a cause of great anxiety during the 50s and 60s. This new fear was embodied by the rise in juvenile delinquency. While any shift in societal behavior is rarely a simple case of cause and effect, parental groups were eager for a target to blame, especially one that would absolve them of any responsibility for this criminal behavior. With the new technology of television and the new music genre rock 'n' roll consuming many teenagers free time, the easy target was mass media. Comic books were specifically targeted by only a few, most notably Dr. Fredric Wertham, but were swept up in the craze that culminated in the Senate hearing on juvenile delinquency. While Senator Estes Kefauver ultimately determined "that juvenile delinquency essentially stems from the moral breakdown in the home and community and, in many cases, parental apathy," the damage to the reputation of comic books was done (qtd. In York, Rebellion 111). A strict Comics Code was established that essentially censored their content while publication dropped off precipitately.

Superheroes were still on tenuous grounds when the X-Men began publication. While Marvel Comics had contributed to a revival in the genre's popularity, they were still under the judgmental scrutiny of adult supervision. So the X-Men became less a reflection of typical American teenagers and more the type of teenagers adults wanted to exist: responsible, fighting only for a just cause, never using slang, never smoking or drinking, and possessing only a chaste version of a libido (Wright 73). The X-Men are always respectful to their teacher, Professor X. When they go out, they are often dressed in suit and tie or very nice casual wear; Marvel Girl, of course, wears a dress. Even their horseplay is carefully monitored. As Professor X observes: "A few minutes of roughhouse is good for all of you... to help you let off some steam!" (*X-Men* #1 8) It is a safe version of the teenage years that would have met with the approval of adults (York, Rebellion 111). In doing so, Lee and Kirby may have been arguing that the juvenile delinquency scare was a non-issue and that teenagers were as capable of acting for the good of humanity as adults were (York, *Fantastic Four* 207).

In *The X-Men* #8, "The Uncanny Threat of... Unus, the Untouchable!," Beast rescues a young child only to have the crowd of onlookers turn on him. "'I've heard there are many such mutants in hiding... Waiting to take over the world!' 'Did you see how he ran past us?? Like he was afraid of us... Like he knew he's out enemy!' 'He probably saved that kid just to throw us off guard... To make us think mutants aren't dangerous!'" (174). Despite characters having referenced prejudice against mutants, this is the only actual instance of fear of mutants being displayed in the first two years of *The X-Men*. But the rhetoric of the crowd also aligns with the threat of a communist spy. However, in equating evil mutants with communists, the X-Men do complicate the Cold War narrative. If evil mutants are a stand in for communists and there are evil mutants and good mutants, would that mean there are good communists? This type of ambiguity towards the Cold War consensus is rife throughout the early years of the X-Men's publication, reflecting concerns that would eventually blossom into the countercultural movement (Costello 61).

One of the best examples of this ambiguity is from Quicksilver and the Scarlet Witch. Despite being members of the Brotherhood of Evil Mutants, they constantly question Magneto's methods to the point that Quicksilver races back to dismantle one of Magneto's nuclear bombs in Santo Marco (#4, 96). They would eventual defect and join the Avengers. This is a polyvalent message. If the evil mutants are to be equated with communists, it shows that not all communists are evil and some wish to defect and enjoy the American way of life, here shown as becoming a superhero. But there is also a generational element of youth rebelling against an authority figure being shown as a positive message.[5]

There is also the issue of brainwashing. This fictional technique of altering the way someone thinks so that they will betray their values preyed on the paranoia of the Cold War. However, in the *X-Men*, it is Professor Xavier who does the brainwashing. He uses his telepathy to erase knowledge for the minds of the Vanisher and the Blob (#2 45, #3 72). By subverting the use of brainwashing, are the creators showing that the ends justify the means?

In *The X-Men* #7, "The Return of the Blob!," Beast and Iceman make their first of many visits to a Greenwich Village coffee house where they encounter jazz, experimental dancing, modernist art, and beatnik poetry. On seeing the size of Beast's feet, they declare: "'Don't move stranger! I've got to make a sketch of those feet! They should be immortalized on canvas!' 'Wait till Bernard sees them! He'll write a new poem immediately!' 'This could start a whole new cult—We'll call ourselves Barefoot Beats!'" (158). While this is the most direct reference to the counterculture, the X-Men increasingly negotiated countercultural ideas in their second year of publication while moving away from the Cold War.

In *The X-Men* #9, "Enter, The Avengers!," the X-Men battled the Avengers while Professor X stopped the alien Lucifer from unleashing "A giant thermal bomb!! Large enough to blow up a continent!" (199). While superheroes battling each other over some misunderstanding at their first meeting is a common comic book trope, this has the added generational element of teenagers fighting authority figures such as Captain America, Iron Man and Thor. *The X-Men* #11, "The Coming of... Ka-Zar!," features the teens attempting to pre-emptively recruit Ka-Zar before Magneto before fighting their way through the prehistoric Savage Land.

The theme of antagonists outside of mutants continues in "The Triumph of Magneto!" (*The X-Men* #11). When a new mutant appears on Professor X's mutant tracking computer Cerebro, the X-Men and Magneto both race to recruit him. But the figure turns out to be the cosmic being the Stranger, who whisks Magneto and the Toad off into space. This seemingly ends the menace of Magneto, albeit only temporarily. As for the Stranger, he could be read as the introduction of some New Age philosophy to the Marvel Universe, something more frequently explored in the pages of *Doctor Strange* than *X-Men*.

The second year finished with a two-part story, "The Origin of Professor X!" and "Where Walks the Juggernaut!" (Issues #12 and #13). The X-Men must face the unstoppable Juggernaut (Cain Marko), who is Professor Xavier's half-brother. Juggernaut it not a mutant but rather receives his power from a mystic gem, perhaps another reference to the New Age ideas. The confrontation over a sibling rivalry might also be interpreted as a commentary on the Vietnam War, the younger generation fighting the battles started by the older one, but this may be stretching things a bit. The fact remains that antagonists like the aliens Lucifer and the Stranger or the mystically powered Juggernaut exist outside the initial mutant agenda of the series and are increasingly empty signifiers. They fall somewhere between the gap of the consensus culture and the counterculture but are evidence of Marvel Comics attempting to negotiate the trends of the day.

This changed in "Among Us Stalk... The Sentinels!" *The X-Men* #14 introduces the robotic mutant-hunting Sentinels and marks a clear shift towards embracing the inherent mutants as minority metaphor. But why did this not occur sooner? The idea that mutants were hated a feared was stated in the first issue. Professor X explained: "But, when I was young, normal people feared me, distrusted me! I realized the human race is not ready to accept those with extra powers! So I decided to build a haven... A school for X-Men!" (11). Despite this, there was only the one example from issue #8 of a mutant being hated just for being a mutant.[6]

Part of the problem undoubtedly would have been the challenge of having five middle-to-upper class WASP-ish teenagers serve as a commentary on the great minority struggle of the day, the Civil Rights movement. The Civil Rights movement exposed the lie beneath the implied homogeneity of 50's consensus culture by highlighting those who were not allowed to participate in that American way of life. The public debate and news coverage undoubtedly informed the creators in the initial conception of the series (Darowski 83). However, superheroes are inherently conservative in nature, fighting to preserve the status quo rather than promote change. The Civil Rights movement, and other counterculture ideology, were promoted by a vocal portion of society but lacked support of the majority either through opposition or, more likely, ambivalence (Johnson 97).

This changed with passing of the Civil Rights Act of 1964 (Johnson 95). By becoming the law of the land, it was now part of the status quo and the creators felt at liberty to address what had previously been the subtext of the series. This newfound liberty lead the X-Men to becoming a metaphor for any person who felt disenfranchised by society, which in turn made them one of the most popular comic book series of all time.

X-Men: First Class director Matthew Vaughn stated of the film: "1962 is far more grounded in the world of the 50s. I think it takes about five years for a decade to really start getting its identity,..." (Leyland). Though the film was ostensibly inspired by, but bore little resemblance to, the early adventures of the X-Men, the Cuban Missile Crisis was crucial to the plot, bringing a Cold War narrative to the forefront of the film. In this it did reflect the first two years of the X-Men's publication, which had served as a dialogue between the hegemonic ideology of consensus and containment of the 1950s and the questions and values that complicated that grand narrative and resulted in the countercultural movement of the 1960s (York and York 10). In negotiating the prominent trends of the time, *The X-Men* offer an illuminating reflection of an important period in American history.

NOTES

1. At this time Marvel Comics was distributed by Independent News Company, which was owned by DC Comics. They agreed to distribute eight Marvel titles a month. To maximize their output, Marvel published 16 titles on a bi-monthly basis (Wright 201).

2. *The Avengers* has the same publication date of Sept. 1963, but was a team created from pre-existing heroes.

3. Cover date Sept. 1963. There has always been a discrepancy between the cover date and when the book was actually released. In the 1960s, this was usually 4 months. Because release dates are harder to track, the cover date is used to indicate publication (Darowski 44).

4. Nine of the 13 adventures were within U.S. borders. The exceptions are Santo Marco in #4 (which looks suspiciously eastern European), an island in the north Atlantic in #6, Bavaria in #9 and the Savage Land in #10.

5. At this point Magneto is only viewed as the leader of the Brotherhood of Evil Mutants. He would later be revealed as the father of Quicksilver and Scarlet Witch.

6. In issue #5, the Toad disguises himself and participated in a track meet where he is attacked as a cheater, not necessarily because he is a mutant.

WORKS CITED

Costello, Matthew J. *Secret Identity Crisis: Comic Books and the Unmasking of Cold War America*. New York: Continuum, 2009.

Darowski, Joseph. "Reading *The Uncanny X-Men*: Gender, Race, and the Mutant Metaphor in a Popular Narrative." Diss. Michigan State University, 2011.

Gabilliet, Jean-Paul. *Of Comics and Men: A Cultural History of American Comic Books*. Trans. by Bart Beaty and Nick Nguyen. Jackson: University of Mississippi Press, 2005.

Gardner, Jeanne Emerson. "'Dreams May End, But Love Never Does': Marriage and Materialism in American Romance Comics, 1947–1954." In *Comic Books and American Cultural History: An Anthology*. Matthew Putz, ed. New York: Continuum, 2012.

Getner, Robert. "'With Great Power Comes Great Responsibility': Cold War Culture and the Birth of Marvel Comics." *The Journal of Popular Culture* 40.6 (2007): 953–978.

Johnson, Jeffery K. *Super-History: Comic Book Superheroes and American Society*. Jefferson: McFarland, 2012.

Lee, Stan, and George Mair. *Excelsior! The Amazing Life of Stan Lee*. New York: Fireside, 2002.

Lee, Stan (w) and Jack Kirby (a). "X-Men." *The X-Men* #1 (Sept. 1963). In Cory Sedlmeier, ed., *Marvel Masterworks: The X-Men Volume 1 Nos. 1–10*. New York: Marvel Comics, 2003.

_____ and _____. "No One Can Stop the Vanisher!" *The X-Men* #2 (Nov. 1963). In Cory Sedlmeier, ed., *MarvelMasterworks: The X-Men Volume 1 Nos. 1–10*. New York: Marvel Comics, 2003.

_____ and _____. "Beware the Blob!" *The X-Men* #3 (Jan. 1964). In Cory Sedlmeier, ed., *Marvel Masterworks: The X-Men Volume 1 Nos. 1–10*. New York: Marvel Comics, 2003.

_____ and _____. "The Brotherhood of Evil Mutants!" *The X-Men* #4 (Mar. 1964). In Cory Sedlmeier, ed., *Marvel Masterworks: The X-Men Volume 1 Nos. 1–10*. New York: Marvel Comics, 2003.

_____ and _____. "Trapped: One X-Man!" *The X-Men* #5 (May 1964). In Cory Sedlmeier, ed., *Marvel Masterworks:The X-Men Volume 1 Nos. 1–10*. New York: Marvel Comics, 2003.

_____ and _____. "Sub-Mariner! Joins the Evil Mutants!" *The X-Men* #6 (July 1964). In Cory Sedlmeier, ed., *Marvel Masterworks: The X-Men Volume 1 Nos. 1–10*. New York: Marvel Comics, 2003.

_____ and _____. "The Return of the Blob!" *The X-Men* #7 (Sept. 1964). In Cory Sedlmeier, ed., *Marvel Masterworks: The X-Men Volume 1 Nos. 1–10*. New York: Marvel Comics, 2003.

_____ and _____. "The Uncanny Threat of... Unus, the Untouchable!" *The X-Men* #8 (Nov. 1964). In Cory Sedlmeier, ed., *Marvel Masterworks: The X-Men Volume 1 Nos. 1–10*. New York: Marvel Comics, 2003.

_____ and _____. "Enter, the Avengers!" *The X-Men* #9 (Jan. 1965). In Cory Sedlmeier, ed., *Marvel Masterworks:The X-Men Volume 1 Nos. 1–10*. New York: Marvel Comics, 2003.

_____ and _____. "The Coming of... Ka-Zar!" *The X-Men* #10 (Mar. 1965). In Cory Sedlmeier, ed., *Marvel Masterworks: The X-Men Volume 1 Nos. 1–10*. New York: Marvel Comics, 2003.

_____ and _____. "The Triumph of Magneto!" *The X-Men* #11 (May 1965). In Cory Sedlmeier, ed., *The X-Men Omnibus Volume 1: Collecting The X-Men Nos. 1–31*. New York: Marvel Comics, 2009.

Lee, Stan (w), Jack Kirby and Alex Toth (a). "The Origin of Professor X!" *The X-Men* #12 (July 1965). In Cory Sedlmeier, ed., *The X-Men Omnibus Volume 1: Collecting The X-Men Nos. 1–31*. New York: Marvel Comics, 2009.

Lee, Stan (w), Jack Kirby and Werner Roth (a). "Where Walks the Juggernaut!" *The X-Men* #13 (Sept. 1965). In Cory Sedlmeier, ed., *The X-Men Omnibus Volume 1: Collecting The X-Men Nos. 1–31*. New York: Marvel Comics, 2009.

_____, _____ and _____. "Among Us Stalk... The Sentinels!" *The X-Men* #14 (Nov. 1965). In Cory Sedlmeier, ed., *The X-Men Omnibus Volume 1: Collecting The X-Men Nos. 1–31*. New York: Marvel Comics, 2009.

Leyland, Matthew. "X-Men: First Class Sequel Plans Revealed." *Total Film*. Accessed

4 Nov., 2013, at http://www.totalfilm.com/news/x-men-first-class-sequel-plans-revealed.

Payne, Phillip G., and Paul J. Spaeth. "Agent of Change: The Evolution and Enculturation of Nick Fury." In *Comic Books and American Cultural History: An Anthology*. Matthew Putz, ed. New York: Continuum, 2012.

Wright, Bradford W. *Comic Book Nation: The Transformation of Youth Culture in America*. Baltimore: The Johns Hopkins University Press, 2001.

York, Chris, and Rafiel York. "Introduction: Fredric Wertham, Containment and Comic Books." In *Comic Books and the Cold War, 1946–1962: Essays on Graphic Treatment of Communism, the Code and Social Concerns*. Chris York and Rafiel York, eds. Jefferson: McFarland, 2012.

York, Rafiel. "*The Fantastic Four*: A Mirror of Cold War America." In Chris York and Rafiel York, eds., *Comic Books and the Cold War, 1946–1962: Essays on Graphic Treatment of Communism, the Code and Social Conerns*. Jefferson: McFarland, 2012.

_____. "Rebellion in Riverdale." In *Comic Books and the Cold War, 1946–1962: Essays on Graphic Treatment of Communism, the Code and Social Concerns*. Chris York and Rafiel York, eds. Jefferson: McFarland, 2012.

Call for Community:
Charles Xavier's School
for Gifted Youngsters as
Hippie Community Experience

Jean-Philippe Zanco

Superheroes in the Family

Superman's childhood can be seen as a picture of the ideal family. The orphan hero finds security within a replacement family cell which also became the medium for integration into human society. However, the adult age Clark Kent had to break out with his foster home so he could both fulfill his super-hero destiny and clear his roots. As a superhero, Superman had no true family life, like many of the Golden Age superheroes, from Batman (another orphan hero) to Captain America.

In the sixties, for a new generation of superheroes, family life became a way to anchor them in social reality and a way to make the readers identify more easily with their heroes. Peter Parker's personal history shared a lot with Clark Kent's (the loss of biological parents, a foster family instilling the key values which inspire the character), but contrary to Superman, family life was the cornerstone of Spiderman's social existence and of his daily life.

When Stan Lee and Jack Kiby's created the Fantastic Four in 1961 their foremost purpose was to provide the publisher with a competitive team of superheroes in light of DC's Justice League. But, while the Justice League members were united by martial solidarity ("male" solidarity, notwithstanding the presence of Wonder Woman), Stan Lee and Jack Kirby connected the Fantastic Four by family relationship, so as to make the readers identify themselves more strongly with their heroes.

The Fantastic Four became the only superhero family team built on a historical and cultural specific pattern : the nuclear family pattern. This pattern was defined by the sociologist Emile Durkheim as soon as the end of the nineteenth Century:

> We are in the presence of a new family type. Since the only permanent elements are the husband and wife, since all children leave home sooner or later, I propose to call it conjugal family. [...] This included the father, the mother and all the generations born to them, except the girls and their descendants. The conjugal family includes no more than the husband, the wife, and unmarried minor children."

This "new" family type at the time Durkheim wrote had become the norm a few decades later in industrial societies. In 1970, married couples, with or without children, represented more than 70 percent of American families. It is not so surprising to see superheroes defend this unit of society directly or indirectly.

The Commune as a Counterpoint

In their very first adventures, the X-Men were a curiosity. Charles Xavier's "Gifted Youngsters" shared adventures and training, like many others superheroes groups, but they also lived together. They shared such symbolic activities as birthday parties (*X-Men* #4, Mar. 1964) or daily dinner (*X-Men* #6, Jul. 1964). They didn't share a martial association (like the Avengers), nor a full family (like the Fantastic Four), but they were more than a fellowship. While the Fantastic Four symbolized the modern model of the American family life, can the X-Men be seen as their counterpoint, as a resurgence of what Emile Durkheim again called the primitive "family commune?"

The X-Men organization sounds paternalist, with the figure of Professor Charles Xavier, as a tutor and a teacher, whose wisdom, age and disability command respect. However, respect, affection, and even love, are not enough to build the traditional family relationship of this era, for, as Durkheim wrote, "Marriage both founds and comes from family." Rather than a family, the X-Men take on more what Durkheim called "the corporation," or from the primitive "community" in Ferdinand Tönnies' meaning:

> It is an aggregate of consciousness so strongly clustered that none can move independently. [...] What actually holds individuals in unity and mixity is [...] the silent and spontaneous agreement of many consciences feeling and thinking the same, which are open to each other, which share sensations, joys and pains, in one word, which vibrate in unison. [...] To make the consciences so mingle, so that they participate in each others' life, they might be of the same natures,

or they must have at least great similarities, and that is why the community of blood is the definitive source of all kinds of community. [...] What insures the cohesion of domestic society in addition of inbreeding, is the fact of living together, close to each other, in the same location ; it is also the community of memories as a necessary consequence of shared existence. [...] It rises brother-hoods, political, economic or religious corporations, in which assemble all those who go in the same functions, the same beliefs, who feel the same needs, etc. [Durkheim].

There is no inbreeding in the X-Men, their communalism is a chosen communalism.

X-Men and "Teen-Youth Culture"

The X-Men communal process reflects a social phenomenon of the Fifties and the Sixties. Youth "gangs" appeared in all major cities of Western countries, including the United States, embodying values borrowed from mass culture (rock'n'roll, films). A "teen-youth culture" (so-called by Edgar Morin) rose in counterpoint of the adult world dominant culture. This movement can be defined in counter-norm and counter-value terms, for it identified with anti-heroes like James Dean in *Rebel Without a Cause* (1955) or Marlon Brando in *The Wild One* (1953), while adult society took its benchmarks with mature, con-servative heroes like John Wayne. Teen-youth culture built up unity, helping the group to close ranks. Youth gangs, Morin wrote, "tend to be clan-based up."

The spread of youth culture counter-values led to bourgeois (adult) cul-ture contestation, which flourished in the beatnik movement, and then radi-calized and politicized in the mid-sixties. The Berkeley Free Speech Movement protest (1964–1965) certainly rose from an American student youth malaise, but it was quickly structured and organized against the University teaching model and governance. The Berkeley rebellion echoed in France in May 1968 and in many academic centers in London, the Netherlands, Scandinavia, and South America.

While protests blew out in Berkeley, the X-Men were living their very first adventures, and they shared some of the values of counterculture youth. In *X-Men* #7 (Sep. 1964) we see Hank McCoy, or the Beast, listening to jazz music and beatnik poetry at a Greenwich Village coffee shop, "enjoying a taste of the bohemian side of New York" (Lee). He is soon acclaimed by long-haired beatniks as "The king of the barefoot beats" (Lee). But, despite this, the young superheroes seemed rather conformist when submitting to the very paternal authority of Professor X. The School for Gifted Youngsters seemed to be a refugee for teenagers breaking out with their biological family, a goal Professor

X announced: "I realized the human race is not yet ready to accept those with extra powers! So I decided to build a haven... a school for X-Men!" (*X-Men* #1, Sep. 1963). The mutant commune appears as the natural consequence of labeling individuals as "deviants." As Howard Becker explains:

> A final step in the career of a deviant is movement into an organized deviant group. [...] From a sense of common fate, from having to face the same problems, grows a deviant subculture: a set of perspectives and understandings about what the world is like and how to deal with it, and a set of routine activities based on those perspectives.

Membership in such a group solidifies a deviant identity.

The X-Men as an Organized Deviant Group

Like in youth gangs, age is a criteria for X-Men membership in this era. It assigns a status, the pupil status that is differentiated from Professor X. But the definitive criterion is the *stigma* of mutation. The first X-Men were a perfect illustration of the stigmatization of individuals as examined in Erving Goffman's *Stigma*:

> The Greeks [...] originated the term stigma to refer to bodily signs designed to expose something unusual and bad about the moral status of signifier. The signs were cut or burnt into the body and advertised that the bearer was a slave, a criminal, or a traitor—a blemished person, ritually polluted, to be avoided, especially in public places [Goffman].

Cyclops' blindness, the Beast's simian feet and hands, Angel's wings, and even Professor X's paralysis: obvious "bodily signs" of a pathological status, in the classical meaning of Emile Durkheim. The Beast's stigma became more obvious when he gained a blue-haired, animal-like appearance in the early 1970s. Genetic anomaly both separates the mutants from the rest of humanity, and builds group cohesion. It creates a deviant-mutant subculture transcending the socio-cultural differences between the X-Men.

However a stigma is not necessarily exclusive:

> [D]oes the stigmatized individual assume his differentness is known about already or is evident on the spot, or does he assume it is neither known about by those present nor immediatly perceivable by them ? In the first case one deals with the plight of the discredited, in the second with that of the discreditable [Goffman].

The Beast is a *discredited* individual while Professor X, Marvel Girl, and Magneto are *discreditable* ones. Although Magneto *chose* to reveal his mutation, making so of himself a discredited individual. "Instead of cowering, the stigmatized individual may attempt to approach mixed contacts with hostile bravado, but this can induce from others its own set of troublesome reciprocation" (Goffman). In most cases, the mutant

> will find that there are sympathetic others who are ready to adopt his standpoint in the world and to share with him the feeling that he is essentially normal in spite of appearances and in spite of his own self-doubts. [...] The first set of sympathetic others is of course those who share his stigma. Knowing from their own experience what it is like to have this particular stigma, some of them can provide the individual with instruction in the tricks of the trade and with a circle of lament to which he can withdraw for moral support and for the comfort of feeling at home, at ease, accepted as a person who really is like any other normal person [Goffman].

The Political Aim of the Commune

Professor Xavier's dream was not only to protect the mutants from ostracism, it was to educate people to accept mutants as much as to teach the mutants the way to use their powers to serve humanity, reconciled and united beyond genetic differences. "We must use our powers to bring about a Golden Age on Earth," claimed Professor X in *X-Men* # 4 (Mar. 1964). The peaceful and utopian implication of Professor X's project may suggest the aspirations of the beatnik movement, while the evil mutants movement led by Magneto, because of its violence, echoed the marxist and anarchist student movements radicalism. The evil mutants' rejection of Homo Sapiens and the promotion of Homo Superior (the mutant) are a metaphor of the rejection of the bourgeois society by the Youth which clearly displays its intent to reverse power links. As Magneto proclaims in *X-Men* #4 (Mar. 1964), "We are born to rule the Earth ! The humans must be our slaves! They are our natural enemies...." Magneto was not only a destructor, he proposed a political project. "Moving into an organized deviant group," writes Howard Becker, "has several consequences for the career of the deviant. First of all, deviant groups tend, more than deviant individuals, to be pushed into rationalizing their position... Most deviant groups have a self-justifying rationale (or 'ideology')."

X-Men: An Undergound Commune or a Middle-Class Subgroup?

It is hard to see Professor X as an avatar of Gary Snyder or Allen Ginsberg. His rational-scientific culture and his wealth remove him from the mystical-artistic and anti-bourgeois aspirations of the underground culture that James Spates and Jack Levin defined as follows:

> In their antithetical reaction to the dominant culture, the members of the underground say they are exposing the overriding problems which a virtually total and increasingly instrumental view of the world produces . To sum up their position: the middle-class value system, by its overbearing emphasis on all forms of achievement [...], rational behaviour [...], and economic endeavour [...].

Although stigmatized and gathered in a deviant community, the X-Men aspire to join the American society which norms and values they intend to protect through their fights. This is why the desire to see the mutation "cured" is frequently expressed: an another evidence of the "pathological" nature of the mutants. It is difficult to see in the X-Men an emerging mutant counter-culture: they are all in all quite conformist.

On the other hand, the Brotherhood of Evil Mutants' actions match up more to the Spates & Levin's definition of underground. The utopian dimension of Magneto's political project is significantly larger than Professor X's "educational" aim. While the X-Men seem to respond more to the instrumental cultural dominant model, the Brotherhood of Evil Mutants is more in line with the expressionist action.

> In contradistinction to the future-oriented instrumental orientation, expressive action is present-oriented and "cathectic," an attempt to satisfy a need-disposition for its own sake "rather than subordinating gratification to a goal outside the immediate situation or to a restrictive norm" [PARSONS, 1951]. To put it slightly differently, the expressive orientation values activity as an end in itself rather than as a means to an end, as is the case in the instrumental pattern [Spates and Levin].

"Pedagogical" communes are more individualistic than other types of communities. According to the French sociologist Hélène Chauchat's study,[1] the phenomenon of conformity to the group subculture is significantly weaker than it is in political or religious communities, for example.

Charles Xavier the pedagogue vs Magneto the guru? Each of them expresses a different form of the Weberian legimacy: rational for the first, charismatic for the second. The rivalry between the X-Men and the Brotherhood of Evil Mutants is the confrontation between two different philosophies of community experience, between two forms of protest of the dominant American culture.

NOTE

1. In his 1975 study on communities, French sociologist Hélène Chauchat identifies six types of communities: religious communities, oriental communities, politic commu-

nities, artistic communities, pedagogical communities, rousseaust communities. Hélène CHAUCHAT, *La voie communautaire Pourquoi vivre en communauté ?* [Paris]: Publications de la Sorbonne, 1975.

WORKS CITED

Abrams, Philip, and Andrew McCulloch. *Communes, Sociology & Society.* Cambridge: Cambridge University Press, 1976.

Becker, Howard. *Outsiders.* Glencoe, IL: The Free Press of Glencoe / MacMillan Publishing Co., 1963.

Chauchat, Hélène. "Doctrine Officielle et Déclarations Individuelles: Les Motivations à Vivre en Communauté." *L'Année Psychologique.* 80.1 (1980).

Durkheim, Emile. "Communauté et Société Selon Tönnies (1889)." *Textes 1—Eléments d'une Théorie Sociale.* Ed. Emile Durkheim. Paris: Les Editions de Minuit, 1975. Trans. Jean-Phillipe Zanco.

_____. "La Famille Conjugale (1892)." *Textes 3—Fonctions Sociales et Institutions.* Ed. Emile Durkheim. Paris: Les Editions de Minuit, 1975. Trans. Jean-Phillipe Zanco.

_____. *"Les Règles de la Méthode Sociologique* (1894)." 1960. Paris: Presses Universitaires de France, 2013. Trans. Jean-Phillipe Zanco.

Goffman, Erving. *Stigma: Notes on the Management of Spoiled Identity.* NY: Simon & Schuster, 1963.

Morin, Edgar. "Culture Adolescente et Révolte Etudiante." *Annales. Economies, Sociétés, Civilisations* (1969): 765–776. Trans. Jean-Phillipe Zanco.

Spates, James L., and Jack Levin. "Beats, Hippies, the Hip Generation, and the American Middle Class: An Analysis of Values." *International Social Science Journal.* 24.2 (1972).

Wright, Bradford W. *Comic Book Nation: The Transformation of Youth Culture in America.* Baltimore: The Johns Hopkins University Press, 2001.

When Business Improved Art: The 1975 Relaunch of Marvel's Mutant Heroes

Joseph J. Darowski

Observers of American popular culture are likely aware of the impact the X-Men franchise has had, even if they've never read a comic book. Besides dozens of comic book titles and myriad mini-series there have been cartoons, video games, feature films, and merchandise that have made the X-Men a popular and profitable franchise. However, despite this modern widespread popularity, the comic book series initially failed to find an audience. Launched by the legendary Jack Kirby and Stan Lee, the series achieved only mediocre sales and soon began rotating writers and artists. Lacking a consistent tone and purpose, the series never achieved the success of *The Fantastic Four* or *The Amazing Spider-Man*. The X-Men would be cancelled after 66 issues, a respectable run, but not indicative of the massive franchise the X-Men would eventually become for Marvel Comics.

Near the end of the X-Men's first run, Roy Thomas returned to the series as writer for a second run and was paired with the artist Neal Adams. Thomas and Adams were more successful than any creative team since Lee and Kirby, but the end of the series seemed to have already been decided. As Gerard Jones and Will Jacobs explained, fans who had been frustrated by less-than-compelling in X-Men comics now found "complex character interactions, big adventure, and a harrowing tone of paranoia. And as soon as they'd tasted it, it was snatched from them." (136). Low sales doomed the X-Men and the company's publisher, Martin Goodman, canceled the series after *The X-Men* #66 (Mar. 1970) (Howe 105).

Despite being canceled, the series and characters did not disappear entirely. After several months Marvel continued to publish X-Men comics, but they were simply reprints of the earlier stories. So *The X-Men* #67 (Dec. 1970) reprinted the story from *The X-Men* #12 (Jul. 1965). These reprints continued on through *The X-Men* #93 (Apr. 1975). Thomas has argued that these reprints are evidence that the work he and Adams had done near the end of the series resonated with fans and caused an uptick of interest in the series. "The proof of the pudding is that Goodman very soon brought *X-Men* back as a reprint title... something he didn't do with other comics that he cancelled. It was almost—but not quite—his way of admitting he'd made a mistake" (Murray 18).

Additionally, during these reprint years the team or individual characters would occasionally guest star or even feature in other Marvel titles. Significantly, the Beast appeared in *Strange Tales* in a series of solo adventures that saw him transform from a fairly normal looking human to a more ape-like creature with fur sprouting out all over his body (originally gray fur, later blue). These guest-appearances and the Beast's brief solo adventures were the exceptions to the rule and the X-Men appeared very infrequently between 1970 and 1975 outside of their reprinted adventures.

In 1975 the X-Men franchise was relaunched. A comic book titled *Giant-Size X-Men* #1 (May 1975) introduced a new team of mutant characters. Plans for *Giant-Size X-Men* #2 were scrapped, and instead the story was split in two and published as *The X-Men* #94 (Aug. 1975) and *The X-Men* #95 (Oct. 1975). From then on the X-Men title ceased publishing reprints and only contained new adventures. This 1975 relaunch is what would establish the X-Men franchise as a power in the comic book industry and a key to Marvel's success. Soon, the X-Men side of the Marvel Universe would include ongoing titles such as *Dazzler*, *New Mutants*, and *X-Factor*, to be followed by many more series over the decades.

It is generally agreed that the X-Men comic books increased greatly in quality with the 1975 relaunch. The early issues did introduce the loaded concept of mutants to the Marvel Universe and were rife for potential, but as Charles Hatfield argued, "Kirby and Lee did not fully exploit this potential" (131). Hatfield goes on to say that "the series cast about undertainly for subplots, hooks, and distinctive characterizations" and became "dully repetitive" (131). Scott Bukatman argues that the Lee and Kirby X-Men comics "lacked the grandeur" of the Fantastic Four and Thor comics or the "nerdy charm" of Spider-Men, but there "was something of interest in the series" (50). This "something of interest" would become the key to the series in the 1970s. Lee and Kirby's concept had the seeds of fantastic concepts waiting to bear fruit; it would just take more than a decade before they began to be fully realized.

But why was this new version so much more spectacularly successful than the failed 1960's version of the title? One key reason may have had little to do with creative freedom and more to do with a business mandate from the publisher. This mandate, applied to the X-Men, simultaneously (and perhaps inadvertently) gave the series narrative and thematic heft and nuance that had been missing from the earlier series. In the early-to-mid–1970s the comic book industry was experiencing a decrease in overall sales. The domestic market was yielding fewer sales, and the president of Marvel, Arthur Landau, believed increasing foreign sales was the best way shore up Marvel's shrinking profits. Gerard Jones and Will Jacobs write of this period in the industry, when fans complained that quality seemed to be slipping as quickly as sales, explaining:

> No matter what genres or gimmicks were tried sales kept contracting and contracting. [...] Comics needed a miracle and it didn't look like anyone in charge was capable of producing one. Marvel President Arthur Landau's idea of a money-making idea was this: create a team of international superheroes representing all the major foreign markets in which he could sell Marvel product [205].

Specifically, Landau "realized that European and Asian markets would have great international value," so the company president charged the editor-in-chief with "devising a superteam of non–Americans" (Howe 153). Landau made his suggestion for an international superhero team in 1974 (Murray 18). Roy Thomas, who had written 35 issues of *The X-Men* in its original run, had become the editor-in-chief of Marvel. He explains,

> ...the idea of a revived "international" X-Men was my idea in 1974, after the company's president, Al Landau, suggested that it would be good to create a group of heroes from different countries we sold comic[s] to. I put writer Mike Friedrich and artist Dave Cockrum on it, with instructions to use a few old X-Men and create a few new ones, and left them to it. I quit the editor-in-chief job not long afterward, so had no further connection with it [...] [Thomas, "Follow Up"].

Dave Cockrum, the original artist of the X-Men's relaunch, recalls that Thomas proposed that the new X-Men would be like "mutant Blackhawks," a reference to an international group of World War II era pilots that had appeared in an eponymous comic book series (DeFalco 85). The goal was to have the new characters represent markets where Marvel Comics already had a significant presence. Because the distribution systems were already in place in these foreign markets, no new business costs would be incurred, but Landau hoped that featuring a local character on the cover would increase sales.

Shortly before the relaunch, Roy Thomas stepped down as editor-in-chief of Marvel Comics. Len Wein and Marv Wolfman were both promoted to high level editor jobs, Wein over color comics and Wolfman over Marvel's black-and-white publications. This reshuffling proved opportune for several young staffers, including a twenty-four-year old freelance writer named Chris Claremont who was promoted to the position of assistant editor (Amash 51). Though Cockrum and Wein were responsible for *Giant-Size X-Men*, Claremont would take over writing duties on the subsequent issues when Wein had to drop writing a title in order to better manage his editor job. Claremont would become one of the definitive X-Men writers, and his scripts helped to refocus the series with the idea that the X-Men are group defined by a fight to protect a world that hates and fears them.

Wein and Cockrum's new X-Men team was indeed international, but Thomas says that "somehow or other, by the time Len [Wein] was writing the book, the whole idea of having the new heroes be from countries where Marvel sold a lot of comics got lost" (DeFalco 34). Cockrum confirmed that "the new team didn't really wind up being what Marvel expected" (DeFalco 85). The new members of the X-Men would include a Russian and a Kenyan, hardly markets where Marvel was selling lots of comics 1975.

The new team members were Nightcrawler (a German teleporter named Kurt Wagner), Storm (Ororo Munroe, a weather controller from Kenya), Colossus (the Russian Peter Rasputin who could turn his flesh to organic steel), Banshee (the Irishman Sean Cassidy who had a sonic scream), Warpath (John Proudstar, an Apache with super-strength), Sunfire (a fire-wielder from Japan named Shiro Yoshida), and Wolverine (the Canadian with claws and a healing factor known only as Logan). Not all of these characters would remain X-Men for long, but this relaunch firmly established the X-Men as a team that embraced international characters in a way that other Marvel superhero teams, such as the Avengers or the Fantastic Four, rarely have. This tradition would continue as new characters were added to the roster over the years or spin-off series were launched. Frequently the new characters were non–Americans or represented racial minorities in America, a trend that adds welcome diversity to the American superhero genre.

One reason that the X-Men may have struggled so much to find an audience in their initial issues could be that they lacked key elements of the prejudice metaphor that the series addressed in storylines and dialogue. Some of the modern success of the X-Men franchise has been attributed to the "mutant metaphor" which allows the fictional mutants of the Marvel Universe to stand-in for minorities who feel somehow different from the larger culture and society around them. This metaphor can potentially be applied to anyone who feels different from the dominant culture around them, whether it is due to race, gender, sexuality, religious beliefs, personal ideologies, economic class, or even age.

All of the original X-Men were white, middle-to-upper-class Americans. This was a very WASP-ish group to be struggling against prejudice in a minority metaphor. Further complicating this particular group as representative of a racial metaphor is the fact that none of these mutants were in any way distinguishable from white Americans. While later mutants would often have distinctive features which would set them apart from all of humanity, such as fur, horns, or different skin pigmentation, the original X-Men could pass as non-mutants whenever they wished. Not only could the X-Men pass as non-mutants, they could pass as white humans, thus eliminating the institutionalized and social prejudices ethnic minorities faced. The 1960's era X-Men appeared to belong to the cultural majority in most ways. They were all white and middle-to-upper class citizens. Most members of the team were male. The few members of the original team who had outward signs of being a mutant could hide that difference to pass as normal humans. Cyclops wore special sunglasses that contained his eyeblasts, Beast's overly large feet weren't very conspicuous, and Angel would strap his wings down in such a way that they could be hidden under his shirt. Marvel Girl never appeared to be a mutant, and Iceman could choose to have a normal human form or an ice body (or a more fluffy, snowman-esque body in the earliest issues).

Besides not bearing the physical appearance of American minorities, the stories told in the X-men's earliest adventures do not touch on the ideas of mutants functioning as cultural "others" or facing persecution very often. Yes, the Sentinels, a government sponsored means of containment, are introduced and there are some instances of normal humans expressing either fear or hatred of mutants, but the majority of issues are more in line with the traditional superhero fare from the time and not the more allegorical tales that many associate with X-Men comic books. The consistent anti-prejudicial theme that would become easily identifiable in later years was not yet running through the series in the 1960s. Roy Thomas, who wrote the majority of the X-Men issues before the hiatus, has confessed that he "just wasn't that big into the mutant thing at that time" (DeFalco 23). The X-Men comic books written by Claremont and drawn by Cockrum and John Byrne in the mid-to-late '70s fully embraced the mutant aspect of the X-Men, adding thematic heft to the series as well as more diverse characters. This is the period when the popularity of the series increased dramatically, though it wouldn't become a massive franchise until the 1980s and 1990s. But in the issues from the 1960s, the X-Men did not look like a group that would be suffering from prejudice in America.

A hypercorrection of this omission of characters of color and non–American characters occurred when the new team was introduced in the 1975 relaunch of the X-Men title. There was not a single white American among the new members of the team, and many of the minority groups represented had been the subject of widespread prejudice in the United States, much of it institutionalized by the government. Germans were mistrusted after World

War II and the well-publicized horrors of the Holocaust. Africans have a long history of suffering from prejudice in America beginning with the slave trade. The general feelings toward Russians during the Cold War were far from friendly, and having an Eastern European accent could lead to accusations of Communism. Anti-Irish sentiment was strongest in the mid–1800s in the United States when discrimination in the workplace included the posting of NINA signs in want ads (No Irish Need Apply). Native Americans have been mistreated within the United States since settlers first reached the country's shores, and the forced movement onto reservations is only one of a long list of grievances. During World War II the federal Government forced Japanese Americans to live in internment camps because of mistrust.

The only exception to this trend of new characters being added to team from groups who had been subjected to prejudice in America is the Canadian Wolverine (excepting the War of 1812 and occasional efforts by far-right politicians and commentators to hold up Canada as an example of a too-liberal government, America's relationship with Canada has largely been amiable). However, Wolverine was a pre-existing character, having already appeared in issues of *The Incredible Hulk*. Len Wein had created Wolverine (with input from John Romita, Sr. and Roy Thomas) while writing *The Incredible Hulk*, and brought the character over to his new project, *Giant-Size X-Men*. Wolverine does take on the role of the outsider on the team, and adopts cowboy imagery, such as a cowboy hat, and mannerisms. The cowboy is an iconic image of a lonesome societal outsider, and traditionally the cowboys in American pop culture are white men who have no racial or gender barrier to acculturation, but nonetheless function outside of society.

The new team quickly lost some of its diversity. After one adventure, Sunfire quit the team and returned to Japan. Thunderbird was killed during the team's second adventure together, removing an American Indian presence from the group. The core group quickly became Cyclops, Wolverine, Storm, Nightcrawler, Banshee, and Colossus. Storm was the sole character of color in the group and Nightcrawler was the first mutant who could not easily pass as a normal human on the team. The team was not as homogenously White and American as it had been in the 1960s, but nor was it as diverse as it was set up to be in *Giant-Size X-Men* #1. The increased diversity in terms of race and nationality aided in establishing the power of the "mutant metaphor" in the series.

While highlighting the new, more diverse line up of the X-Men, Randy Duncan and Matthew J. Smith also surmise that the X-Men's popularity may have come about because of a "successful formula of matching realistic themes with a popular creative team" (63). One of the most iconic pairings of writer and artist is Chris Claremont and John Byrne, the regular team on *The*

Uncanny X-Men after Dave Cockrum left the series. Claremont and Byrne were "one of the most highly regarded collaborations in the field" of superhero comic books (62). Many of their tales are considered classics of X-Men and superhero comic books and are still referenced by fans, adaptations, and in current X-Men stories. Though the revitalization of the X-Men began with Wein and Cockrum, Claremont and Byrne have been credited, rightfully, with transforming "a second-tier bi-monthly series to the best-selling title in the industry" (Wright 263). Even after Claremont took over the writing duties from Wein, the series remained bi-monthly under Cockrum until Byrne took over as artist. Byrne has said that Cockrum "is such a wonderful artist, but he couldn't put out a monthly book," which is one of the reasons Byrne was brought on to the series (DeFalco 102). Claremont would script the series until 1991. As John C. Snider put it, "If Stan Lee is the father of the X-Men, then Chris Claremont is their godfather" (qtd. in Rhodes 107). Claremont remains the writer most closely associated with the franchise, though other writers such as Grant Morrison and Joss Whedon have made their mark with their own classic runs on the series. It is, of course, possible that without Claremont guiding the series to new creative heights with his artistic collaborators that the X-Men may have disappeared again into the back catalogue of Marvel characters, appearing periodically as guest-stars when creators nostalgically brought in fondly remembered concepts from Marvel's past. Such has been the fate of other series and characters such as the Inhumans, the Champions, and the Defenders.

Regarding the relaunch and subsequent success of the X-Men characters, it seems clear that the company president, Arthur Landau, made a request for a team with more international characters (ideally originating from countries where Marvel was already distributing comic books). Marvel's editor-in-chief, Roy Thomas, suggested that they use the X-Men because it was an established property that was not being used at the time. Though the requested series went through several creators, eventually Len Wein and Dave Cockrum used a blend of pre-existing and new characters to establish the new X-Men in *Giant-Size X-Men* #1. This new team, particularly after writing duties were taken over by Chris Claremont, established the X-Men franchise as one with a unique and easily identifiable hook, the "mutant metaphor." This aspect of the franchise, which had been unevenly applied to the X-Men in the 1960s, would come to define Marvel's mutant characters in subsequent spin-off series and media adaptations. Though the journey from initial idea to final product may have been convoluted, it was a specific business-oriented request that initiated the company's reimagining and relaunching of the X-Men franchise and gave the series significantly more depth and meaning than its original incarnation had demonstrated with any consistency.

Interestingly, Joe Quesada, the editor-in-chief of Marvel Comics for a decade in the early 2000s has offered a different interpretation of the reasoning behind the X-Men's relaunch. Quesada's version relies less on the bottom line and more on thematic resonance:

> The plan was to create a team of characters that were not only diverse in their powers; their diversity would be compounded by their ethnicity, genders, political views and preferences within. A super-powered team that reflected the diversity of a world that was shrinking by the minute. A world whose future could be glorious if we all learned the lessons of tolerance and acceptance, or could end up as a black pit of despair if we let fear rule our lives. Needless to say, this struck a chord within all of us, and the X-Men were reborn [4].

There are several possible reasons Quesada's description of the relaunch varies so much from the version described by Jones and Jacobs and confirmed by Thomas and others. First, Quesada wrote his description in 2003, almost thirty years after the event. While he is a prominent figure in the comic book industry today, his first published work in the comic book industry, as an artist, was released in 1994. His interpretation is most likely based as much on hindsight as anything else. And in hindsight, what he described is what happened with the X-Men, even if it was not originally intended when discussion of the project began. Additionally, as editor-in-chief of Marvel Comics, when speaking publically he may have been interested in recounting a version of history that was driven by creative concerns more than business concerns. While fans of popular culture know that money drives many decisions, the illusion that less-mercenary concerns are behind the production of our entertainment is often promoted by the entertainment industry. This romanticized and even sterilized version of events places primacy on the themes we have come to associate with the X-Men, not the money a company can make from a popular property. Because Thomas was in the room where the meeting took place, it is far more likely that the relaunch of the X-Men was a matter of convenience where a pre-existing property, with all the trademark and copyright concerns that entailed, could fulfill a business-driven mandate. This is one instance where purely monetary concerns improved the quality and thematic nuance of a creative project.

WORKS CITED

Amash, Jim. "Writing Comics Turned Out to Be What I Really Wanted to Do with My Life: Roy Thomas Talks About Writing—and Editing—for Marvel in the 1970s." *Alter Ego 70*. July 2007.3–62. PDF.

Bukatman, Scott. *Matters of Gravity: Special Effects and Supermen in the 20th Century*. Durham, NC: Duke University Press, 2003.

Claremont, Chris, and Len Wein (w) and Dave Cockrum (a). "The Doomsmith Scenario." *X-Men* #94 (Aug. 1975), *The Uncanny X-Men Omnibus Volume 1: Collecting Giant-Size X-Men No. 1, The X-Men Nos. 94–131*. Eds. Mark D. Beazley and Cory Sedlmeier. NY: Marvel Comics, 2009. 47–65. Print.

_____, and _____ and _____. "Warhunt!" *X-Men* #95 (Oct. 1975), *The Uncanny X-Men Omnibus Volume 1: Collecting Giant-Size X-Men No. 1, The X-Men Nos. 94–131*. Eds. Mark D. Beazley and Cory Sedlmeier. NY: Marvel Comics, 2009. 66–85. Print.

DeFalco, Tom. *Comics Creators on X-Men*. London: Titan Books, 2006.

Duncan, Randy, and Matthew J. Smith. *The Power of Comics: History, Form & Culture*. NY: Continuum, 2009.

Hatfield, Charles. *Hand of Fire: The Comics Art of Jack Kirby*. Jackson: University Press of Mississippi, 2012.

Howe, Sean. *Marvel Comics: The Untold Story*. NY: Harper Collins, 2012.

Jones, Gerard, and Will Jacobs. *The Comic Book Heroes: The First History of Modern Comic Books from the Silver Age to the Present*. Rocklin, CA: Prima Publishing, 1997.

Murray, Will. "The Extraordinary but Star-Crossed Origins of the X-Men." *Alter-Ego 120* (Sep. 2013): 3–20. PDF.

Quesada, Joe. "Introduction," *Marvel Encyclopedia Vol. 2: X-Men*, Eds. Beazley, Mark D. and Jeff Youngquist. NY: Marvel Comics, 2003: 4. Print.

Rhodes, Shirrel. *A Complete History of American Comic Books*. NY: Peter Lang, 2008.

Thomas, Roy. "Re: Follow Up Question." Message to Joseph Darowski.31 October 2013. E-Mail.

Thomas, Roy (w) and Sal Buscema (a). *X-Men* #66 (Mar. 1970), "The Mutants and the Monster!" *Marvel Digital Comics Unlimited*. 27 Jan. 2010. Online.

Wein, Len (w) and Dave Cockrum (a). "Second Genesis!" *Giant-Size X-Men* #1 (May 1975), *The Uncanny X-Men Omnibus Volume 1: Collecting Giant-Size X-Men No. 1, The X-Men Nos. 94–131*. Eds. Mark D. Beazley and Cory Sedlmeier. NY: Marvel Comics, 2009. 10–46. Print.

Wright, Bradford W. *Comic Book Nation: The Transformation of Youth Culture in America*. Baltimore, MD: The Johns Hopkins University Press, 2001.

From Kitty to Cat: Kitty Pryde
and the Phases of Feminism

MARGARET GALVAN

"This chapter is an argument for *pleasure* in the confusion of
boundaries and for *responsibility* in their construction."
—Donna Haraway, "A Cyborg Manifesto"

Why would Chris Claremont and John Byrne, the creative team behind
The Uncanny X-Men in the late 1970s and early 1980s, make a young teenage
girl the newest member of the international group of superheroes? Over the
first half of the 1980s, both fans and fellow characters questioned whether
Kitty Pryde, not only on the basis of her age, but also her inexperience—the
unknown potential of her mutant abilities, coupled with her immature attitude
and its consequences in fights—was more of a liability than an asset to the
team. Professor Xavier even momentarily demotes her from the X-Men because
she is "too young" and "too little is known about [her] powers" in *The Uncanny
X-Men* #167 (Mar. 1983). In a fan letter, Daniel Kaufman agrees with Xavier's
assessment, but expands these sentiments into a harsher critique by adding
gender to the list of disadvantages: "I always found it hard to believe a 14 year
old kid whose only powers are phasing, looking cute and drooling over Colossus could pull the X-Men's fat out of the fire as it seems she's done almost
every issue" (*The Uncanny X-Men* #173 [Oct. 1983]). Although Kaufman belit-
tles Pryde by calling her a "kid" and naming her flirtations with Colossus as
among her "only powers," he cannot help but admit that she often aids the
X-Men in victory. Pryde may seem innocuous, but she challenges these superficial evaluations with each success. When she earns back her spot on the team
in *The Uncanny X-Men* #168 (Apr. 1983), she proves herself to Xavier not by
acting more mature and demonstrating the full potential of her mutant abilities. Rather, she defeats her enemies with her youthful persistence and her

wits when an enemy temporarily deactivates her powers. Fighting against expectations, Pryde extends the field of what powerful superheroines look and act like.

Claremont, the writer on *The Uncanny X-Men* for nearly two decades (1975–1991), is known for helping to develop a number of powerful female heroines during his tenure. Jean Grey and Storm stand out as two of these iconic heroines, and, as Ramzi Fawaz astutely tracks in an article in *American Literature* (2011) that focuses on the beginning of "The Phoenix Saga" in 1977, these characters "[dramatize] two distinct but overlapping feminist projects of the mid–1970s... the desire for female autonomy and self-actualization and the development of alternative intimacies and solidarities outside of the scheme of heteropatriarchy" (374, 376). Fawaz aligns the former project with Grey as a stand-in for a "white liberal feminist worldview" and the latter with Storm and "radical women of color" (376). Importantly, in his analysis of "The Phoenix Saga," Fawaz draws out how Grey's drastic transformation into Phoenix, representative of the race-and-class-blind drive for female liberation, alienates not only her black female teammate, but her male teammates, as well.[1] In this storyline's denouement, Fawaz locates the possibility for reconciliation as Storm offers up her life to help save Grey (380). This exchange, however, is far from equal: one gives, one takes.[2] The unevenness of this dynamic underlines the incompatibility of these feminisms and signals the sea change of the 1980s where disenfranchised feminists insist that difference must be at the heart of any conception of feminism. It is in this evolving milieu that Pryde comes of age.

When Claremont and artist Byrne added Pryde to the team in *The Uncanny X-Men* #138 (Oct. 1980), not only was she the first new addition to the X-Men since the team changed its roster dramatically in *The Uncanny X-Men* #94 (Aug. 1975), but she also represented a clear replacement for Grey, who died in the previous issue. Like Pryde, Grey also started her tenure while still a teenager as Marvel Girl before blossoming into the empowered Phoenix that Fawaz aligns with a particular strain of 1970s feminism. Even though Pryde is young, her determined spirit distinguishes her from Marvel Girl who Fawaz labels as a "shrinking violet persona" before Claremont dramatically reconceives her when he begins writing the series in 1975 (373). By marked contrast, Pryde, in her first appearances before she even joins the team and has any formal training, ably evades capture, infiltrates enemy headquarters, and alerts Nightcrawler that other X-Men have been detained (*The Uncanny X-Men* #129–130 [Jan.-Feb. 1980]). While her ability to phase through solid objects initially may make her seem like a mysterious wallflower when she disappears through barriers, with this power, Pryde actively challenges notions of stability at their most basic, physical level. How she employs these trans-

gressive powers in concert with a plucky persona make Pryde an often overlooked powerhouse and a figure of the multivalent feminism that thrived in
the 1980s.

In attitude and age, Pryde easily matches the young, feisty females who
take over the silver screen in 1980s teen films. When Xavier says that he will
demote her because of her youth, Pryde responds by intoning, "Professor
Xavier is a jerk!" in a memorable one-page splash opening *The Uncanny X-
Men* #168 (Apr. 1983). This outburst echoes Molly Ringwald as Andie's excla-
mation, "Duckie, you're being a real jerk!" in *Pretty in Pink* (1986). Moreover,
just like the teenagers in most of John Hughes' films, Pryde hails from the
Chicago suburbs.[3] The plot of the comics often highlights Pryde's youth by
showing her daily habits, including reading comics, studying, and attending
dance practice, amidst her responsibilities to the X-Men. Her youthful energy
also radiates from her face: in early issues, Pryde is most often depicted in
close-up, emoting or reacting to something rather than showing off her powers.
This premise holds even in "Demon," an issue where Pryde defeats a N'garai
demon while she's alone in the X-Mansion on Christmas Eve (*The Uncanny
X-Men* #143 [Mar. 1981]). Although she uses her phasing abilities in combination with her technical aptitude to triumph over the enemy, her emotional
reactions as she figures out her next course of action visually dominate the
panels instead. Not only do these visual cues mark her as Brat Pack *avant la
lettre*, but they distinguish her from Storm, whose offensive tactics are on display in the issue's flashback splash page that shows her full body in flight battling a group of N'garai.[4]

But, even if Pryde superficially matches these peers, her identity as a
mutant sets her apart. Her mutant identity closely aligns with this surface, evidenced by a text box in the issue where she officially joins the team: "She's
13½, cute, bright, spunky—and she walks through walls" (*The Uncanny X-Men*
#138 [Oct. 1980]). These primary descriptors could name any number of Brat
Pack characters, but Pryde's difference lies in the hyphen that introduces her
powers. It is at the point of these mutant abilities that her narrative diverges
from the John Hughes paradigm. Although Molly Ringwald often plays the
role of an empowered misfit, she ably discards this identity by the film's end.
When one of the rich characters derisively refers to Ringwald's Andie as a
"mutant" in *Pretty in Pink* and chastises his friend for speaking with her, such
a mark is an ephemeral insult. In the last shot of the film, Andie's locking lips
with the rich guy of her dreams.[5] In theorizing Ringwald's strong female characters in her Brat Pack films, Anthony C. Bleach argues that the characters fit
within a post-feminist paradigm as they decide to leverage female empowerment for capitalist social advancement (28).[6] However, as a genetic mutant
who lives apart from society, such gains are never fully available for Pryde.[7]

Although she comes from a good family in the suburbs, Pryde's mutant identity limits her ability to latch onto the upwardly mobile trajectory opened up by straight white feminists in the 1970s. In fact, Grey's death signals the shortcomings of 1970s white liberal feminism to achieve a sustainable vision. By marked contrast, Storm thrives in the 1980s, redefining herself (*The Uncanny X-Men* #173 [Oct. 1983]) and besting Cyclops for leadership even during a period of powerlessness (*The Uncanny X-Men* #201 [Jan. 1986]), all of which underscores the flourishing of multicultural feminism that takes place in the decade. In forging a relationship with Storm respectful of her wisdom and leadership, Pryde represents a new breed of feminist who operates horizontally in how she transgresses boundaries and builds partnerships. When Pryde is introduced in January 1980, the narrative text box surrounding her form intones, "Katherine Pryde is heading home from dance class. She's 13 years old, going on fourteen—and her world is slowly falling apart." (*The Uncanny X-Men* #129). On the surface of the plot, the dissolution of "her world" signals the impending divorce of Pryde's parents, but it rests alongside and thereby resonates with the moment where Pryde first experiences her mutant abilities that will necessarily distance herself from both her parents—divorce or no.[8] As she negotiates a family imploding from all angles, any sense of a unified feminism was crumbling in the real world.

In some ways, the 1980s is a decade stuck between the second-wave of 1970s feminists and the third-wave that arises in the early 1990s. Pryde is both a product and a figure of this liminality. But, what occupies the space between these waves? If Pryde is a 1980s feminist, what does that mean? As Erica E. Townsend-Bell summarizes in a 2012 article reviewing the voices of diverse feminists in the 1970s and 1980s, "The writing of the 1980s focused even greater attention on the question of coalitions, interrogating the basis for assumed unity" (129).[9] This skepticism about the possibility of coalition, joined particularly around the contentious issues of sexuality and race. By decade's end, Kimberlé Crenshaw coined the idea of intersectionality in "Demarginalizing the Intersection of Race and Sex" (1989) to argue for an attention along and valuation of all lines of identity difference, but, as Jasbir Puar notes in a 2011 article, arguments for a nuanced and multifaceted approach to identity in feminism resonated throughout the 1980s (par. 2). Puar pinpoints Audre Lorde's essay, "Age, Race, Class, and Sex: Women Redefining Difference," first delivered as a paper in 1980 and then published in the 1984 collection, *Sister Outsider*, as thinking through these issues (par. 2).

Within this milieu of heightened identity politics, feminist theorists Gloria Anzaldúa and Donna Haraway produce work that seeks to find synthesis across difference. Their desires to think more capaciously about identity and difference lead them both to theorize the liminal identities of the mestiza and the cyborg, respectively, who, like Pryde, are challenged by and themselves challenge theoretical and physical borders and boundaries. Haraway, in "A Cyborg Manifesto," first germinated as a conference paper in 1983 and then developed and published in *Simians, Cyborgs, and Women* (1991) and Anzaldúa in *Borderlands/La Frontera* (1987), question the permeability of social barriers and how identities in-between get marked by them. These thinkers seem apt theoretical companions for a superheroine who actively transgresses supposedly stable physical boundaries. Moreover, not only must Pryde continually fight critiques that undervalue her on the basis of superficial criteria, but she also holds three minority positions as Jewish female mutant. All of these simultaneously ever-present identities embody the concerns of 1980s feminism by putting pressure on monolithic ideas of identity. While this chapter will focus on the intersection of her mutant and female selves, her Jewishness is a rich area that invites further research and reflection.

Pryde's body itself illustrates the difficulty of negotiating multiplicity through the seemingly superficial teenage indecisiveness that surrounds her appearance and code name. In the early years of Pryde's existence, her look radically shifts continuously enough to prompt frustrated fan responses to silly costume changes and proposals for different looks (*Uncanny X-Men* #156 [Apr. 1982]; *Uncanny X-Men* #168 [Apr. 1983]). Printing these proposals in the pages of the comic creates further multiplicity, not less. Although the response to a fan letter in #156 (Apr. 1982) chalks up Pryde's ridiculous costume in #149 (Sep. 1981) to the vagaries of youth, every new look challenges desires for stasis, for two-dimensional characters in one-dimensional looks. While Pryde's personality evolves gradually, her uneven appearance resonates with a decade in flux. Her subversive malleability reaches a fever pitch when she more powerfully manipulates her look to help save the team in *Uncanny X-Men* #157 (May 1982). While she and Nightcrawler are hostages of the alien Shi'ar in *Uncanny X-Men* #155–157, she discovers a Shi'ar device that can change not only her clothes, but also her makeup and hairstyle. Her first transformations are superficial and silly, including a Darth Vader costume that exasperates Nightcrawler (*Uncanny X-Men* #155 [Mar. 1982]). She, however, ultimately wields the device in combination with her powers to change into a ghost-like Phoenix who can disappear through walls, which allows her and Nightcrawler to stop the Earth's destruction by terrifying the Shi'ar (*Uncanny X-Men* #157 [May 1982]). This moment as Phoenix emphasizes how Pryde not only challenges physical structures by penetrating them with her body, but how she breaks down barriers between and within identities.

In extending her transgressive force beyond simply phasing through walls, Pryde employs a feminist worldview that reshapes both her environment and herself. Building from Pryde's potential to capaciously wield her powers, we will now turn to consider Pryde as a feminist blazing the trail against anti-mutant sentiment, starting with the two-issue "Days of Future Past" story-line (*The Uncanny X-Men* #141–142 [Jan.-Feb. 1981]) and opening up across the 1980s. Following this exploration of Pryde as mediator and freedom fighter in concert with her teammates, we will explore how Pryde confronts and rebuilds her own sense of self in *Kitty Pryde and Wolverine*, a six-issue miniseries (Nov. 1984–Apr. 1985). These storylines develop Pryde's complexity while always footnoting her youth, emphasizing her multimodal identity and underscoring the fact that she is a feminist making her way in the 1980s.

"Days of Future Past" complicates Pryde's hitherto immature character by introducing an older version of Pryde, Kate Pryde, who psychically travels back in time and temporarily switches minds with her younger self to help prevent a murder that puts into motion anti-mutant sentiment and creates a dystopian world in Kate's future. Although these two Prydes only encounter each other in passing through time, this evocation of multiple selves echoes Joanna Russ's famed feminist science fiction novel, *The Female Man* (1975). In this text, four characters, who are variations on a theme of each other and shaped by their societal circumstances in their alternate timescapes, meet and reevaluate gender roles in their own worlds based on the experiences of the others. Russ's text, as much rhetoric as it is narrative, parallels her own feminist theorizing, where she suggests that the science fiction genre offers unparalleled opportunities to create well-rounded female characters with complex narrative trajectories.[10] Following Russ's line of reasoning, integrating speculative elements into *The Uncanny X-Men* allows Pryde to ultimately discard the plot offerings and trajectories of a more conventional tale, giving her the freedom to break away from the Brat Pack.

We see such possibility in how the future Pryde inhabits her younger self's form with a particular seriousness. Gone are the up-close reaction shots that generally accompany Pryde's actions. Rather, we see her full-body in profile, running interference to prevent the assassination. With Pryde at the center of the plot, this narrative anticipates and acts as a more progressive, feminist version of James Cameron's *Terminator* (1984).[11] Rather than a son coming back from the future and teaching his mother to have fighting spirit, this comic ignores such twisted heteropatriarchal dynamics by putting a future Pryde at the center of the action, performing a one-to-one swap with herself. Moreover, it is significant that Pryde, who is still so young and who only begins her training as an X-Man right before the temporal swap, is the protagonist in this dystopian future as one of the few surviving X-Men. Despite her status as the newest and youngest member of the team in the present, her survival and leadership role in the future furthers her character's multiplicity while also emphasizing her strength and the accompanying viability of her feminist politics.

But more than just establishing her complexity, this storyline wields Pryde to illustrate the hateful and apocalyptic course of anti-mutant sentiment. Although the X-Men often deal with animosity from humans, this story centralizes the high stakes of this prejudice. Moreover, while this storyline and subsequent ones that evoke this dystopia make future discrimination present,[12] the introduction of the Morlocks, a subterranean community of mutants who hide themselves from humanity on account of their harrowing appearances and powers, in *The Uncanny X-Men* #169 (May 1983) foregrounds the presence and price of discrimination in the present. Pryde involves the X-Men in this narrative when she becomes infected and captured by the Morlocks in *The Uncanny X-Men* #169–171 (May–Jul. 1983) and later kidnapped in *The Uncanny X-Men* #178–179 (Feb.-Mar. 1984). Whether as freedom fighter or captive, Pryde forces the X-Men to engage issues of discrimination.

Pryde's highlighting of these uncomfortable issues, bringing them across the boundaries of the future or the sewers into the forefront of the narrative, further aligns her, in particular, with the work of Anzaldúa in *Borderlands/La Frontera*. While this critical work was both a success when it was published in the late 1980s and remains in the critical consciousness today, AnaLouise Keating, editor of *The Gloria Anzaldúa Reader* (2009), asserts in her introduction that some of the provocative or uncomfortable parts of Anzaldúa's oeuvre remain underexamined (5). In one of these overlooked chapters in *Borderlands*, "*La herencia de Coatlicue*/The *Coatlicue* State,"[13] Anzaldúa explores her mysticism, its connection to her body, and how such a relationship marks her as an outcast:

> I was two or three years old the first time *Coatlicue* visited my psyche, the first time she "devoured" me (and I "fell" into the underworld). By the worried look on my parents' faces I learned early that something was fundamentally wrong with me. When I was older I would look into the mirror, afraid of *mi secreto terrible*, the secret sin I tried to conceal—*la seña*, the mark of the Beast. I was afraid it was in plain sight for all to see. The secret I tried to conceal was that I was not normal, that I was not like the others. I felt alien, I knew I was alien. I was the mutant stoned out of the herd, something deformed with evil inside [64–65].

Anzaldúa's delineation of this phenomenon equates not only to Pryde's own experience of her mutant identity, but also to the harrowing experiences of mutant discrimination in the 1980s that we encounter through Pryde's mediation. In this autobiographical vignette, Anzaldúa describes the negative parental reaction to difference and the embrace of self-hatred, secrecy, and fear that grows out of this initial response by seeking to protect the self from further rejection and retribution on account of this selfhood.

In fact, Anzaldúa's autobiographical snippet here could easily be the back-story of any number of outcast mutants, and the potential consequences of such actions are explored in *New Mutants* #45 (Nov. 1986). In this issue, Pryde befriends a young man named Larry, who's bullied by his school peers and called a mutant on account of his intelligence. Successfully hiding his mutant identity but stressed to the limit by the verbal abuse of his peers, he commits suicide.[14] On the last page of the issue, Pryde delivers the eulogy for Larry, transforming the moment into a public service announcement that attempts to expansively encompass all coalitions of outcasts and pariahs in a call to disavow "the label, the brand, [the] personal 'Scarlet Letter'" that people use to mark and exile each other. We do not see the many bodies that Pryde invokes here in words, aside from her own that she identifies at the beginning of her speech as "a four-eyed, flat-chested, brat, chick, brain, hebe, stuck-up Xavier's snob freak!" However, we do see Pryde's body represented from multiple angles as she delivers her speech at a podium. Both this eulogy and its representation is feminist: Pryde puts her own body on the line as she speaks for multiplicity and inclusion, actively recognizing and making (her) difference visible.[15] Moreover, just like "Days of Future Past" where she's in the center of the fray preventing the murder and thus hopefully quashing future anti-mutant sentiment, right after this speech she springs into action alongside the X-Men in *The Uncanny X-Men* #211–212 (Nov.–Dec. 1986) to fight the Marauders, a team of mutant assassins, who are massacring the Morlocks. In putting her politics into direct action, she incurs a serious injury whereby she cannot become solid matter and remains in a phased state.[16] She eventually heals, but this battle injury resonates with the increasing gravity of radical politics in the latter half of the decade as the AIDS crisis devastates a marginalized populace, who must rally even as their bodies fail them.[17]

Establishing how Pryde functions within the team as a force of feminism, we now must consider how Pryde more personally and bodily operates along the tenuous tenets of 1980s feminism. Haraway's musings on the figure of the cyborg are particularly evocative here, for, in a certain sense, Pryde fulfills many of Haraway's cyborg criteria, which Haraway describes succinctly near the outset of her manifesto: "From another perspective, a cyborg world might be about lived social and bodily realities in which people are not afraid of their joint kinship with animals and machines, not afraid of permanently partial identities and contradictory standpoints" (154). Starting with the two most physical elements in this construct, Pryde has strong alliances with both "animals and machines" that often crucially help her succeed. For example, in the aforementioned "Demon" issue, Pryde employs the technologies of both the Danger Room and the Black Bird jet to defeat her enemy. Her skills supplement her physical prowess in allowing her to dispense with an intruder.

Likewise, during a confrontation with the Brood in *The Uncanny X-Men* #166 (Feb. 1983), a small purple dragon helps save Pryde and becomes her long-time companion and side-kick in future fights when she smuggles it back to Earth with her. In addition to these important kinships that push Pryde's body ever past the bounds of her own flesh, I want to circle back to Pryde herself and ask how her bildungsroman miniseries, *Kitty Pryde and Wolverine*, formally illuminates what it means to be a cyborg feminist and what possibilities it suggests for younger women, who grew up amidst the second-wave of the 1970s, but who came into their own during this following decade.

Although *Kitty Pryde and Wolverine* unsurprisingly features Wolverine, no other X-Men play a sustained role in this six-issue miniseries. Rather, the narrative takes both characters out of the United States as Pryde follows her father to Japan after eavesdropping on a business meeting and realizing he is in trouble with Japanese gangsters (*Kitty Pryde and Wolverine* #1 [Nov. 1984]). Wolverine trails her to Japan, but before he can find her, she's brainwashed by an evil ninja master named Ogun in cahoots with the Japanese gangsters threatening Pryde's father (*Kitty Pryde and Wolverine* #2 [Dec. 1984]). In her brainwashed state, Pryde dons Ogun's demonic facemask and battles Wolverine with expert ninja skill. When he knocks off her mask and is shocked to see her face, she unhesitatingly stabs him through the chest and nearly kills him (*Kitty Pryde and Wolverine* #3 [Jan. 1985]). As he recovers, Wolverine serves as her mentor, training her physically so that she can develop the strength to fully overcome the brainwashing and reclaim her will (*Kitty Pryde and Wolverine* #4 [Feb. 1985]). The final two issues feature Pryde heading back to Tokyo to defeat the gangsters and Ogun (*Kitty Pryde and Wolverine* #5–6 [Mar.-Apr. 1985]).

In these final issues, as she travels to face her foe and thereby test herself, Pryde articulates a new and more nuanced sense of purpose and identity. Although the form of the bildungsroman almost requires this moment of realization and growth, the comic also pushes back against a sense of linear character development through its very covers. In each of the six covers, a vertical line runs down the center, dividing each cover into two halves. In the first cover and a number of the following covers, Pryde's body straddles that divide, emphasizing from the outset and throughout her always transgressive form. As Haraway argues that her manifesto exists as "an argument for pleasure in the confusion of boundaries and for *responsibility* in their construction," these covers illustrate those dynamics as Pryde continually and determinedly confuses boundaries (150). It is not a matter of Pryde learning to do away with that sense of fragmentation, but learning how to responsibly embrace it. In the first issue, Pryde impulsively plunges from Chicago to Tokyo, which is depicted on the cover where half of the page shows each locale. Her distressed facial expression on this first cover recurs on the sixth cover, where again the cover's divide visually cuts her body in half. Here she stands between Ogun and Wolverine, who both penetrate her body with their metal weapons. Given the fierceness of her brainwashed visage in the third cover where she confronts Wolverine and a more determinedly aggressive stance in both the fourth and fifth covers as she trains with Wolverine and then departs to confront Ogun, this sixth cover seems to signal an unfortunate regression.

Yet, what we see here on the sixth cover is not downfall for Pryde, but, rather, a valuing of the initial self that leads Pryde to Tokyo in the first place. In the sixth issue, most of which covers the match-up with Ogun, Pryde's inability to physically carry out the murder of Ogun paradoxically signals her release from Ogun's mental hold as it foregrounds a loyalty to her core values and a retention of her childlike innocence. The last panel of the miniseries makes this point extremely well as it illustrates Pryde in perhaps the most juvenile pose in the story as she, wide-eyed as ever, grins over a huge sundae. Yet, the Pryde who eagerly indulges in ice cream is simultaneously the Pryde who takes to Wolverine's training and hones her battle skills to a fine point. That she can capaciously encompass this multiplicity is part and parcel of what makes her most especially a figure of the genealogy of 1980s feminism.

Even though there's a recursiveness built into the narrative's end, this experience grounds Pryde more fully in her multivalent sense of self. This evolution is most evident in the fifth issue where, in preparing for her faceoff with Ogun, we see her calmly and confidently negotiating both her old mutant powers and her new ninja skills in an easy synthesis. In one panel that spans much of the bottom half of a page, she expertly walks on air above Tokyo in full ninja garb as she describes in the accompanying narrative boxes her powers and how they have opened up a different world for her. In these boxes, she confidently acknowledges her triumphs, doing so in a varied register where the seriousness of how she "slide[s] the molecules of [her] body between" is accompanied by the casual conclusion that this phasing is a "pretty neat trick, huh?" As soon as she safely makes it across the air to the roof of the next skyscraper, the inset panel at the bottom right of the page depicts her partially removing her ninja mask to reveal her youthful visage, visually stressing her multiplicity as she reflects, "I'm glad it's almost over." She is both youthful and mature, klutzy and powerful, nurturing apparent contradictions in order to thrive, embracing "new couplings, new coalitions" as any feminist in Haraway's cyborg vein does (170). Such an expansive embrace is fairly unique in this divisive decade. Her rare posture is illustrated visually in her ability to bridge impossible gulfs, just as feminists in this coalitional spirit attempted to do throughout the 1980s, particularly in anthologies like the fittingly titled, *This Bridge Called My Back* (1981).[18]

Following this key moment is yet another epiphany, another climax of
self-definition that resonates more forcefully off of the pages of the comic and
into the society that produces them. As she boards the Tokyo subway to dispense with Ogun after facing some lower-level threats, she again muses on her
past as she stares at her reflection in the subway window. As she hypothetically
ruminates on the potential paths open to her, her reflection morphs into the
easily relatable wide-eyed past self and then into an action shot of her present
ninja self scaling buildings. Across this apparent chasm of selves, her thoughts
intone, "Would it have been so bad to live a normal ordinary life? Is it too late
to try?! Go to college, meet some guy, have 2.4 kids, live happily ever after.
That's what other women do—lots of them—why not me?! Except—normal
people don't sky-dance." This active eschewing of the "normal" narrative for
"other women" puts pressure on that construct, as she, actively blurring both
reflections by fogging up the window with her hot breath, resolves, "Even without any super-powers, I'll never settle for what society—or my parents—
expects of me." Her action and her thoughts create a *tabula rasa* from which
a more complicated self can emerge.

On the fogged window, she marks her presence with an X as she names
herself: "I'm not a kitty anymore—much as I wish differently—I've grown up.
I'm a cat. And I like the shadows a whole lot more than the daylight. Shadowcat. I like it. Suits me better than Ariel or Sprite, that's for sure." Just as she
previously dispenses with the identities that parents or society lined up for
her, here she rejects previous codenames given to her by fellow teammates and
fashions her own moniker out of the bits and pieces of herself. Discarding
these nominal ties allows her to draw greater strength from within herself, as
is evident during her fight with Ogun where she evokes Shadowcat as an identity solely under her control, completely separate from the girl Ogun brainwashed. In latching onto this name as battle cry, Pryde performs the same
rhetorical moves that Haraway and Anzaldúa do when they theorize the potential of the cyborg and mestiza identities to challenge and overcome the borders
and boundaries that try to marginalize these subject positions.

Part of how Pryde can so complexly operate as an agent of 1980s feminism
is due to her existence as a popular, recurring character in a monthly comic
title. The import of such stability in developing a multivalent, transgressive
figure can be seen if we look to underground feminist comics production in
the period. Given page limitations in the feminist series where many female
artists published, the ability to develop a character arc was circumscribed,
and many artists produced timely one-off vignettes for their contributions.[19]
By developing over the course of the decade, Pryde can be more than a flat
character and can rally for multiple rights, calling on her various collectivi-
ties as needed. She acts as a complex, multifaceted character who does not

simply regurgitate feminist politics, but who actively engages in feminist practice and continually subverts patriarchal expectations with her transgressive
body.

NOTES

1. Fawaz scrutinizes how the cover of *X-Men* #101 (Oct. 1976) illustrates Grey's alienation from her teammates as her empowered rise out of the water threatens them with
drowning (374–376).

2. This pattern where the white woman takes from the woman of color echoes
throughout woman of color feminism critical of the tunnel-vision dynamics of 1970s
feminism and seeking to create a more equitable collectivity. In "Age, Race, Class, and
Sex: Women Redefining Difference" (1980), Audre Lorde spells out how women of
color face the burden of always having to make themselves legible to white feminists:
"In other words, it is the responsibility of the oppressed to teach the oppressors their
mistakes. I am responsible for educating teachers who dismiss my children's culture in
school. Black and Third World people are expected to educate white people as to our
humanity. Women are expected to educate men. Lesbians and gay men are expected to
educate the heterosexual world. The oppressors maintain their position and evade responsibility for their own actions. There is a constant drain of energy which might be better
used in redefining ourselves and devising realistic scenarios for altering the present and
constructing the future" (114–115).

3. In addition to *Pretty in Pink* (1986), the suburbs of Chicago or Chicago itself
appears in a number of Hughes' other hit films like *Sixteen Candles* (1984), *The Breakfast
Club* (1985), *Ferris Bueller's Day Off* (1986). Pryde's suburban background also echoes
the "all-white suburban cast" of the original X-Men, as opposed to the new international
recruits introduced in *Giant-Size X-Men* #1 (May 1975) (Fawaz 363).

4. Although, retrospectively, it makes sense to understand Pryde alongside the Brat
Pack as the popular figure of 1980s adolescence, she actually predates the grouping by a
number of years. The first Brat Pack film, *The Outsiders*, was released in 1983, and the
concept of the Brat Pack was defined in a 1985 *New York* magazine article.

5. By contrast, Pryde's romantic attachment to Colossus ends in failure as he becomes
unwillingly attracted to another and breaks up with Pryde in *The Uncanny X-Men* #183
(Jul. 1984).

6. With this argument, Bleach proposes a more nuanced version of Susan Faludi's
idea of backlash culture articulated in *Backlash: The Undeclared War Against American
Women* (1991) whereby pop-culture's post-feminism does not mean the defeat of feminism, but that there can be feminism woven into a narrative that may, ultimately, choose
post-feminist trajectories (Bleach 27).

7. José Esteban Muñoz's off-the-cuff assessment of the X-Men as "social pariahs" in
Cruising Utopia (2009) resonates here and fruitfully suggests the space for more queerly
theoretical considerations of these characters (130).

8. The use of "alongside " here resonates with Eve Kosofsky Sedgwick's non-dualistic
approach to criticism that she lays out in *Touching Feeling* (8–9).

9. For a comprehensive overview of 1980s feminism, see also Chela Sandoval's "U.S.
Third World Feminism" in *Methodology of the Oppressed*.

10. See Russ's essay, "What Can a Heroine Do? or Why Women Can't Write."

11. Certainly, scholars have argued for a feminist understanding of the *Terminator* franchise through Sarah Connor's gradual empowerment. To read interpretations along these lines, see Diana Dominguez's "'It's Not Easy Being a Cast Iron Bitch'," Jeffrey A. Brown's "Gender and the Action Heroine," and Donald Palumbo's "The Monomyth in James Cameron's *The Terminator*." Noted queer scholar Jonathan Goldberg performs a reading along LGBT lines in "Recalling Totalities."

12. Throughout the 1980s, various storylines pick back up on this dystopian future as Rachel Summers time-travels backwards in "The Past of... Future Days" (*The Uncanny X-Men* #184, Aug. 1984) and an extremely powerful mutant-hunting nemesis, Nimrod, follows Summers back to try to exterminate all mutants in that present timescape, starting in *The Uncanny X-Men* #191 (Mar. 1985).

13. In *The Gloria Anzaldúa Reader*, Keating contrasts this chapter from *Borderlands/ La Frontera* with the frequently anthologized "*La conciencia de la mestiza*/Towards a Mestiza Consciousness." Of "*La herencia de Coatlicue*/The *Coatlicue* State," she argues: "Given its provocative linkages between spirituality, sexuality, revisionary myth, and psychic experience, it's not surprising that scholars rarely examine 'La herencia de Coatlicue.' However, these issues were crucial to Anzaldúa herself and represent some of the most innovative, visionary dimensions of her work" (5). To not attend to these insights is to miss the heart of Anzaldúa's theory.

14. The closeted nature and precarity of mutant life, highlighted by this teenage suicide, necessarily resonates with the struggle against discrimination faced by lesbian and gay youth in the 1980s. As Eve Sedgwick asserts in "How to Bring Your Kids Up Gay," originally composed for a 1989 Modern Language Association panel, "it's always open season on gay kids" (155).

15. By naming herself with slurs, Pryde embraces the fraught nature of her identity. Similarly, both Lorde and Anzaldúa often cataloged their various identities, refusing to disassociate from unpopular positions or privilege one identity above the others. Like Pryde confronts an audience with her in-your-face catalog, so does Lorde: "Perhaps for some of you here today, I am the face of one of your fears. Because I am woman, because I am Black, because I am lesbian, because I am myself—a Black woman warrior poet doing my work—come to ask you, are you doing yours?" (41–42). In "The New Mestiza Nation," Anzaldúa highlights how the mestiza continually negotiates and recognizes all identities: "Using *mestiza* as an umbrella term means acknowledging that certain aspects of identity don't disappear, aren't assimilated or repressed when they are not in the foreground" (211).

16. Although this injury takes her out of the X-Men line-up for the rest of the 1980s, her departure nearly coincides with the joining of some new members, including the heroines, Psylocke in *The Uncanny X-Men* #213 (Jan. 1987) and Dazzler in *The Uncanny X-Men* #214 (Feb. 1987), helping ensure that the X-Men retain a diverse and deep roster.

17. See Eve Kofosky Sedgwick's "Interlude, Pedagogic" in *Touching Feeling* (2003) for a pithy consideration of the coalitional possibilities among different marginalized bodies that arose in political organizing during the AIDS crisis.

18. Other important anthologies in this 1980s coalitional feminist vein include *But Some of Us Are Brave* (1982) and *Home Girls* (1983). The formation of Kitchen Table, a woman of color activist press, in 1980, served as a home for some of this work. The

press itself was founded on the principles of coalition as Barbara Smith describes in a short essay: "...most people of color have chosen to work in their separate groups when they do media or other projects. We were saying that as women, feminists, and lesbians of color we had experiences and work to do in common, although we also had our differences" (11). After *This Bridge* struggled with its first publisher, Persephone Press, a white feminist venture that foundered, Kitchen Table Press coordinated the second edition and rerelease of the book.

19. Two well-known exceptions to this are Aline Kominsky-Crumb and Alison Bechdel, both of whom are extensively analyzed in Hillary Chute's landmark *Graphic Women* (2010), one of the first critical texts in comics studies to make female artists the primary focus. Over the course of her career, Kominsky-Crumb produced many autobiographically-inflected comics of different lengths that satirized herself as The Bunch, which have been collected in *Love That Bunch* (1990) and *Need More Love* (2007). Bechdel, who began her career after the downturn in underground comics production and did not publish primarily in those venues, began drawing *Dykes to Watch Out For* as a strip with a cast of recurring characters and story arcs in the mid 1980s and was successfully syndicated in many newspapers.

WORKS CITED

Anzaldúa, Gloria. *Borderlands/La Frontera: The New Mestiza*. Third Edition. San Francisco: Aunt Lute Books, 2007. Print.

_____. *The Gloria Anzaldúa Reader*. Ed. AnaLouise Keating. Durham: Duke University Press Books, 2009. Print.

_____. "The New Mestiza Nation: A Multicultural Movement." *The Gloria Anzaldúa Reader*. Ed. AnaLouise Keating. Durham: Duke University Press Books, 2009. 203–216. Print.

Bleach, Anthony C. "Postfeminist Cliques?: Class, Postfeminism, and the Molly Ringwald-John Hughes Films." *Cinema Journal* 49.3 (2010): 24–44. Print.

Blum, David. "Hollywood's Brat Pack." *New York*. 10 June 1985.

The Breakfast Club. Dir. and screenplay by John Hughes. Universal Studios, 1985.

Brown, Jeffrey A. "Gender and the Action Heroine: Hardbodies and the 'Point of No Return.'" *Cinema Journal* 35.3 (1996): 52–71. Print.

Chute, Hillary L. *Graphic Women: Life Narrative and Contemporary Comics*. New York: Columbia University Press, 2010. Print.

Claremont, Chris (w) and Alan Davis (a). "Psylocke." *The Uncanny X-Men* #213 (Jan. 1987). New York: Marvel Comics. Print.

Claremont, Chris (w) and Allen Milgrom (a). "Lies." *Kitty Pryde and Wolverine* #1 (Nov. 1984). New York: Marvel Comics. Print.

_____ and _____. "Terror." *Kitty Pryde and Wolverine* #2 (Dec. 1984). New York: Marvel Comics. Print.

_____ and _____. "Death." *Kitty Pryde and Wolverine* #3 (Jan. 1985). New York: Marvel Comics. Print.

_____ and _____. "Rebirth." *Kitty Pryde and Wolverine* #4 (Feb. 1985). New York: Marvel Comics. Print.

_____ and _____. "Courage." *Kitty Pryde and Wolverine* #5 (Mar. 1985). New York: Marvel Comics. Print.

_____ and _____. "Honor." *Kitty Pryde and Wolverine* #6 (Apr. 1985). New York: Marvel Comics. Print.

Claremont, Chris (w) and Barry Windsor Smith (a). "With Malice Toward All." *The Uncanny X-Men* #214 (Feb. 1987). New York: Marvel Comics. Print.

Claremont, Chris (w) and Dave Cockrum (a). "The Doomsmith Scenario!" *The Uncanny X-Men* #94 (Aug. 1975). New York: Marvel Comics. Print.

_____ and _____. "And the Dead Shall Bury the Living." *The Uncanny X-Men* #149 (Sep. 1981). New York: Marvel Comics. Print.

Claremont, Chris (w), Dave Cockrum (a), and Bob Wiacek (a). "First Blood." *The Uncanny X-Men* #155 (Mar. 1982). New York: Marvel Comics. Print.

_____, _____, and _____. "Pursuit!" *The Uncanny X-Men* #156 (Apr. 1982). New York: Marvel Comics. Print.

_____, _____, and _____. "Hide 'n' Seek!" *The Uncanny X-Men* #157 (May 1982). New York: Marvel Comics. Print.

Claremont, Chris (w) and John Byrne (a). "God Spare the Child...." *The Uncanny X-Men* #129 (Jan. 1980). New York: Marvel Comics. Print.

_____ and _____. "Dazzler." *The Uncanny X-Men* #130 (Feb. 1980). New York: Marvel Comics. Print.

_____ and _____. "Elegy." *The Uncanny X-Men* #138 (Oct. 1980). New York: Marvel Comics. Print.

_____ and _____. "Days of Future Past." *The Uncanny X-Men* #141 (Jan. 1981). New York: Marvel Comics. Print.

_____ and _____. "Mind out of Time!" *The Uncanny X-Men* #142 (Feb. 1981). New York: Marvel Comics. Print.

_____ and _____. "Demon." *The Uncanny X-Men* #143 (Mar. 1981). New York: Marvel Comics. Print.

Claremont, Chris (w) and Jackson Guice (a). "We Were Only Foolin.'" *New Mutants* #45 (Nov. 1986). New York: Marvel Comics. Print.

Claremont, Chris (w), Jim Sherman (a), and Bob McLeod (a). "X-Men Minus One." *The Uncanny X-Men* #151 (Nov. 1981). New York: Marvel Comics. Print.

Claremont, Chris (w) and John Romita, Jr. (a). "Hell Hath No Fury...." *The Uncanny X-Men* #178 (Feb. 1984). New York: Marvel Comics. Print.

Claremont, Chris (w), John Romita, Jr. (a), and Bret Blevins (a). "Massacre." *The Uncanny X-Men* #211 (Nov. 1986). New York: Marvel Comics. Print.

Claremont, Chris (w), John Romita, Jr. (a), and Dan Green (a). "What Happened to Kitty?" *The Uncanny X-Men* #179 (Mar. 1984). New York: Marvel Comics. Print.

_____, _____, and _____. "He'll Never Make Me Cry." *The Uncanny X-Men* #183 (Jul. 1984). New York: Marvel Comics. Print.

_____, _____, and _____. "The Past... of Future Days." *The Uncanny X-Men* #184 (Aug. 1984). New York: Marvel Comics. Print.

_____, _____, and _____. "Raiders of the Lost Temple!" *The Uncanny X-Men* #191 (Mar. 1985). New York: Marvel Comics. Print.

Claremont, Chris (w) and Paul Smith (a). "Live Free or Die!" *The Uncanny X-Men* #166 (Feb. 1983). New York: Marvel Comics. Print.

_____ and _____. "The Goldilocks Syndrome! (or: Who's Been Sleeping in My Head?)" *The Uncanny X-Men* #167 (Mar. 1983). New York: Marvel Comics. Print.

_____ and _____. "Professor Xavier is a Jerk!" *The Uncanny X-Men* #168 (Apr. 1983). New York: Marvel Comics. Print.

_____ and _____. "Catacombs." *The Uncanny X-Men* #169 (May 1983). New York: Marvel Comics. Print.

_____ and _____. "Dancin' in the Dark." *The Uncanny X-Men* #170 (June 1983). New York: Marvel Comics. Print.

_____ and _____. "To Have and Have Not." *The Uncanny X-Men* #173 (Sep. 1983). New York: Marvel Comics. Print.

Claremont, Chris (w) and Rick Leonardi (a). "Duel." *The Uncanny X-Men* #201 (Jan. 1986). New York: Marvel Comics. Print.

_____ and _____. "The Last Run." *The Uncanny X-Men* #212 (Dec. 1986). New York: Marvel Comics. Print.

Claremont, Chris (w) and Walt Simonson (a). "Rogue." *The Uncanny X-Men* #171 (Jul. 1983). New York: Marvel Comics. Print.

Crenshaw, Kimberlé. "Demarginalizing the Intersection of Race and Sex: A Black Feminist Critique of Antidiscrimination Doctrine, Feminist Theory, and Antiracist Politics." *The University of Chicago Legal Forum Volume: Feminism in the Law: Theory, Practice and Criticism.* (1989): 139–167. Print.

Dominguez, Diana. "'It's Not Easy Being a Cast Iron Bitch': Sexual Difference and the Female Action Hero." *Reconstruction* 5.4 (2005). Print.

Faludi, Susan. *Backlash: The Undeclared War Against American Women.* New York: Random House, 1991. Print.

Fawaz, Ramzi. "'Where No X-Man Has Gone Before!' Mutant Superheroes and the Cultural Politics of Popular Fantasy in Postwar America." *American Literature* 83.2 (2011): 355–388. Print.

Ferris Bueller's Day Off. Dir. and screenplay by John Hughes. Paramount Pictures, 1986.

Goldberg, Jonathan. "Recalling Totalities: The Mirrored Stages of Arnold Schwarzenegger." *Differences* 4.1 (1992): 172–204. Print.

Haraway, Donna J. "A Cyborg Manifesto: Science, Technology, and Socialist Feminism in the Late Twentieth Century." *Simians, Cyborgs, and Women: The Reinvention of Nature.* 1st ed. New York: Routledge, 1991. 149–181. Print.

Hull, Gloria T., Patricia Bell Scott, and Barbara Smith, eds. *All the Women are White, All the Blacks are Men, But Some of Us Are Brave: Black Women's Studies.* New York: Feminist Press, 1982. Print.

Kominsky-Crumb, Aline. *Love That Bunch.* First Edition. Fantagraphics Books, 1990. Print.

_____. *Need More Love: A Graphic Memoir.* M Q Publications, 2007. Print.

Lorde, Audre. "Age, Race, Class, and Sex: Women Redefining Difference." *Sister Outsider.* New York: Ten Speed Press, 1984. 114–123. Print.

_____. "The Transformation of Silence into Language and Action." *Sister Outsider.* New York: Ten Speed Press, 1984. 40–44. Print.

Moraga, Cherríe L., and Gloria Anzaldúa, eds. *This Bridge Called My Back: Writings by Radical Women of Color.* First Edition. Watertown, MA: Persephone Press, 1981. Web. 8 Feb. 2011.

Muñoz, José Esteban. *Cruising Utopia: The Then and There of Queer Futurity.* New York: NYU Press, 2009. Print.

The Outsiders. Dir. by Lewis John Carlino. Orion Pictures, 1983.

Palumbo, Donald. "The Monomyth in James Cameron's *The Terminator*: Sarah as Monomythic Heroine." *The Journal of Popular Culture* 41.3 (2008): 413–427. Print.

Pretty in Pink. Screenplay by John Hughes. Dir. Howard Deutch. Paramount Pictures, 1986.

Puar, Jasbir. "'I Would Rather Be a Cyborg Than a Goddess': Intersectionality, Assemblage, and Affective Politics." *transversal* (2011). Web.

Russ, Joanna. *The Female Man*. New York: Bantam Books, 1975. Print.

_____. "What Can a Heroine Do? or Why Women Can't Write." *To Write Like a Woman: Essays in Feminism and Science Fiction*. Bloomington: Indiana University Press, 1995. 79–93. Print.

Sandoval, Chela. "U.S. Third World Feminism: Differential Social Movement I." *Methodology of the Oppressed*. Minneapolis, MN: University of Minnesota Press, 2000. 41–64. Print.

Sedgwick, Eve Kosofsky. "How to Bring Your Kids Up Gay: The War on Effeminate Boys." *Tendencies*. Durham: Duke University Press, 1993. 154–164. Print.

_____. *Touching Feeling: Affect, Pedagogy, Performativity*. Durham: Duke University Press, 2003. Print.

Sixteen Candles. Dir. and screenplay by John Hughes. Universal Pictures, 1984.

Smith, Barbara. "A Press of Our Own Kitchen Table: Women of Color Press." *Frontiers: A Journal of Women Studies* 10.3 (1989): 11–13. Print.

_____, ed. *Home Girls: A Black Feminist Anthology*. New York: Kitchen Table—Women of Color Press, 1983. Print.

Terminator. Dir. and screenplay by James Cameron. Orion Pictures, 1984.

Townsend-Bell, Erica E. "Writing the Way to Feminism." *Signs* (Autumn 2012): 127–152. Print.

Wein, Len (w) and Dave Cockrum (a). *Giant-Size X-Men* #1 (May 1975). New York: Marvel Comics. Print.

Days of Future Past:
Segregation, Oppression and Technology in X-Men and America

CLANCY SMITH

The year is 2013. Amid the despair and ruin of the once glorious city of New York, the last remaining X-Men gather together for one final, desperate attempt to save a world on the brink of nuclear annihilation. In the shadows of a citywide concentration camp, a wheelchair-bound man emerges from the shadows, the leader of the X-Men: Erik Lehnsherr, the mutant known as "Magneto." It has all come to this. He whispers, gravely, "If there were an alternative... *any* alternative ... we would take it. But if we do nothing, by tomorrow, the world will be at war. And the day after tomorrow ... the world will be dead" (Claremont, "Days").

In 1981's "Days of Future Past," one of the most iconic storylines in the long history of the X-Men franchise and one of the most celebrated tales in comics history, writer Chris Claremont and artist John Byrne show us a glimpse of the future that awaits the X-Men should Professor Charles Xavier fail to prevent a war between humanity and mutantkind. It provides a definitive answer to the questions: what if the X-Men lost? What sort of world would be created if humanity's hatred and fear compelled them to commit the most horrific atrocities against mutantkind? Claremont creates a dystopian future where those few mutants who survive are confined to concentration camps in a world governed by the iron fist of an armada of robotic, mutant-hunting Sentinels created by humanity to provide the final solution to the mutant "problem."

Claremont presents two parallels narratives: the present (1981) and the future (2013). In the present, tensions simmer between the United States government and the perceived mutant "threat" as Xavier seeks to stem the rising tide of anti-mutant legislation at a Congressional hearing. In the future, the Sentinel regime threatens to instigate a nuclear response from what little remains of humanity, heralding the potential end of all life on earth. Procuring advanced technology, the last vestiges of the X-Men, led by their one-time antagonist Magneto, send Kate Pryde's consciousness back in time to inhabit the body of her younger self in a desperate effort to avert an assassination by the Brotherhood of Evil Mutants at the very same Congressional hearing Xavier is attending. The Brotherhood's attack, the catalyst for increased aggression towards mutantkind, culminates in the dark future which our heroes experience in 2013.

Rather than exploring this theme through the eyes of one of the more established and iconic X-Men characters, Claremont makes a shrewd and ingenious choice: we get to see this narrative of horror unfold through the eyes of the innocent. Kitty Pryde, a wide-eyed neophyte, joins the team just prior to the events of "Days of Future Past." Naïve, idealistic and full of hope, the use of Pryde as the protagonist of the tale adds another dimension to Claremont's exploration of this dystopian future by directly juxtaposing Pryde's hopeful optimism as a child, and the jaded, battle-worn "Kate" Pryde of that future. We come to see the death of innocence itself.

Zeitgeist: Times They Are a-Changin'

"Come senators, congressmen / please heed the call / don't stand in the doorway / don't block up the hall / for he that gets hurt / will be he who has stalled / there's a battle outside / and it is ragin' / it'll soon shake your windows / and rattle your walls / for the times they are a-changin'" (Dylan, 1964). Written thirteen years prior to the publication of "Days of Future Past," Bob Dylan's iconic lyrics captured the zeitgeist of the age, a testament to the rapidly changing American political landscape. Chris Claremont was eighteen years old when it written, beginning his degree in political theory at Bard College[1] in upstate New York in a socio-political atmosphere unlike any our nation had seen before. His background in political theory is manifest throughout every page of his dystopian vision in "Days of Future Past," combining relentless action with profound reflections on a variety of themes: otherness, discrimination[2] and technology. Claremont's run with the series, beginning in 1975 and lasting until 1991, breathed new life into this alternative corner of the Marvel universe and brought the X-Men into their own[3] as one of the best-selling comic franchises of all time.[4]

Although the height of the Civil Rights movement had passed by the time of its publication, the title, itself, "Days of Future Past," may be read as not only a reflection of the ongoing struggle for freedom and equality but, too, an ominous warning against the threat of the past repeating itself in the future. The concentration camps of Germany and the Japanese internment camps in America, are reflected in the dystopian future of Claremont's vision. And the battle in the Senate, the pivotal moment in the narrative, echoes the dire warning of Dylan's song as Senator Kelly stands in the way of equality, and the "battle," indeed, comes to him; the walls of the courthouse are quite literally "rattled" to the ground. It is a testament to the enduring struggle of any minority group fighting for equal rights within a legal system beyond their control. It is a timeless theme that provides *X-Men* with its timeless appeal. As Claremont says, "*X-Men* has always been about finding your place in a society that doesn't want you " (Claremont interview).

Claremont, though born in London, was only three years old when he came to America in 1953. The political landscape around his early years saw rapid shifts in both race relations and advances in technology. Claremont's America saw the heights of the Civil Rights movement: the legislation enacted throughout the late 50s and early 60s aimed at the dissolution of racial segregation in America, bolstered by the march on Washington and King's iconic "I Have a Dream Speech" in 1963. So, too, did it see the horrors of hatred and racism that accompanied this battle, the assassination of Malcolm X in 1965, the Watts Riots, and the assassination of King in 1968. Beyond racial discrimination and violence, the years leading up to the publication of "Days of Future Past" saw both the shootings at Kent State in 1970 and the assassination of Harvey Milk, the first openly gay politician to be elected in the state of California, in 1978.

At the same time, technology began to rapidly advance in terrifying and liberating ways. Space exploration took off in 1957 with the Russian launch of Sputnik and a year later with the founding of NASA. The world was becoming increasingly mechanized as computer and entertainment technology were becoming more affordable, entering into nearly every American household. Concurrently, nuclear weaponry continued to proliferate as east and west dug in for a long, cold war.

The year "Days of Future Past" was published was the same year Ronald Reagan became the 40th president of the United States. Reagan inherited the struggles of his predecessors, having to face both enduring discrimination and advances in technology that continued to push us to the brink of a nuclear war with the Soviet Union. Reagan's relationship with issues of racial discrimination was immensely complex and anything but clear. Though he was frequently cited as being a strong opponent of any form of racial discrimination in public addresses,[5] historians have often associated some of his legislative policies as a subtle, subversive[6] form of racial discrimination shrouded in the language of economics.[7] To what degree these specific events contributed to Claremont's "Days of Future Past" is a matter of speculation. What is *not* as speculative is the zeitgeist in which Claremont was raised and his degree in political theory, demonstrating both an interest in and ability to engage with, the preeminent socio-political issues of his age.

Otherness: Fighting for a World That Hates and Fears Them

No matter how valiantly the X-Men fight, ultimate victory ever eludes them. In essence they are undone by the very terms of their purpose, the very bind of their existence: they fight for a world that *hates* and that *fears* them. The greatest enemy the X-Men face doesn't wear a mask or a gaudy costume: their enemy *is* hate and their enemy *is* fear. Until the means of perpetuating hate and fear are dissolved, the X-Men can never fully achieve the victory they seek. As *X-Men* editor Marc Powers notes, "there's a certain darkness, because the X-Men's true enemy is hate, which is something that's never going to go away" (Claremont interview).

What *is* the "Other?" Traditionally, on the most fundamental level, the Other is all that is *not myself.* It is the resistance I encounter from outside myself that demarcates where *I* end and where what is *not myself* begins. As such, it plays a pivotal role in how I define myself, seeing myself as I *am*, seeing myself as what I am *not* (I am not the Other), and, important to our investigation here, seeing myself *through the eyes* of this Other, coming to know myself as I'm seen by the Other and attempting to reconcile that with how I see myself.[8] For some, encountering the Other is necessary for growth and development, for it is only through productive dialogue that we, together, may move towards heightened realms of truth and understanding.[9] For some, the Other represents an obstacle that must be overcome, a hindrance that foils my plans and threatens my subjectivity. For the villains in many of Claremont's X-Men stories, mutants are seen as this sort of obstacle, a challenge to the hegemony of mankind, and the individuation of each, specific representative of that mutantkind are reduced to the terms of bare Otherness. Senator Kelly does not see a difference between the X-Men and Brotherhood, hero and villain, simply the blanketing Otherness that represents, in his mind, a genuine threat to his own kind's hold on power. The term "freaks" (Claremont, "Mind"), for example, used by Senator Kelly to describe mutants, only has meaning at all in so far as it measured against what he perceives as "normal."

What constitutes normativity is in large part culturally conditioned but always reflects the traits of this power class. These are the traits of what Martin

Luther King, Jr. called "the power majority" ("Letter"), forming what scholars like George Yancy have called "the transcendental norm" (3) of human experience, against which all else is judged, specifically, the traits that power minorities do not share with those of the majority: "whiteness," "maleness," etc. The power majority utilizes a two-fold method of ensuring their enduring dominion over society: they use legislative means to ensure the Other has no say in the governing of that society, and they proliferate the belief that the Other is *essentially* (by their nature) somehow inferior. Both tactics played key roles in the struggle for Civil Rights throughout Claremont's life. King responded to segregation statutes by defining them as unjust laws, "a code that a numerical or power majority group compels a minority group to obey but does not make binding on itself. This is difference made legal" ("Letter"). The proliferation of a false and artificially constructed self-identity, what scholars often refer to as an "imago," an "an elaborate distorted image" (Yancy, 110), helped convince minorities of their essential inferiority. This sense of inferiority was both in the eyes of the majority (seeing the Other as essentially inferior) and, far more devastating, instilling a sense of inferiority in the minorities themselves whenever they see themselves through the eyes of the majority. As Frantz Fanon once noted, "not only must the black man be black; he must be black in relation to the white man" (Fanon, 110). As Claremont notes, "The X-Men are hated, feared and despised collectively by humanity for no other reason than that they are mutants. So what we have here, intended or not, is a book that is about racism, bigotry and prejudice" (Godoski).

The imago for mutantkind seems clear enough: mutants are dangerous, criminal, and threaten mankind through their very existence. The proliferation of that imago, the engine for the perpetuation of the hate and fear that the X-Men fight so desperately to overcome, can be seen throughout "Days of Future Past." Consider, for example, the language that humans use in referencing mutants throughout Claremont's tale. During the pivotal courtroom scene, as Senator Kelly delivers his pitch for mutant registration to his fellow Congressmen, we hear whispers from the reporters and camera crew as they discuss "muties" (Claremont, "Days"),[10] a derogatory terms for "mutants" (even more so than the word "mutant," itself, which contains plenty of negative connotations without any further help). When the Brotherhood bursts into the courtroom, Senator Kelly responds angrily by saying "this is monstrous! How *dare* you freaks turn the United States Senate into a battlefield?! How dare you threaten me! Marshals, arrest those ... people!" (*The Uncanny X-Men*, #142 [Feb. 1981]). The word "people" may as well have been spat upon the courtroom floor and the term "freak" is aimed both at the Brotherhood and the X-Men who arrive just in time to foil the Brotherhood's assault. The Senator is incapable of making such distinctions, despite Storm's protest that "mutants, like people, are both good and bad. You would do well to remember that, Senator, before you seek to condemn us *all*" (Claremont, "Mind"). Kelly sees mutants in their pure Otherness, they are *all* alike, essentially villainous, and universally seen as antagonists to the human race. Rather than demonstrating his gratitude towards the X-Men for saving his life, he responds: "if there were no mutants, period, my life wouldn't have been threatened at all" (Claremont, "Mind").

Consider, too, the heart of his speech in favor of mutant registration. He says, "there is no place for *ordinary* men and women" in world of mutants who have "abilities which set them apart—some would say *above*—the rest of humanity" (Claremont, "Days"). Humanity fears allowing the Other the recognition the Other desires, for if left free, the Other may rise past humanity, enslave it, perhaps, as Kelly fears, even destroy it. In short, he fears allowing mutantkind to do to humanity what humanity is already doing to mutantkind.

The X-Men, as ever, fight for a world that hates and fears them. But why do this? The X-Men and the Brotherhood share the same goal: a world where mutants live free from the fear of human persecution. The Brotherhood believe they can force this outcome by teaching humanity to fear mutants *even more* than they currently do, to instill so much fear that humanity would never dare to challenge mutant autonomy. This is why Xavier is key to the X-Men's project, not simply because he was the founder and former leader of the group but, far more importantly, his vision, which is referred to as "Xaver's dream" throughout the long run of the comic, is uniquely situated against the Brotherhood's agenda. If hatred is based on this fear of Otherness, to increase that fear (as the Brotherhood plans) will only increase the hatred that is fueled by it. To dissolve the fear that founds humanity's hatred, for Xavier, is the only way to achieve mutant equality, and this requires means directly contrary to the Brotherhood's reliance on forceful coercion.

The parallel with King's role in the Civil Rights movement is immediately clear and profoundly compelling. Acting as the "gadfly" ("Letter"), a term he took from Plato's iconic protagonist Socrates, King's project was to shake America free from the passive acceptance of such imagos and the unacceptable status quo of inequality. King's method was one of nonviolence, not wanting to add to the false imago of the essential brutishness, aggressiveness and irrationality of black Americans, he appealed, instead, to compassion, education and civil disobedience in the idiom of one of his greatest influences, Mahatma Gandhi. As Andrew Godoski notes, like King, Xavier does not advocate proactive violence for it "only serves to further divide humans and mutants and drive the fear that brings about his brethren's persecution. That's not to say he doesn't believe in violence, but only when necessary and usually in the form of protecting humanity from other mutants seeking to harm it" (Godoski). Consider the team that Claremont assembles for the story, itself a vibrant display of diversity.[11] For the most part, their powers are uniquely designed for non-lethal combat.[12] Only Wolverine violates this pattern: his entire comportment, from his training to his razor sharp adamantium claws, is designed, specifically, to take lives, which, in *"Days of Future Past,"* becomes a point of a great contention in the narrative. Storm (the field leader of the X-Men at this point in the narrative) not only insists that the only acceptable form of violence is the defense of Senator Kelly,[13] but she even prevents her ally from taking the life of one of the Brotherhood in the ensuing melee. A few moments later, Storm, again, confronts Wolverine, his claws thirsting for blood: "sheathe them—or use them on *me*... you should not need your claws except in the most extreme of situations and most powerful of foes" (Claremont, "Mind").

Thus, in sharp contrast to the Brotherhood's agenda, Xavier quite closely followed the non-violent path of King who dreamed of a world where "the sons of former slaves and the sons of former slave owners will be able to sit down together at the table of brotherhood" ("I Have a Dream"). A world where "children will one day live in a nation where they will not be judged by the color of their skin but by the content of their character" ("I Have a Dream"). Indeed, the association between King and Xavier is anything but coincidental, as Claremont himself notes in an interview with Alec Foege for *New York* magazine: "To use Martin Luther King's idea," says Claremont, "judge them by the content of their character, not the color of their skin." He pauses. "Or the number of arms they have" (Claremont Interview).

Concentration Camps: The X-Men's Dark Future, Our Dark Past

As the situation in Congress continues to deteriorate, Moira MacTaggert turns to Xavier, whispering ominously, "registration of mutants today, gas chambers tomorrow" (Claremont, "Days"). Xavier, however, knows how to combat this discrimination: "be charitable, Moira," he replies, "he's scared. We must teach him that his fear is unfounded" (Claremont, "Days"). Xavier has lived through the Second World War and knows all too well the horrors of an authoritarian power that demands the annihilation of the Other. The horror of the mutant holocaust comes to mirror our own dark past, as shades of Auschwitz and the memory of Japanese internment on American soil are visible on every page of Claremont's foreboding dystopia.

In the future portion of the narrative, the scene opens with our protagonist, Kate Pryde, a jaded, hardened warrior making her way through New York City, now barely more than an abandoned wasteland, doubling as a citywide concentration camp for those few remaining mutants. "...A slum abandoned, derelict, dying—much like ... the country, the planet around it" (Claremont, "Days"). The decay of the future city parallels the decay of our protagonist herself.[14] Every member of society is forced to have a single letter emblazoned on their clothing, "'H' for baseline human—clean of mutant genes, allowed to breed," "'A' for anomalous human—a normal person possessing mutant genetic potential, forbidden to breed," and "'M,' for mutant, the bottom of the heap, made pariahs and outcasts by the Mutant Control Act of 1988" (Claremont, "Days"). The use of such branding was likely a calculated move by Claremont, reflecting the badges emblazed on the prisoners' clothes in Nazi concentration camps.[15] Humans and mutants alike become enslaved to the technology forged of humanity's hatred and fear.

The parallels between the mutant concentration camps in "Days of Future Past" and the concentration and internment camps during World War II have profound thematic ramifications for this story and the X-Men franchise as a whole. Consider, for example, the X-Men's most iconic antagonist, the mutant known as "Magneto." Before he became "Magneto,"[16] Erik Lehnsherr was born to a relatively affluent German Jewish family just prior to World War II.[17] Ultimately, Erik's entire family was slaughtered by the Nazi regime and "Magneto" was born, forged in the fires of bigotry and hatred unlike anything the world had seen before. It can be argued that Magneto's entire motivational spectrum stems from his early experiences with Nazi occupation and his desire to ensure that mutantkind does not suffer the same fate as his Jewish people. As such, his role as "villain" has become increasingly problematized. No longer numbered among the sociopathic, costumed lunatics clamoring for power and world domination for the sheer, one-dimensional glory of villainy, Magneto is the product of mankind's ultimate moment of hatred and intolerance. He embarks upon a quest to ensure, at any cost, that history does not repeat itself with the incarceration or eradication of mutants, that the days of the future do not come to repeat the days of the past. Magneto, born of these horrors, adopts a more cynical attitude towards the potential realization of Xavier's dream. Magneto, lacking faith that mankind will ever embrace equality without forceful coercion, finds a more plausible solution in the violent suppression of humanity. Although I maintain it is easier to draw parallels between Xavier and King than it is between Magneto and Malcolm X, certainly in their distinct attitudes towards the use of violence in the fight for equality, some productive comparisons may be drawn.

King and Malcolm X often placed themselves in opposition to one another, despite the fact that they seemed to share a common goal.[18] In his "Letter from a Birmingham Jail," for example, after King makes abundantly clear that "nonviolence" has become "an integral part of our struggle." Though not referencing Malcolm X by name, he ominously notes that "if this philosophy had not emerged, by now many streets of the South would, I am convinced, be flowing with blood" and that "if our white brothers ... refuse to support our nonviolent efforts, millions of Negroes will, out of frustration and despair, seek solace and security in black nationalist ideologies—a development that would inevitably lead to a frightening racial nightmare." In direct response to this ideology, Malcolm X said that "concerning nonviolence: it is criminal to teach a man not to defend himself when he is the constant victim of brutal attacks" ("A Declaration of Independence") and that one ought to "be peaceful, be courteous, obey the law, respect everyone; but if someone puts his hand on you, send him to the cemetery" (*Malcolm X Speaks*, 12).

These diametrically opposed positions are at the forefront of "Days of Future Past." Kate Pryde reveals that the catalyst for the dystopia is the assassination of Senator Kelly, Moira McTaggert and Professor Xavier by the Brotherhood "to teach humanity to fear and respect the power of *homo superior*. Their plan backfired. Mutants became objects of fear and *hatred*" (Claremont, "Days"). Quite simply, Claremont demonstrates that the Brotherhood's method *cannot*, on principle, attain the goal it sets out to achieve. If the hatred humanity feels towards mutants is based upon fear, and if that fear is fueled by the exertion of violence, violence will only further perpetuate that fear and, with it, increase humanity's hatred of mutantkind.

Nevertheless, the Brotherhood remain convinced of the efficacy of their course of action and attack the Senate, a powerful image of their anti-authoritarian position, destroying the very site, a symbol, of human law. Note, especially, what the Blob, a member of this Brotherhood, says as he disrupts the proceedings: "you been babblin' a lot about the mutant menace, Kelly. We're here to teach ya the error o' your ways" (Claremont, "Days"). It is interesting to note here that both Xavier and the Brotherhood used the word "teach" in response to Kelly's form of discrimination. For Xavier, it was the promise of enlightenment through peaceful dialogue. For the Brotherhood, it was a thinly veiled threat of force and coercion to set an example of Kelly and to demonstrate that mutants would not passively accept humanity's intolerance. Intriguing, then, to see Magneto's role in the dark future portion of the story: he has become the leader of the X-Men, even coming to mirror Xavier's physical comportment, bound to a wheel-chair, an image that Claremont and Byrne use to complete the reversal of Magneto's fundamental ideology.

Rise of the Sentinel: Technocracy and Dystopia

This world that hates and fears them fights back against a threat they feel they can no longer deny: the first attempt, the Mutant Control Act, was struck down by the Supreme Court as unconstitutional, so "the administration responded by reactivating the Sentinels" which were "given an open-ended program, with fatally broad parameters, to 'eliminate' the mutant menace once and for all" (Claremont, "Days"). In a familiar horror trope,[19] the creation rebels against its creator and brings about a world that no one, not even their human masterminds, could have ever desired. "They destroyed not only mutants, but non-mutant super-beings—both heroes and villains. By the turn of the century the North American continent was under their complete control" (Claremont, "Days").

In very broad strokes, the relationship between humanity and technology has long been viewed in two often opposing ways. On the one hand, it is seen as a means of emancipation from toil and the eradication of scarcity to bring about a free, flourishing future for mankind. On the other, it has been seen as the realm wherein mankind was not meant to venture far, invariably leading to enslavement or annihilation. In the post-industrial world, this dichotomy has remained at the forefront of philosophical thought. Some saw technology's emancipatory potential: machines that can eliminate the scarcity that fuels war and can free us from our endless labor to pursue loftier goals of self-cultivation and the betterment of mankind. Others saw the potential for further indoctrination and alienation: weapons of greater destructive force and the technological means of proliferating the propaganda of hate and fear. Critical theorists of the Marxist school, for example, saw technology's advance as complementary with the advance of authoritarianism, not merely through the creation of weapons of mass destruction, but through the insidious ways in which technology infiltrated every aspect of our waking lives. Herbert Marcuse, for example, one of the most iconic critical theorists during the Civil Rights movement, noted, "technology ... as the totality of instruments, devices and contrivances which characterize the machine age" has become "a mode of organizing and perpetuating (or changing) social relationships, a manifestation of prevalent thought and behavior patterns, an instrument for control and domination" (Marcuse, 110–111).

Over time, this technology begins to take on a life of its own. No longer in the direct control of its creators, it begins to dictate the direction of our entire culture. It takes on a terminal momentum all its own, dictating how we take our leisure, the purpose of higher education, the jobs we must get in order to have money enough to engage in a standard of living itself determined by technological innovation, even determining the means with which we engage in social interaction. Technological innovations have become "independent of the purpose for which they are employed. Our tools have become the environment in which we live; increasingly, we are incorporated into the apparatus that we have created, and we are subordinated to its rhythms and demands" (Feenberg, 214).

The Sentinels were initially an instrument of human hegemony, the final solution to the mutant "problem," but the momentum of the Sentinels' "open-ended program" comes to enslave even their human masters, bringing the world to the brink of nuclear annihilation. Humanity, incapable of overcoming mutantkind through sheer force of might, turned to technology as leverage in the confrontation, ultimately dooming them all to the same horrific fate.

Hope

Claremont presents a potential solution in the form of going back into the past to alter the present (the present, that is, for the future narrative). At first, this may seem naïve and deeply problematic: as a social commentary, we, in our world, cannot go back into the past and alter the trajectory of the time leading up to the present. But a more charitable reading (and, I believe, a more interesting one) does not advocate the impossible task of returning to the past but, rather, offers a cautionary tale about avoiding such events in order to prevent that future from ever unfolding. We see the signs: as technology advances, the language of hate and discrimination, sometimes overt, sometimes couched in the language of economics and politics, continues to proliferate and continues to objectify Otherness, marginalizing and criminalizing it. And yet still we fight: we know where hatred comes from, we know the source of this fear, and with this knowledge, perhaps, we can avoid this potential dark future. Avoid it not by *altering* the past, but by *remembering* it, and ensuring that it never repeats itself; that the days of the past never become the days of the future.

There will always be outsiders, those who are different, and those who struggle and fight for recognition and equality in a world that seems stacked against them. And the X-Men will always represent those of us who don't fit neatly into the norm. Xavier's dream will never die, a "dream" that parallels King's own. To never abandon the fight for genuine equality and a world free from the fear of persecution regardless of the color of your skin or, as Claremont said, the number of arms you have.

"Looking at the story again from years ago when I was thinking about finishing it, I suddenly realized: How can you have a hero who's helpless?" [Claremont] asks with a knowing smirk. "What the X-Men were about ten years ago was being against forces beyond their control. What they're about now is transcending that—finding a way to win no matter what. Even in the face of the greatest adversity, the key is to never lose hope, never lose sense of the dream that drives you. That whatever happens, we'll find a way to win" (Claremont interview).

NOTES

1. Claremont graduated from Bard College in 1972. The town where Bard is located, Annandale-on-Hudson, features in multiple issues of *Uncanny X-Men, X-Men, X-Men Origins* and others. I graduated from Bard College precisely 30 years after Claremont graduated.

2. Noel Murray notes that Claremont's work dealt heavily with the theme of "bigotry" and that even "his multicultural team was itself an understated plea for tolerance" (Murray, 2013).

3. As Alec Foege notes, Claremont "transformed a single underachieving comic into the best-selling superhero franchise of its time. From 1975 to 1991, Claremont wrote bimonthly and then monthly installments of an edgy, ambitious, often grandiose epic that eventually spawned eleven continuing related series" (Claremont interview, 2000).

4. "Under Claremont's stewardship—aided by a string of young artists who also made their reputations on the book—*The Uncanny X-Men* became a chart-topper, spinning fan-favorite story lines that have since been adapted into the various animated "X-Men" cartoons, and nodded to in the recent blockbuster "X-Men" movies" (Murray, 2013).

5. "We need unity, not divisiveness to see us through. If we're to remain strong and free and good, we must not waste the talents of one mind, the muscle of one body, or the potential of a single soul. We need all our people—men and women, youngand old,individuals of every race—to be healthy, happy, and whole." Ronald Reagan, remarks at a White House Reception for the National Council of Negro Women (July 28, 1983).

6. As *New York Times* columnist Bob Herbert notes, "the truth is that there was very little that was subconscious about the G.O.P.'s relentless appeal to racist whites." He argues that, motivated by "an opportunity to renew itself by opening its arms wide to white voters who could never forgive the Democratic Party for its support of civil rights and voting rights for blacks," Reagan, "opposed both the Civil Rights Act and the Voting Rights Act of the mid-1960s" (Herbert, 2005).

7. Lee Atwater, for example, said in 1981, the same year "Days of Future Past" was published: "You start out in 1954 by saying, 'N_____, n_____, n_____.' By 1968 you can't say 'n_____'—that hurts you. Backfires. So you say stuff like forced busing, states' rights and all that stuff. You're getting so abstract now [that] you're talking about cutting taxes, and all these things you're talking about are totally economic things and a byproduct of them is [that] blacks get hurt worse than whites. And subconsciously maybe that is part of it. I'm not saying that. But I'm saying that if it is getting that abstract, and that coded, that we are doing away with the racial problem one way or the other. You follow me—because obviously sitting around saying, 'We want to cut this,' is much more abstract than even the busing thing, and a hell of a lot more abstract than 'N_____, n_____'" (cited in Herbert, 2005).

8. George Yancy, taking a cue from W.E.B. DuBois' conception of a "double-consciousness," grants a phenomenological experience of being seen, as a black man, through

the eyes of a member of the white power majority: "despite what I think about myself, how I am for-myself, her perspective, her third-person account, seeps into my consciousness. I catch a glimpse of myself through her eyes and just for that moment, I experience some form of double consciousness" (Yancy, 5). He sees himself as he believes himself to be and, simultaneously, he sees himself in his Otherness through the eyes of a member of the racial power majority.

9. King championed this idea, saying, "I have earnestly opposed violent tension, but there is a type of constructive, nonviolent tension which is necessary for growth. Just as Socrates felt that it was necessary to create a tension in the mind so that individuals could rise from the bondage of myths and half truths to the unfettered realm of creative analysis and objective appraisal, so must we see the need for nonviolent gadflies to create the kind of tension in society that will help men rise from the dark depths of prejudice and racism to the majestic heights of understanding and brotherhood. The purpose of our direct action program is to create a situation so crisis packed that it will inevitably open the door to negotiation. I therefore concur with you in your call for negotiation. Too long has our beloved Southland been bogged down in a tragic effort to live in monologue rather than dialogue" ("Letter from a Birmingham Jail," para. 9).

10. The same term is used in the future portion of the story by the villainous human underground known as the "Rogues" when they encounter Kate Pryde (*The Uncanny X-Men* #141 [Jan. 1981]).

11. The team is comprised of Storm, Colossus, Wolverine, Nightcrawler, Angel and Kitty Pryde. Storm is of African descent, Colossus is Russian, Wolverine hails from Canada, and Nightcrawler is a blue-skinned German, Angel is a white American, and Kitty Pryde is Jewish American.

12. Angel has wings, Storm controls the weather, Colossus is impervious to harm with his metal skin, Nightcrawler can teleport, and Kitty Pryde can turn intangible.

13. "If you mean to harm Senator Kelly, Mystique ... you'll have to go through us to get to him," says Ororo (*The Uncanny X-Men* #141 [Jan. 1981]).

14. My thanks to Gilbert Huerta for this keen insight. Along with Tim Elliot, he produces a podcast on *X-Men* comics called "CrossX."

15. Perhaps the most elaborate system of badges was used at the Dachau concentration camp, an intricate and complicated set of multicolored triangles demarcating the individual's supposed "offense" and letters indicating their nationality, reminiscent of the system Claremont depicts.

16. The character's origins have evolved over time, but this is the common, contemporary tale as it is presented today.

17. See X-Men: Magneto Testament #1

18. Malcolm X said: "Dr. King wants the same thing I want—freedom!" Malcolm X with Louis Lomax on Cleveland television station KYW, aired April 4, 1964.

19. Similar to that of the Judaic golem legends, Mary Shelley's *Frankenstein*, science fiction plotlines akin to the *2001: A Space* Odyssey, *The Terminator*, *The Matrix*, and so forth.

Works Cited

Claremont, Chris. "The X-Men Files: As the X-Men Prepare to Do Box-Office Battle, the Men Behind the Comic-Book Mutants Are Counting on the Myth-Making Powers of the Very Mild-Mannered Chris Claremont." Interview by Alec Foege. *New York Magazine* (July 17, 2000): Web.

Claremont, Chris (w) and John Byrne (a). "Days of Future Past." *The Uncanny X-Men* #141 (Jan. 1981). New York: Marvel Comics.

_____ and _____. "Mind Out of Time." *The Uncanny X-Men* #142 (Feb. 1982). New York: Marvel Comics.

Dylan, Bob. "The Times They Are a-Changin'." *The Times They Are a-Changin'.* Columbia Records, 1964. Record.

Fanon, Frantz. *Black Skin, White Masks.,* trans. Charles Lam Markmann. New York: Grove Press, 1967.

Feenberg, Andrew. "The Critique of Technology: From Dystopia to Interaction." In *Marcuse: From New Left to Next Left.* Ed. John Bokina and Timothy J. Lukes. Lawrence, Kansas: University Press of Kansas, 1994. Print.

Godoski, Andrew. "Professor X and Magneto: Allegories for Martin Luther King, Jr. and Malcolm X." Web. *Screened.* June 1, 2011.

Herbert, Bob. "Impossible, Ridiculous, Repugnant." *The New York Times* (October 6, 2005): Web.

King, Martin Luther, Jr. "I Have a Dream." Lincoln Memorial, March on Washington. August 28, 1963.

_____. "Letter from a Birmingham Jail." April 16, 1963.

Malcolm X. "A Declaration of Independence." March 12, 1964.

_____. *Malcolm X Speaks: Selected Speeches and Statements.* Ed. George Breitman. New York: Grove Press, 1994.

Marcuse, Herbert. "Some Social Implications of Modern Technology." In *Collected Papers of Herbert Marcuse Volume 1: Technology, War and Fascism.* Ed. Douglas Kellner. New York: Routledge, 1998. Print.

Murray, Noel. "'X-Men: Days of Future Past': Claremont's Tales Set Uncanny Agenda." Web. *Los Angeles Times: Hero Complex.* March 20, 2013.

Yancy, George. *Black Bodies, White Gazes.* New York: Rowman and Littlefield, 2008. Print.

"Mutant hellspawn" or
"more human than you?"
The X-Men Respond to Televangelism

Jacob Rennaker

The late 1970s and early 1980s witnessed the rapid increase in popularity and power of televangelists—pastors emphasizing "that old-time religion" embraced modern media, resulting in droves of Americans tuning in religiously to view their sermons. This was the golden age of Oral Roberts, Jimmy Swaggart, Jim and Tammy Faye Bakker, Jerry Fallwell, and Pat Robertson. It was in this milieu that Chris Claremont and Brent Anderson produced the graphic novel *God Loves, Man Kills* (1982). In a rare story where the superhero team known as the X-Men does not fight a costumed villain, *God Loves, Man Kills* focuses on the threat posed by Reverend William Stryker, whose vitriolic anti-mutant message mobilized Americans against mutants. In a revelatory moment, Reverend Stryker turns out to be the father of a mutant, introducing an element of both hypocrisy and irony. Such a storyline highlighted the potential dangers of televangelists wielding substantial religious and political power by warning of its abuse. This story turned somewhat prophetic when in the late 1980s a number of prominent televangelists were exposed for committing the very acts against which they had been preaching. By identifying intersections between the graphic novel and public opinion during the 1980s, it will become clear that *God Loves, Man Kills* was an active participant in the discussion of televangelism in the United States as well as its possible future. In spite of its sometimes skeptical view of televangelism, *God Loves, Man Kills* responded to this complex situation with a heroic sense of hope that ultimately empowered its readers to make positive, lasting changes in the world.

A Very Short Introduction to Religious Broadcasting

From its inception, broadcasting has been associated with religion. When Reginald Fessenden sent the first successful voice transmission on Christmas Eve in 1906, he chose to include not just sacred music, but also a reading of passages from the New Testament (Hadden 114). By the 1920s, diverse groups were scrambling to have their voices heard on the air, among them, religious organizations. One author alliteratively described this period in public broadcast history as a "frenzied frequency free-for-all" (Neuendorf 73). The first religious broadcaster to amass a large audience was a Roman Catholic priest, Father Charles E. Coughlin. After broadcasting his sermons locally in 1926, his popularity boosted him to the national stage in 1930 when his program was picked up by CBS Radio, reaching approximately 45 million Americans weekly by 1932 (Hadden 115). His "bellicose attacks on communists, socialists, international bankers, Jews, labor union leaders and, finally, President Franklin Roosevelt led many to fear Coughlin more than Germany's Hitler" (Hadden 125). As a result, broadcasting companies became much more reserved in selling airtime to religious organizations, and the National Association of Broadcasters created a code of ethics that banned "controversial" speakers (Hadden 125).

However, with the development of FM and daytime-only AM radio in the 1950s, the amount of religious broadcasts increased dramatically, especially among the more religiously conservative organizations (Howley 25). With the development of television, Roman Catholics led the way as Archbishop Fulton J. Sheen was first to televise a sermon in 1940 (Korpi and Kim 410). These groups took full advantage of advances in technology, quickly moving from the use of filmstrips (which were expensive and time-consuming to produce) to VHS tapes (which were easier to copy and distribute) to satellite transmission, which finally allowed for live broadcasts of religious messages (Hadden 119). In the 1970s, satellite and cable television spurred the creation of full-time religious broadcast services, whose on-air solicitations for donations provided funding for an ever-expanding market (Howley 25).

Because of their theological focus on proselytizing, it was largely evangelical[1] Christian organizations that were willing to put so much time and effort into running such large and far-reaching broadcast services. Pat Robertson's Christian Broadcasting Network was the first to utilize satellite broadcasting for religious programming, which was quickly followed by Paul Crouch's Trinity Broadcasting Network, and Jim Bakker's "Praise the Lord" PTL Network (Hadden 120). This movement gained so much momentum that theologian Harvey Cox described the blossoming relationship between evangelicals and the electronic media as the most significant religious event in the United States during this period (Cox 43–44).

The X-Men Respond to Televangelism

For author Chris Claremont, *God Loves, Man Kills* is the distillation of what has made X-Men graphic novels socially relevant. In a recent interview, he stated:

> If you wanted one book to summarize all that the X-Men is about, in terms of character and conflict and theme, I'd have to say that [*God Loves, Man Kills*] was it. If you could only read one X-Men [graphic novel], start with that. Because for me, the X-Men is not about superheroes and super-villains; it is about people, and how you deal with the challenge of life and the choice you have to make every day [Claremont].

While other storylines dealing with such challenges are much more metaphorical in nature, *God Loves, Man Kills* describes a conflict where the X-Men are confronted by a human devoid of any super power (let alone a flashy costume). Instead, they struggle to fight a single man with a message, which introduces plot complexities that could not be easily dealt with in other settings. These complexities were tied up in American public discourse, and this story reflects the author's familiarity with and responses to that discourse.

There was a wide spectrum of opinion regarding the televangelism movement—at one end of that spectrum, there were those who were fearful, skeptical, and hostile toward televangelists and all those who tuned in to their sermons. On the other end of the spectrum were a rather sizable number of people who found fulfillment and happiness through the easily-accessible Christian messages broadcast from these remote pulpits. The viewpoints expressed in *God Loves, Man Kills* fall somewhere in the middle, but more often than not express a skeptical view of these religious leaders and their adherents. In the end, the author presents a story about something more than the X-Men confronting organized religion; he creates a story portraying socially responsible people fighting against certain strands of religious extremism.

The story begins with a lynching. Two children (presumably black) flee from unidentified pursuers late at night. Their parents have been killed for no apparent reason, and these frightened children are running for their own lives. Their assailants, who describe themselves as "Purifiers" catch up with them and shoot one of the children. It is at this point that the child's eyes begin to glow, revealing his identity as a mutant before the Purifiers execute him. When the second child asks why they are being targeted, the head "Purifier" shoots her before responding: "because you have no right to live." The children are then hung from a schoolyard swing with signs reading "MUTIE" fastened to their chests. Beginning the story in this way prepares the reader to deal with the theme of bigotry that runs throughout, while remaining ambiguous as to the specific motivations of the killers.

This ambiguity is resolved in the next scene. It begins with a panel stretching the page's entire height of an expensive-looking high-rise building, explained as "The Stryker Building, Headquarters of the Worldwide Evangelical Stryker Crusade." Reverend Stryker is in his office, reading the following passage aloud from the Bible: "If there be found among you ... man or woman, that hath wrought wickedness in the sight of the LORD thy God, in transgressing his covenant, and hath gone and served other gods, and worshipped them ... [thou] shalt stone them with stones, till they die" (Deuteronomy 17:2–5). Having read this, the audience now begins to understand the killing in the previous scene as one motivated by a particular religious worldview, setting the stage for a rather lengthy discussion of televangelism that runs throughout *God Loves, Man Kills.*

In the scene that immediately follows, yet another recurring theme is introduced. X-Men member Kitty Pryde is shown fighting with a young man because of his support for Revered Stryker's anti-mutant position. Fellow X-Men member Colossus breaks up the fight, and when his comrade Wolverine asks Kitty why she's bruised, she responds: "I wasn't fighting an evil mutant, or super-villain, or murder machine ... just a kid with a big mouth. It was no big deal." A few pages later, the stakes of such a conflict with ideas (as opposed to specific super-villains) are articulated by the leader of the X-Men, Professor Xavier: "An evil mutant—such as our arch-foe Magneto—can be confronted physically. We have no such option with Stryker, whose stocks-in-trade are words and ideas. We can only counter them with saner, gentler words of our own ... and hope for the best" (Claremont, *God Loves*). While the X-Men have been trained in hand-to-hand combat, they are much less experienced in arenas of public relations, philosophy, and theology (the X-Men's technologically advanced combat training "Danger Room" appears not to have a "debate" setting). Perhaps this is why *God Loves, Man Kills* is so intriguing—the X-Men are taken from a world of physicality and thrust into a world of ideology.

From the outset, Claremont makes clear that the villain, Revered Stryker, is a televangelist. Toward the beginning of the story, Professor Xavier engages in a televised debate with Reverend Stryker, who is described by a news anchor as "The Reverend William Stryker, founder of the Stryker Crusade, one of the foremost—and most influential—electronics evangelical ministries" (Claremont, *God Loves*). The use of the phrase "electronics evangelical ministries" puts Stryker squarely in the arena of televangelism, not just any church group. For instance, a 1980 Forbes magazine article on televangelism carried the title "The Electronic Pulpit" (Sloan and Bagamery), and one of the earliest influential leaders of the televangelist movement wrote a book entitled *The Electric Church* (Armstrong). As a confirmed televangelist, Stryker serves as a symbol for what this sort of organization is capable of.

In *God Loves, Man Kills,* even the television studio control room operators participate in this larger dialogue about televangelism. As the debate
between Reverend Stryker and Professor Xavier continues, one of the operators
says, "Stryker knows television—and he's playing to the audience. He comes
across as such a nice, personable guy... Too bad—'cause the man's message is
pretty damn scary" (Claremont, *God Loves*). As televangelism became more
and more popular among Americans, some, like these fictional television operators, were worried that the televangelists were "playing to the audience" and
therefore not being completely genuine in their sermons. Contemporary
authors voiced similar concerns—one analysis of 1980s televangelists observed
that they were required to "adjust what they preach to accommodate the struc-
turally established needs of a modern television ministry" (Hughey 34). The
author went on to write, "To raise the huge sums needed for TV production
costs, televangelists have turned to some of the more specialized techniques
of the retail trade and, as might be expected, to advertising strategies" (35).[2]
This sort of fear was apparently confirmed to skeptics when the Executive
Director of the National Religious Broadcasters stated, "you can get your share
of the audience only by offering people something they want" (Krohn 26).

These carefully crafted televangelist sermons drew in what was, for some,
an alarming number of followers. While watching Revered Stryker make a
religious statement about mutants being less-than-human in his debate with
Professor Xavier, Kitty says, "It seems impossible, but Stryker's so popular.
Millions of people believe his every word" (Claremont, *God Loves*). According
to some figures, American viewership of religious programming went from
around 5 million in the late 1960s to almost 25 million by the mid–1980s
(Hadden 120). While the reasons behind such phenomenal growth were varied,[3] the sheer number of consumers was startling and served as a cause for
concern for those who wondered why seemingly intolerant televangelists were
amassing such large audiences. Similarly, it wasn't just the number of viewers
that surprised Kitty; it was the blatantly negative tone of Stryker's arguments.

Following the debate, X-Men member Cyclops voiced similar concerns
to his teammate Storm when he said, "We were slaughtered... [Professor
Xavier] was speaking to people's ideals, Stryker to their fears" (Claremont,
God Loves). This echoes the concerns of contemporary skeptics regarding the
seemingly fear-inducing messages of televangelists. One author wrote:

> Modern televangelists generally imply that Hell is reserved for others. The view-
> ing audience is usually assumed to belong to the ranks of the "Righteous We," to
> the saving remnant of the virtuous, while responsibility for any moral or other
> deficiencies in the larger society are pointedly attributed to "Sinful Others" who
> are the enemies of the godly—i.e. to abortionists, pornographers, homosexuals,
> rock stars, secular humanists, and liberals in general [Hughey 42].

This served the double purpose of affirming the faith of those already committed, as well as creating a compelling storyline for viewers to follow. In other words, "a message of love, universal brotherhood, and Christian humility may be a pleasant message, but it makes for boring television viewing. By contrast, assailing the sinful adds dramatic tension to sermons, provides a sense of urgency to the televangelist's message, and helps to hold the viewer's attention" (Hughey 42–43).

This rhetoric of the "Sinful Others" employed by some televangelists and its ultimate effects are paralleled throughout *God Loves, Man Kills* by Claremont's subtle references to the Jewish Holocaust. In the fight between Kitty and the young man referred to above, the artist clearly shows her wearing a Star of David necklace (which is consistently shown whenever Kitty isn't wearing her costume).[4] The X-Men's arch-nemesis Magneto plays a prominent role in this story, and his involvement and frequent appearances in this particular religiously-charged story is significant. His role in this conflict reminds readers that just the previous year in *The Uncanny X-Men* #150 (Oct. 1981), Magneto revealed that he lived as a child at the Auschwitz concentration camp where "the guards [were] joking as they herded my family to their death"[5] (Claremont, "I, Magneto"). In the current story, when Magneto discusses the murders committed by Reverend Stryker's Purifiers, he comments dryly, "Once more, genocide in the name of God" (Claremont, *God Loves*). When Magneto later enters into an argument with Cyclops about the futility of helping humanity and suggests creating a world regulated by mutants instead, Cyclops says, "Is your way any better? A mutant dictatorship?" Magneto responds: "Do not take that tone with me, boy. I have lived under a dictatorship ... and seen my family butchered by its servants" (Claremont, *God Loves*). Magneto emerges here as a complex character whose motivations to create a different world—at all costs—emerged from a childhood where he witnessed the wholesale slaughter of his family and his people, and as such, is wary when others use religious language to enforce a discriminatory worldview. American televangelists were not calling for extermination. However, Claremont attributes this motive to Stryker in order to demonstrate what might be on the horizon if certain types of televangelists continued to flourish.

Throughout the narrative, Reverend Stryker quotes Bible passages that seem to reinforce his view that mutants are evil and must, therefore, be killed. In fact, the first words that come out of Stryker's mouth in the narrative come from Deuteronomy and in a subsequent discussion with Professor Xavier, Stryker quotes the following passage: "Think not that I am come to send peace on earth: I came not to send peace, but a sword. For I am come to set a man at variance against his father ... he that loveth son or daughter more than me is not worthy of me" (Matthew 10:34–35, 37). Toward the end of the story,

Stryker quotes several Bible passages at Magneto: Ecclesiastes 12:13, Isaiah 1:4, and Ezekiel 18:20, culminating in his own summary: "We have sinned. And must atone for our transgressions ... with blood! [implying the blood of mutants]" (Claremont, *God* Loves). These passages provide Stryker (and his audience) with a religiously-authorized rationale for violence—a rationale rooted not in religion per se, but rather in a perverted sense of justice that uses religious overtones for its own purposes. This extreme form of proof-texting demonstrates that biblical passages could be dangerous if taken out of context. It is in Stryker's final sermon, however, that the Reverend most completely lays out the scriptural and ideological framework for his position that mutants should be exterminated.

The final chapter of *God Loves, Man Kills* begins with a news anchor announcing that shortly, "Reverend Stryker will give what is being heralded as the most significant sermon of his ministry" (Claremont, *God Loves*). This culminating, concluding sermon deserves special attention for a number of reasons—not the least of which is that this sermon is set in Madison Square Garden (no small venue). Stryker outlines his hyper-literal interpretation of the Bible's creation narrative, his views on the theory of evolution, and the implications of this view for a world where mutants exist. Stryker begins by quoting the biblical account of earth's creation (Genesis 1:1, 27), followed by the creation of humanity by God (Genesis 2:7). He continues:

> We are beings of divine creation, yet there are those among us whose existence is an affront to that divinity. God created man—the human race! The Bible makes no mention of mutants. So where do they come from? Some—so-called scientists, humanists—say they are part of the natural process of evolution... Are we now to let those who put forward the proposition that we are descended from apes tell us that our descendents—our children—will be born monsters?! And that this is natural?!? I say, no! I say, never! We are as God made us! Any deviation from that sacred template—any mutation—comes not from heaven, but hell! [Claremont, *God Loves*].

Stryker's extreme view not only served to vilify an entire race, but endorsed an antagonistic posture against scientific endeavours. During the 1980s, several authors were concerned that American televangelism would foster a sense of hostility toward the scientific community. One observer stated that he was "fascinated by the seemingly effortless employment of the most modern skills of the technological age in the service of the positively antideluvean [*sic*] ideal of a pre-enlightened mentality, and repelled by the unapologetic assertion of beliefs presumed dead since Darwin" (Green 136). While this view is rather reductionist and extreme, it nevertheless reveals the thoughts and feelings of some in the public square who feared that the televangelist movement was opposed to modern science and would somehow impede beneficial scientific research.

The second reason why Reverend Stryker's final sermon is noteworthy is that it reflects the public concern that the televangelist movement could—and would—influence, if not highjack, the political process because the opinions of its loyal followers were being shaped by the increasingly influential televangelists. Before Stryker delivers his sermon, a news anchor notes that "invitations have been sent to every major national political figure—of both parties—and the few refusals are eloquent testament to the Crusade's clout" (Claremont, *God Loves*). This point is emphasized further when some of these "political figures" are shown in the story. During Stryker's sermon, an unnamed United States Senator asks a presidential aide how the President feels about Stryker's views: "Does the President have any idea what Stryker's saying?! Does he support it?!" The aide responds with the following: "The President is a fair-minded man. He believes the reverend's views deserve a hearing" (Claremont, *God Loves*). The suggestion that so many politicians—and even a United States president—would be interested in a televangelist's message is worth exploring.

During the 1980s, a frequent topic of conversation and contention was church-state relations. According to one study published during this period, "there is a contentious movement to change the relation between religious values and government actions.... Recent actions by the Christian Right ... concerning private religion and public duty have aroused considerable criticism" (Tamney and Johnson 3). The televangelist movement became an increasingly significant political force in America, as many observers noticed an "insatiable urge on the part of some [televangelists] to mix religion and politics to the point that the two become virtually undifferentiated" (Hadden 121). A number of factors contributed to the "political clout" of televangelists, which are summarized by Litman and Bain:

> While religious broadcasting traces back to the earliest days of radio, the recent swing toward political conservatism, escalation of the public debate about moral issues such as abortion and prayer in public schools, and the pervasiveness of television have created a favorable arena for these preachers to spread their influence and, for [prominent televangelist] Pat Robertson, to run for the president [329].

The convergence of these factors created a social, technological, political, and religious environment where strong-willed and charismatic preachers could not only influence election and ballot results, but could also run for the office of president. As seen above, *God Loves, Man Kills* deals with the issue only in passing, but nevertheless acknowledges this very real concern.

The third and final reason why Reverend Stryker's last sermon is significant foreshadows one of the contributing factors behind televangelism's eventual decline: the fear of hidden motives and hypocrisy. As his sermon reaches its crescendo, Stryker exclaims, "Are we now to let [others] ... tell us that our descendents—our children—will be born monsters?! And that this is natural?!? I say, no! I say, never!" (Claremont, *God Loves*). In the context of the sermon, this mention of children is somewhat unexpected. However, this impassioned plea to prevent the births of mutant children takes on a much deeper significance in light of Stryker's past.

As a U.S. Army Ranger, William Stryker was on a special assignment to the military's nuclear testing facility. Following this assignment, Stryker and his pregnant wife were involved in a car accident in the Nevada desert. Forced to deliver his own child, Stryker sees that the child is a "monster," and "faced with that abomination, [he] did what had to be done." After killing his newborn child, Stryker then kills his wife and attempts to kill himself. He survives the suicide attempt, however, and lives in a constant state of depression and anger, eventually losing his high position in the military. Later, when he reads a magazine article written by Professor Xavier about mutants, Stryker makes the following realization:

> After months of torment, I knew what the monster was. A mutant. But—could I have fathered such a creature? Was my life so wicked that the Lord sought to punish me through my son? And if so, why then let me live? If I was evil, shouldn't I have been condemned to eternal damnation? I prayed for guidance. It was given me. The evil—the sin—was [my wife's], not mine. She was the vessel used by God to reveal unto me Satan's most insidious plot against humanity— to corrupt us through our children, while they were still in the womb. The Lord created man and woman in His image, blessed with his grace. Mutants broke that sacred mold. They were creations, not of God, but of the Devil. And I had been chosen to lead the fight against them [Claremont, *God Loves*].

From these scenes, the reader learns that Reverend Stryker's religious zeal against mutants ultimately arose from the fact that he himself was the parent of a mutant child, whom he killed. Stryker was finally able to view his deplorable condition through a lens that allowed him to place the blame for his reprehensible actions, the murder of his wife and child, on others instead of himself. This particular type of fundamentalist religious framework allowed Stryker to justify what he had done to his own child, while providing him with the motivation to organize a "crusade" against all mutants.

As mentioned above, some Americans in the 1980s feared that lurking beneath the surface of the wildly successful televangelism movement were hidden motives or hypocrisy on the part of its leaders. More specifically, there was a concern that televangelists were preaching against those things that were most alluring to them or things of which they themselves were guilty (see Hughley). These fears began to be realized in 1987 when some very prominent televangelists admitted to committing the very acts against which they themselves were preaching. A prime example of this was the public discovery that

Jim Bakker—televangelist pioneer and superstar—had admitted to "committing adultery, [... hiding] financial irregularities, and homosexual behavior" (Hougland, Billings, and Wood 56). Other well-known televangelists admitted to similar actions, and national news organizations effected a massive change in public opinion. One observer wrote,

> In most news accounts ... [these] episodes ran mainly as sensational stories of personal corruption, as morality plays in which the greed and lust of [the guilty televangelists] caused their dramatic falls from grace and shook the foundations of their evangelical empires. The attention cast on these ... wayward evangelists has caused many to regard all televangelists as corrupt and hypocritical [Hughey 31].

It goes without saying that this was not true of all televangelists, but the tide of public opinion had turned—for instance, one poll found that during this period of scandal "more than half of the respondents said that their respect for television evangelists had decreased" (Houghland, Billings, and Wood 59). Following these events, *all* televangelists were now under suspicion by an increasingly skeptical public.

   God Loves, Man Kills was surprisingly accurate in its prediction of these rather extreme acts of hypocrisy within the televangelist movement, but Claremont also tempered his skepticism by noting that these sorts of actions would be outliers, and not the norm. Preceding Reverend Stryker's speech, a news anchor made it clear that

> ...a growing number of religious leaders—including fundamentalist Evangelical ministers who only a short while ago were Stryker's friends and allies—have begun to question the direction of his Crusade. It is one thing, they note, to criticize government policy and the moral state of the nation, quite another to single out a specific group of people and brand them as literally less than human [Claremont, *God Loves*].

The narrative is not opposed to televangelism per se, and implies that televangelism and religion in general could play a positive role in discussions of politics and morality. This sort of veiled optimism was also realized in the aftermath of the aforementioned scandals of American televangelism—instead of destroying the evangelical movement in America, these scandals in the late 1980s actually served to refocus the movement and bring it into greater alignment with the attitudes of its congregants.[6]

   While Reverend Stryker is concluding his final sermon in the story, the X-Men foil Stryker's hidden plan to brainwash Professor Xavier into using his special powers to eliminate the world's mutant population. At this point, Colossus believes that the X-Men have "won." Cyclops responds by explaining that it wasn't the physical weapons Stryker used that "are dangerous, but the man himself. His beliefs. His ideas. If we don't stand up to those—here and now—then all we've done is delay an inevitable holocaust." Cyclops then leads the X-Men to Stryker's pulpit, where he affirms Xavier's earlier statement that "we can only counter [hateful speech] with saner, gentler words of our own ... and hope for the best" (Claremont, *God Loves*).

Cyclops' speech offers a different approach to the human/mutant, heaven/hell dichotomy that Reverend Stryker has created in his preceding sermon. When Cyclops challenges Stryker on his willingness to kill anyone who is a mutant—even children—Stryker replies: "Whatever a man's color or beliefs, he is still *human*. Those children—and you X-Men—are *not*!" Instead of lashing out physically against such hate, Cyclops proceeds to challenge Stryker's fundamental assumptions:

> Says who? You? What makes your link with heaven any stronger than mine? We have unique gifts—but no more so, and no more special, than those granted a physician or physicist, or philosopher or athlete. It could be due to an accident of nature or Divine providence, who's to say? Are arbitrary labels more important than the way we live our lives, what we're supposed to be more important than what we actually are?! For all you know, *we* could be the real human race ... and the rest of you, the mutants [Claremont, *God Loves*].

This sentiment ties back to the interview with Claremont referred to above, where he stated, "For me, the X-Men is not about superheroes and supervillains; it is about people, and how you deal with the challenge of life and the choice you have to make every day" (Claremont). In Cyclops' statement, we see this principle articulated—how we judge others should not be dictated by labels, but rather by how others live their lives.

God Loves, Man Kills ends with a discussion about the ways one can and should effect change in the world. With Reverend Stryker finally behind bars due to his involvement with the Purifiers' murders, the X-Men regroup at Professor Xavier's mansion. At this point, Magneto enters the room, claiming that their earlier efforts against Stryker were only a hollow victory: "The *man* was beaten. His cause lives on. Already it's being said that Stryker's goal was right, only his methods were flawed. No matter how hard you try, you cannot truly win" (Claremont, *God Loves*). Magneto suggests another solution: Xavier and the X-Men should join his own crusade for the global dominance of mutants by means of force. Xavier is initially persuaded, but once again it is Cyclops that provides the most meaningful response:

> Granted, times are tough for us and they'll probably get a lot worse. Granted, we probably could conquer the world—though the cost in blood would be staggering. But don't you see—either of you—we're human, too! ...Such a fundamental shift in attitude can't be imposed—to have any meaning, it must grow from within. You brought us together to fulfil a dream, [Professor Xavier]—one born

out of hope and the noblest of human aspirations ... I'm not prepared to give up. The means are as important as the end—we have to do this right or not at all. Anything else negates every belief we've ever had, every sacrifice we've ever made [Claremont, *God Loves*].

Xavier sees the merit in this view, and rejects Magneto's method of changing the behavior of others through force. Immediately after recognizing that he was wrong to consider joining Magneto, Xavier says to the X-Men, "I feel so ... ashamed." Cyclops replies: "To be proven only human, as flawed and vulnerable as the rest of us? Where's the shame in that?" (Claremont, *God Loves*). This statement is a subtle response to the air of "holiness" maintained by American televangelists, which was revealed, in some instances, to be nothing but a front. According to Cyclops, the important thing is not to expect perfection from ourselves or others, but rather to understand our own flaws and vulnerability, recognize the same in others, and do one's best to overcome such shortcomings.

The last page of the story concludes with a slightly different articulation of this philosophy. When Storm expresses her admiration for Cyclops' strong words, he replies, "[Xavier] was in need. I helped him. As he would me. That's what it's all about, really. Needing and helping. Caring for one another. And that caring comes from love. Which makes the world go 'round" (Claremont, *God Loves*). Such a view of love and hope was desperately needed in the United States during a period where the public was already anxious about the federal deficit, poverty, and communism (Zinsmeister 111, 117). *God Loves, Man Kills* was a timely reminder of the power that charisma, excitement, and ideas can hold over a population, and warned its readers that a degree of healthy skepticism should be exercised when considering the messages delivered by televangelists and other popular figures. Although the author clearly had reservations about the televangelist movement, he nevertheless acknowledged that televangelism has a proper place in public discourse, and, through the characters of Professor Xavier and Cyclops, held up a standard of respectful dialogue with those who held differing views. *God Loves, Man Kills* demonstrates the positive role that graphic novels can have in public discourse, and stands as a testament to the creative genius—or perhaps inspiration—of its creators.

NOTES

1. In using the term "evangelical," I follow Hadden's definition that includes "the wide spectrum of conservative Christian traditions that are known by and call themselves 'fundamentalist,' 'Pentecostal,' 'charismatic,' and, simply, 'evangelical'" (114). Because of their focus on the use of television broadcasts, these evangelicals became known as "televangelists."

2. For a detailed comparison of contemporary television sales techniques and televangelist's techniques for raising money, see Hughey 34–41.

3. E.g. Korpi and Kim, "The Uses and Effects of Televangelism" and Litman and Bain, "The Viewership of Religious Television Programming."

4. A few years later, Kitty would be shown participating in a special reception at the National Holocaust Memorial to honor her grandfather. See *The Uncanny X-Men* #199 (Nov. 1985).

5. This connection would have only been reinforced by the fact that around the time that *God Loves, Man Kills* was published, readers also discovered in *The Uncanny X-Men* #161 (Sep. 1982) that Xavier and Magneto had originally met and befriended one another as they volunteered at a psychiatric facility for Holocaust survivors.

6. For a full discussion of the evangelical movement's refinement during this period of turbulence, see Janice Peck's *The Gods of Televangelism*.

Works Cited

Claremont, Chris. XII Encuentro del Cómic y la Ilustración de Sevilla. Sevilla, Spain. 26 November 2011. Keynote address.

Claremont, Chris (w) and Brent Anderson (a). "God Loves, Man Kills." *Marvel Graphic Novel No. 5: The X-Men* (1982). New York: Marvel Comics.

Claremont, Chris (w), Dave Cockrum (a), Josef Rubinstein (a), and Bob Wiacek (a). "I, Magneto..." *The Uncanny X-Men* #150 (October 1981). New York: Marvel Comics.

Claremont, Chris (w), Dave Cockrum (a), and Bob Wiacek (a). "Gold Rush!" *The Uncanny X-Men* #161 (September 1982). New York: Marvel Comics.

Claremont, Chris (w), John Romita, Jr. (a), and Dan Green (a). "The Spiral Path." *The Uncanny X-Men* #199 (November 1985). New York: Marvel Comics.

Cox, Harvey. *Religion in the Secular City: Toward a Postmodern Theology*. New York: Simon and Shuster, 1984. Print.

Green, S. J. D. "The Medium and the Message: Televangelism in America." *American Quarterly* 44.1 (1992): 136–145. Print.

Hadden, Jeffrey K. "The Rise and Fall of American Televangelism." *Annals of the American Academy of Political and Social Science* 527 (1993): 113–130. Print.

Hougland, James G., Dwight B. Billings, and James R. Wood "The Instability of Support for Television Evangelists: Public Reactions during a Period of Embarrassment." *Review of Religious Research* 32.1 (1990): 56–64. Print.

Howley, Kevin. "Prey TV: Televangelism and Interpellation." *Journal of Film and Video* 53.2/3 (2001): 23–37. Print.

Hughey, Michael W. "Internal Contradictions of Televangelism: Ethical Quandaries of That Old Time Religion in a Brave New World." *International Journal of Politics, Culture, and Society* 4.1 (1990): 31–47. Print.

Korpi, Michael F. and Kyong Liong Kim. "The Uses and Effects of Televangelism: A Factorial Model of Support and Contribution." *Journal for the Scientific Study of Religion* 25.4 (1986): 410–423. Print.

Krohn, Franklin, B. "The Sixty-Minute Commercial: Marketing Salvation." *The Humanist* 41 (1980): 26–60. Print.

Neuendorf, Kimberly A. "The Public Trust versus the Almighty Dollar." *Religious Tele-*

vision: Controversies and Conclusions. Ed. Robert Abelman and Steward M. Hoover. Norwood: Ablex, 1990. 73. Print.

Peck, Janice. *The Gods of Televangelism.* Cresskill: Hampton Press, 1993. Print.

Tamney, Joseph B. and Stephen D. Johnson. "Church-State Relations in the Eighties: Public Opinion in Middletown." *Sociological Analysis* 48.1 (1987): 1–16. Print.

Zinsmeister, Karl. "America During the '80s: Summing Up the Reagan Era." *The Wilson Quarterly* 14.1 (1990): 110–117. Print.

From Terrorist to Tzadik: Reading Comic Books as Post-Shoah Literature in Light of Magneto's Jewish Backstory

NICHOLAS PUMPHREY

In 1981, Magneto became Jewish. He did not convert to Judaism, but his new Jewish backstory was revealed in *Uncanny X-Men* #150. When Magneto was created by Stan Lee and Jack Kirby, he was drawn as the X-Men's antithesis. While the X-Men practice the philosophy of Uncle Ben, "with great power comes great responsibility," Magneto uses his power for his own selfish purposes. We first see Magneto in *The X-Men* #1 as a megalomaniac who commandeers missiles and attempts to destroy the lesser Homo sapien. He is a terrorist, believing that mutants are Homo superior and with the natural course of evolution, they will inherit the earth. He simply wants to add a catalyst to the natural cycle. However, when Chris Claremont becomes the writer of X-Men, he eventually reimagined Magneto so that he is no longer a terrorist bent on the destruction of a people, but a Jew and a mutant using his power to fight against genocide.

In 1970, three years after the Six Day War, a young Jewish author went to live on a kibbutz in Israel where he met many Shoah survivors who looked at the war with a new found pride in the strength of the Jewish people.[1] When Chris Claremont returned to America and became the writer for X-Men, he asserted his Jewish identity by using it to express the prejudice that mutants encounter. In Magneto, he created a complicated villain with which readers could understand and sympathize. Claremont used the collective consciousness of Israel that embraces Shoah survivors and looks to them as heroes who represented the power of Israel.

In Hebrew, the term *Tzadik* means "righteous one" and traditionally describes a Biblical "sage" or character that holds great wisdom.[2] In Hasidic traditions today, it refers to religious leaders who not only are seen as righteous, but also hold mystical knowledge of the divine. I use *Tzadik* for Magneto after his Jewish history is established. At this time, he is the embodiment of the political and social message of the new Zionist movement created after the Six Day War in response to the Shoah, which was observed by Claremont in Israel. My analysis centers around four comics of the Claremont era: *Uncanny X-Men* #150, *Uncanny X-Men* #161, *Uncanny X-Men* #199, and *Uncanny X-Men* #200. As an extension of this analysis, I propose that comic books written by Jews should be examined with sensitivity to the history and religious traditions of the Jewish people.

Post-Shoah Literature

Post-Shoah readings often involve an abandonment of religion, a new outlook on G-d,[3] or a cultural shift in Jewish identity within a respective context. Post-Shoah literature is much more nuanced, but for the lack of space in this essay, I only highlight certain aspects. Many texts are theological tracts about how Jews interact with G-d and how G-d now interacts with Jews. Marvin Sweeney states, "The first sustained theological responses to the Shoah began to appear during the 1950s and 1960s, although they tended to be bound up with the broader questions of Jewish understandings of G-d and human beings" (6). These responses appear during Israel's wars and the Eichmann trial, when the public's awareness of the Shoah reached its height.

Culturally, post–Shoah literature is any work that was influenced by, consciously or not, the Shoah either in a theological or experiential way. An example is the memoirs of Shoah survivors and the impact that the event had on their lives. One of the most popular accounts is Eli Wiesel's *Night*, which describes his horrible experiences as well as feelings of abandonment by G-d. Similarly is Art Spiegelman's *Maus*, which describes his father's time in Auschwitz but in comic book form. Spiegelman states, "By the time he comes through the death camps—though he never said this in so many words—it's as if he lost all faith, but for someone brought up so Orthodox, he couldn't become an atheist" (3). Post-Shoah literature shows that Jewish writers are affected by the tragic event and impart that emotion and pain to their readers.

Comic books generally have struggled with recognition as a legitimate art form, educational tool, or even as adult literature. In the 1950s, comics were attacked by psychologist Fredric Wertham for corrupting youth. Later, comics were attacked by the religious-right for depicting satanic imagery. Today, with the blockbuster films and successful cartoons adaptations from comic book sources, the art form cannot be separated from mainstream popular ("lesser") fiction.

The Shoah within the comic discourse creates an even more complicated space. Fredrik Stromberg states, "For many, the Holocaust probably still seems like a topic that should not be dealt with in 'mere' comics, and it did take some time before it was deemed acceptable ... for a long time the subject was more or less taboo, not only in comics but in all forms of media" (132). *Maus* is the most famous depiction of the Shoah in comics; however, Spiegelman does not want to be known for it. For him, *Maus* is his own family's struggle with the death camps and not a statement for a generation. He does not want to fall into his self-named category of "Holokitsch," which is media that profits from the Shoah and sentimentalizes it (70).

In *Maus*, the reader follows Art's struggle with trying to understand the Shoah and why his father counts all his pills, separates his carpenter nails by size, and hordes all his money. Christopher Irving states, "One of Maus' greatest strengths isn't just in his parents' story, but in the story of Art's dysfunctional relationship with his neurotic father, giving the reader a framing sequence that provokes a personal investment in Art's own plight living with a Holocaust survivor" (87). Throughout these scenes, the reader sees Art's father living in Europe and struggling through Auschwitz. Regardless of Spiegelman's opinion of his work, it is paramount not only in legitimizing comics as an art medium but in expressing the affect the Shoah has on Jewish comic writers and artists. Spiegelman started his work on *Maus* in 1972 to have it later produced into a graphic novel in 1985. Jewish kids like Spiegelman were influenced by the raw emotion that their parents and elders were expressing that resulted from Israel's and Judaism's struggle of Shoah identity post–Eichmann trial and post Six Day War. Spiegelman states:

> The subject of *Maus* is the retrieval of memory and ultimately, the creation of memory. The story of *Maus* isn't just the story of a son having problems with his father, and it's not just the story of what a father lived through. It's about a cartoonist trying to envision what his father went through. It's about choices being made, of finding what one can tell, and what one can reveal, and what one can reveal beyond what one knows one is revealing [73].

In the first version of *Maus* published in *Funny Animals*, we indeed see the difficult time a Jewish father has in describing the events to his son. The ironic situation is that it is not only told as a bedtime story, but also that the son is too tired to even understand the magnitude of the situation and quickly falls asleep (Spiegelman 105).

Around the time *Maus* is published, Claremont started working for Marvel. He began writing for Marvel in 1974, but started working on X-Men in 1975. Claremont relates his time living in Israel with Shoah survivors to the prejudice that the X-Men and Magneto experienced. Claremont states, "And that moment in Israel was sort of epiphanic, in the sense of, 'How can you try to convey that?' You know, is there any way to try to convey that … to my audience?" (qtd. in Kaplan 117). To do so Claremont and artist John Byrne created Kitty Pryde, the first Jewish X-Man and produced the famous story arc "The Days of Future Past."[4] With later artistic collaborators, Dave Cockrum and John Romita, Jr., Claremont reimagined Magneto's origins and motivations. Claremont states, "And from a cultural point of view, certainly through my family, I know what it's like to be Jewish! So that became my window through which I could present the youth question, the X-Men universe to a broader audience in terms they could readily and continuously understand" (qtd in Kaplan 121). Thus, Claremont's writing, especially Magneto's evolution under his tenure as writer, represent the cultural change that was specific to Jews living in Israel after 1967 with the new Zionist message of "from Holocaust to revival" (Brog 69).

Israel's Collective Conscious: Shoah, Eichmann, and the Six Day War

Most assume that Israel's stance towards the Shoah has always been one of honoring the victims, uplifting instances of heroism, and proclaiming that it will never happen again; however, in its early stages, Israel's governing body did not want to address the Shoah (Arad 7). Was this a problem for the European Jews or was this a global issue? As a result of the confusion, the amalgamation of Shoah and heroism was not always the unified message in Israel. However, the nation had to address it when 400,000 Shoah survivors arrived in Israel between the 1940s and 1950s (Yablonka 9). In Israel's early stages, the message of the collective was the strength and unity of the people, the Israeli *sabra*.[5] With the Shoah not representing the strength of the nation, the survivors were excluded from the national message. Guile Ne'eman Arad states:

> During the nation-building stage, the Shoah served as a heuristic device to prove the absolute validity of the Zionist prognosis that Israel was the only solution to the "Jewish problem." The lives and memories of the "ordinary" (i.e., non-heroic) victims and survivors were largely disclaimed as an ideological liability; no space was made available in the public sphere to accommodate their tragic ordeals [7].

As a result, the national policy was silence. Arad states further, "Silence was encouraged on both a personal and collective level … for fear that attending to it would daunt the efforts to create a 'new' Jew and a 'normal' nation" (7). Thus, the Shoah was not embraced by Israel yet.

After the Nuremberg trials held between 1945–1946, Israel began to examine the "Shoah problem." At first, Nuremberg represented a German attempt to address the problem with German documents as evidence. However, the trials began a ripple effect amongst Jews that resulted in the Knesset[6] deciding to bring the trials to Israel. First, the message projected by the trials was "sheep to the slaughter" but all changed in 1961 when the Mossad brought Adolf Eichmann from Argentina to stand trial as a primary architect of the Shoah.[7] Hanna Yablonka states, "The Eichmann trial focused on the operative meaning of Jewish sovereignty, the privatization of the Holocaust, and the Holocaust's place in the wider context of World War II" (2). Now, there was a face that the people of Israel could identify instead of the amorphous idea of Nazi and as a result, the Shoah was now in every Jewish home in Israel and abroad.

The Eichmann trial awakened Jews around the world, and in Israel, it acted as a catalyst to the solidification of military strength and the Shoah. Robert Wistrich states, "Indeed many of the refugees were made to feel ashamed that they had even survived. Only after the Eichmann trial ... did the stigma of having gone like 'sheep to the slaughter' begin to fade" (17). Before the trial, Israeli citizens, including many survivors, did not want to discuss or analyze the nightmare that was the Shoah. Yitzhak Zuckerman, a ghetto fighter in Warsaw, avoided his own account for thirty years, even after founding a kibbutz to the commemoration of the Shoah (Marrus 277).[8] The Eichmann trial was so influential simply because of the hyper-publicized nature of the trials and the emotion expressed by witnesses. Spiegelman states that the trial informed him of what his parents endured. As a result, he began looking for books about Eichmann. He said "These gave me my first full and conscious realization that something enormous and devastating had hit my family.... Some of those booklets actually were the models for *Maus*" (15).

The Eichmann trial at times was less about Adolf Eichmann and more about Israel's attempt to cope with the victims of the Shoah. Yablonka states:

> At the time of the Eichmann trial, the Holocaust survivors made up approximately one quarter of the population of Israel and were viewed as immigrants who had arrived in the country at the time of its establishment. The Holocaust was regarded as a tragic, brutal chapter in the history of European Jewry. But the eye witness accounts heard in the Jerusalem courtroom, transformed the public perception of the survivor community [19].

During the trial, each witness was asked, "Why didn't you rebel?" This question asked by the judges echoed the voice of the collective, asking "How can

Jews be a collective strength after going willingly to their death?" In Eichmann's trial "it was the [110] witnesses' stories that shaped Israeli collective memory and Holocaust consciousness in the following years" (Yablonka 19). Given the public nature of the trial, the faces of the survivors could no longer be ignored by the population. Yablonka states, "The trial was regarded as the clearest manifestation that the State of Israel 'represents the entire Jewish people,' and that only by virtue of the state's strength 'had the Jewish people been able to judge its detractors and murderers'" (19). The acceptance of the Shoah survivor as representative of Israel only intensified with the outbreak of the Six Day War, when the Jewish people felt they were under threat of disaster but had the strength to fight back.

Prior to the Six Day War, the nation began representing a heroic, unified Jew as Shoah survivor and IDF soldier. Arad states:

> In 1963, the ministry of education advised to increase to six the number of hours allocated to the history of the Shoah, placing renewed emphasis on its heroic version as exemplified by the ghetto fighters.... The first harbingers of this mind-set came into view in 1967, during the three-week "waiting period" before the Six-Day War, when the Shoah was summoned to validate demands for "war now" and for a "strong man" to lead the nation to victory [13].

The Six Day War was more influential on Israel's collective conscious than the War of Independence, and is evident when double the number of monuments were erected in the first decade "despite the fact that the number of fallen soldiers in the last two wars was only half that of the War of Independence" (Brog 78).

In 1967, after Israel flew air raids into Egypt, a unified power of Arab states responded with an offensive attack against Israel. Within Six Days, Israel crushed the opposition on all fronts. The truce between the two parties resulted in larger borders for Israel and a consciousness of power and safety that said, "We will not suffer the Shoah again." Arad stated, "Israel, it was believed 'must crush the machinations of the new Hitler at the outset, when it is still possible to crush them (the Arabs qua Nazis) and survive'" (13). The aftermath solidified together the commemoration of the Holocaust and the IDF troops.

Now, the fighters of Dachau and Warsaw were synonymous with the soldiers fighting for Israel and the Arab nations suddenly became the Nazi power wanting to rid themselves of Jews.[9] The Six Day War marked a point in the nation's collective conscious where the Shoah would be prevented only through the might of Israel. Arad states, "Unless Israel was to become strong enough to strike back and crush its enemies, it was repeatedly hammered into the collective psyche, what happened during the Shoah could happen. 'Never Again' became Israel's fundamental particularistic lesson, with the Shoah as an absolute signifier of its national ambitions" (14–15). This cultural conscious of "never again" would become the perfect milieu to explain Magneto's troubled past and why he wants to "save" the mutant race.

Magneto Becomes Jewish

In 1970, Chris Claremont spent two months in Israel in a kibbutz near the "Green Line." Meeting the Shoah victims on the kibbutz was a major event in Claremont's life:

> It wasn't religious at all, it was totally secular.... They showed *Judgment at Nuremberg*.... There is a five-or ten-minute sequence in the middle of it, where the prosecuting character, Richard Widmark, shows documentary footage of the liberation of Dachau. And I remember in the dining hall, and it was the first time in my life that I ever understood the concept of silence as an active force [qtd. in Kaplan 117].

Thus, he created many story lines influenced by the Shoah victims he encountered in the kibbutz, but he also included the military influences he saw. He states, "It was an official battle zone. Because there still wasn't any peace with Jordan. There wasn't a day that went by that you didn't see the Air Force flying Phantoms into Jordan, or have Army patrols.... And for someone who was in college in the middle of the Vietnam, [it was] a totally different experience" (qtd. in Kaplan 116). Regarding Magneto, he states, "I was trying to figure out what made Magneto tick. And I thought 'What was the most transfiguring event of our century?' In terms that are related to the whole super-concept of the X-Men, of outcasts and persecution. And I thought, 'Okay! It has to be the Holocaust!'" (qtd. in Kaplan 120). Thus, Magneto embodies the new Jew that was created from the collective subconscious of Israel. This Jew embraces the Shoah victims and uplifts them as heroes, which gives the nation support to crush any attempt to recreate the Shoah.

In the *Uncanny X-Men* #150, the reader gets the first glimpse of Claremont's new Magneto, when he decides that the world would be at peace if ruled by a mutant. Instead of destroying the Homo sapiens, he has now moved to a modus of peace through absolute rule. When Cyclops tells him of Jean Grey's death and states that Magneto could not understand his grief, Magneto harshly replies, "I know something of grief. Search throughout my homeland you will find none who bear my name. Mine was a large family and it was slaughtered—without mercy, without remorse. So speak not to me of grief, boy. You know not the *meaning* of the word" (Claremont, "X-Men VS"). Here, it is only hinted that Magneto experienced the Shoah.

At the end of the issue when the X-Men foil his plot, Magneto lashes out at Kitty Pryde, hitting her with an EMP to the brain. Realizing that he has killed a child, he breaks down:

> Why did you resist? Why did you not understand?! Magda—my beloved wife— did not understand. When she saw me use my powers, she ran from me in terror. It did not matter that I was defending her ... that I was avenging our murdered daughter. I swore then that I would not rest 'til I had created a world where my kind—mutants—could live free and safe and unafraid, where such as you, little one could be happy. Instead I have slain you. I remember my own childhood— the gas chambers at Auschwitz, the guards joking as they herded my family to their death. As our lives were nothing to them, so Human lives became nothing to me [Claremont, "X-Men VS"].

When Storm finds him, she states with rage, "If you have a deity, butcher, pray to it! Magneto replies, "As a boy, I believed. As a boy, I turned my back on God forever. Kill me if you wish, wind-rider. I will not stop you" (Claremont, "X-Men VS"). Here Magneto almost echoes Wiesel's *Night* and his loss of respect to G-d (66). For Claremont, the loss of deity and family during the Shoah is the perfect backstory to explain Magneto's motivation:

> And once I sort of found that point of departure for him, the rest of it all fell into place. Because it allowed me to turn him into a tragic figure, in that his goals were totally admirable. He wants to save his people! His methodology was defined by all that had happened to him.... To take him back within himself to the point where he was that good and decent man, and see if he could start over, and see if he could evolve" [qtd. in Kaplan 121].

The significance of this new Jewish identity makes him a complicated villain with an interesting backstory, which progresses to give him reason for his heinous deeds, not just mindless killing.

In *Uncanny X-Men* #161 (Sep. 1982), we get the famous depiction of Xavier meeting Magneto in Haifa. Both are working at a hospital for people suffering from their experiences in the Holocaust. Xavier first helps Gabrielle Haller, a victim who survived Dachau. When Xavier enters her mind, he finds the images of Nazis but depicted as monsters, terrorizing and raping her. After she regains conscious, the three, Magneto, Xavier, and Gabrielle, tour through Israel. In this time, Magneto states, "Charles, you are an idealistic fool. If mutants exist, humanity will **fear** them and out of that fear, try to **destroy** them" (Claremont, "Gold"). Before long, the Nazis return but in the form of HYDRA led by Baron Strucker looking for a gold horde from the Shoah. The new friends attempt to foil HYDRA's plot, which leads to a parting of ideology between Xavier and Magneto.

Through this window to the past, Claremont weaves the new Magneto with the old. First, Magneto tells Baron Strucker that his powers did not manifest until after the war, but if they had manifested, the war would have ended overnight. Magneto also tells Strucker, "If humanity wishes to follow you to its damnation, so be it. I care nothing for you, or them. And when Homo Sapiens are no more, Homo Superior will claim their rightful place ... as **Lords of the Earth!**" (Claremont, "Gold"). He has yet to embrace a peaceful outlook towards the humans and in the end he kills Strucker and flees with the gold.

As he flees, he tells Charles, "You are far too trusting, Charles, too naïve. You have faith in the essential goodness of man, in time you will learn what I have learned—that even those you love will turn from you in horror when they discover what you truly are. Mutants will not go meekly to the gas chambers. We will fight ... and we will win!" (Claremont, "Gold"). Here, Magneto begins his policy that his people will never suffer again a Shoah. Now his people are mutants. Brog states, "The inevitable psychological relationship of the continuity between death in the Holocaust and death in Israel's wars gave the stories being framed by the Holocaust and the Warsaw Ghetto a cultural context" (69). Just like the Zionist Jews, Magneto's memory of the Shoah became meaningful through his fears of annihilation by humans.

After *Uncanny X-Men* #196 (Aug. 1985), Magneto was leading the X-Men at the request of Xavier, who suspected that he was the target of an assassination attempt. The issue ends with Kitty and Magneto discussing how he knew what to say to stop Rachel Grey from killing the mutant haters, who wanted to assassinate Professor X. He said, "An easy task, Katherine, for one who, like Rachel, has dwelled too long in the valley of the shadow of death. In too many tragic ways, we are kindred souls—survivors of the holocaust, children of the Abyss." Kitty Pryde replies "Maybe the prof's right after all—you do have the makings of a Hero!" Magneto's then states, "No, I am no hero, merely a man ... who has seen and done and endured what can never be forgotten ... or forgiven" (Claremont, "What"). In this issue, it becomes blatant that Magneto's role as villain is but a memory.

In *Uncanny X-Men* #199 (Nov. 1985), it is revealed that Xavier is dying and he wants Magneto to replace him as leader of the X-Men. The issue centers on a reception at the National Holocaust Memorial. During the opening speech, the speaker states, "We must therefore make every effort to teach our children everyone's children what was done—that such a nightmare never occur again! We may forgive but we must **never** forget," echoing Magneto's response to Kitty in #196 as well as the message of Israel after the Eichmann trial and Six Day War (Claremont, "The Spiral"). Lee Forester, who is actually Mystique in disguise, comments on the brutality of humanity. Magneto responds, "Then, Lee, it was the Jews. My nightmare has ever been that tomorrow it will be Mutants" (Claremont, "The Spiral"). The next scene has Kitty Pryde standing at the podium for her grandfather, Samuel Prydeman. He passed away recently, but he wanted to attend the ceremony since he never could find his sister, Chava, after the Shoah.

Coincidentally, Magneto may have known Chava in Auschwitz. As he tells Kitty, two elderly people come up and recognize him. They were in the Warsaw Ghetto Uprising and were sent to Auschwitz with Kitty's great-aunt but she died there. The couple would have died too if it weren't for Magneto who saved some of them. When Kitty asks if he was a hero, Magneto replies, "Hardly, in those days, heroism meant holding onto one's humanity, while the Nazis tried their best to turn us into animals, the way to defy them—to defeat them—was to lie, to hold onto hope, no matter what. Believe me Kitty, I was no one special. If I am a hero, then so is every other man and woman who survived" (Claremont, "The Spiral"). Magneto voices the collective political message of Israel after the Eichmann trials. All of a sudden, Mystique transforms into her true form and after a battle, Magneto willing goes with her to stand trial for his crimes.

The cover of *Uncanny X-Men* #200 (Dec. 1985) is especially telling. Much like the "M" patches worn by mutants during *Days of Future Past*, Magneto is branded with a large "M," alluding to the yellow Star of David worn by Jews in the Shoah. As Claremont states in an interview, this is the turning point for Magneto:

> The X-men is not about superheroes and supervillians. It is about people. And how you deal with the challenge of life and the choice you have to make every day.... That for me is why Magneto is so important. Xavier is spoken for. He already... he has made his choices. He is a hero. Magneto is a work in progress. He is not evil. He is defined by his past. But that definition drives him to disaster. The question for him is..is he the victim of his destiny or can he change it. Can he grow? I'm not sure. I'd like to think he can ["Freakytown"].

Magneto is no longer a villain, but someone who did not wish to plunge into the Shoah again.

As his defendant, Gabrielle Haller explains Magneto's position to Kitty, which also mimics Israel's post-war conscious. She states, "It's easy to run away—or give up, as my parents did. They were lucky. They died in Bergen-Belsen. For them, the pain ended quickly. They've no memories to haunt them no more fears. But we who survived have a duty to make certain the holocaust never happens again, to anyone! We must fight Kitty—We may be defeated, but we must never surrender" (Claremont, "The Trial"). In his statement to the court, Magneto echoes this and fully transforms into the hero like the ones Claremont met in Israel:

> My dream, from the start, has been the protection and preservation of my own kind, mutants. To spare them the fate my family suffered in Auschwitz—and do not tell me such a thing cannot happen again because that is a lie! You humans

slaughter each other because of the color of your skin, or your faith or your politics—or for no reason at all—too many of you hate as easily as you draw breath, what's to prevent you adding us to that list?! I thought I could impose sanity from above—through conquest—but there are too many of you. So I decided, I must try another way. I am the reason mutants are unjustly feared. That is why I am here, why I will abide by the court's decision. My hope is to make the world understand the reasons for my being.... I have seen the error of my ways—can you say the same?! [Claremont, "The Trial"].

Not only does this statement explain the change of attitude in Magneto but contextualizes the prejudices that all humans face that is embodied by mutants.

During the trial, the Fenris twins attack Magneto out of revenge for their father Strucker. Magneto in return saves the court and proves that he has changed; however, Xavier is dying. Xavier makes him promise to take over the school, lead the X-Men, and teach the New Mutants. Magneto reluctantly promises but fears that he will only let the professor's dream down, in which Xavier reminds him that it was Magneto's dream too. Lilandra comes and takes Xavier away with promises that the Shi'ar will heal him. According to an interview with Claremont, this was not his original plan:

> The actual storyline was that Xavier would die in issue #200 ... and Magneto would become head of the school [pause] permanently.... But the idea, that goal was built from the death of Phoenix. The hope was to show that this is ... their lives as X-Men have a real risk. This isn't superhero games. This is reality. In reality good guys sometimes do not win and people die. And that has to be part of their lives otherwise it just becomes a video game ... life isn't like that. And I always thought, my thought was the stories we tell in comics shouldn't be like that either. If there is risk for the reader, then the victory is that much sweeter. And you can, something can happen that can catch you by surprise and can have that much power and heart ["Freakytown"].

The once-terrorist would have been the leader of the X-Men. This could not have been possible without his transformation based on the new Israeli who had the strength to protect his people from the mutant Shoah. Magneto now represented Israel and the Uncanny X-Men.

Reading the X-Men Post-Shoah

Post-Shoah literature is any work influenced by the event or works to react to it; either theologically or culturally. Comic books are known for reacting to current events and, for most of the twentieth century, comics were produced by Jews. As Claremont states, "What was the most transfiguring event of our century?" (qtd. in Kaplan 120). Obviously for Jewish writers of comics, it is the Shoah. Regardless of what Spiegelman wants, his work will always be a watershed for comic books and the Shoah. *Maus* overtly asserted that comic books are not only a legitimate form of media and art, but also they can express very powerful messages and carry weight. Claremont's work also carries this weight.

Between the 1972 issue of *Funny Animals* and the 1985 *Maus*, we have the work of Chris Claremont: the creation of Kitty Pryde, the retconning of Magneto, and "Days of Future Past." All are reactions to Claremont's Jewish identity and his time in Israel with Shoah victims. I propose that works like Claremont's and Spiegelman's should act as standards for scholars to examine comics after the Shoah for comic writers' response to the tragic event, even if the writers themselves did not live through the event.

For Claremont, as stated in an interview, Magneto represented the new Jew attempting to face extinction. He states, "That was what gave Magneto so much of his passion and focus. In terms of defending his people, they really were dancing along the edge of extinction and they really did need someone like him" ("Freakytown"). Magneto would not allow his people to go to the gas chambers again. After the Six Day War in Israel, non–Shoah survivors began to erect "monumental structures placing the emphasis on the national narrative 'from Holocaust to revival'" (Brog 81). Magneto is such a monument. "The role of community commemorations in the process of change is substantial because of public acceptance for Holocaust memory to become a legitimate component in Israeli identity and a subject expressing social solidarity for the collective" (Brog 81). As a result, not only does Magneto become Jewish, but mutant-kind and the fear of annihilation becomes described like Jews hunted down by Nazis. In issue #150, Magneto states, "Because we are different, I and my fellow mutants have been hunted down and slain like wild animals. Those killings will stop. All Killing will stop" (Claremont, "X-Men VS"). Magneto, the righteous *Tzadik,* who survived Auschwitz, will not let his people suffer again.

NOTES

1. The word Shoah means catastrophe and encapsulates the cultural tragedy that happened to the Jewish people during the Nazi regime. Holocaust denotes a burnt offering and has a religious connotation that does not represent every victim or survivor. Art Spiegelman says that he wants to disown Holocaust for this reason (75).

2. For example, Noah is a Tzadik in Genesis 6.9. In Proverbs 10.25, a Tzadik is the foundation of the world.

3. I am using the respectful spelling of G-d given that my essay connects Jewish theology. Orthodox Judaism typically shows respect to the name of their deity and goes so far as to spell G-d with the hyphen.

4. For more on Kitty Pryde please see Margaret Galvan's chapter in this collection. For more on "Days of Future Past" please see Clancy Smith's chapter in this collection.

5. *Sabra*, which is a cactus in Hebrew, was the chosen representative for the Israeli people in the 1930s and 1940s as a tough people willing and capable of surviving harsh conditions. Sabra is also the name of an Israeli superhero in Marvel comics modeled after this same concept.

6. The Knesset is the Israeli legislative body of government.

7. The Mossad is the Institute for Intelligence and Special Operations. The American equivalent is the CIA.

8. Kibbutz literally means gathering and now represents communal groups traditionally based around a agricultural industry. Families live and work for the community, while also producing goods for sale. In the 1970s, it became popular for non–Israeli Jews to visit and work on Kibbutzim for extended periods of time.

9. Obviously the Arab powers did not want to commit genocide; however, this is not the feeling that was perpetuated by Shoah survivors and the Arab media.

WORKS CITED

Arad, Gulie Ne'eman. "Israel and the Shoah: A Tale of Multifarious Taboos." *Taboo, Trauma, Holocaust*. Spec. issue of *New German Critique* 90 (Autumn, 2003): 5–26. Print.

Brog, Mooli. "Victims and Victors: Holocaust and Military Commemoration in Israel Collective Memory." *Israel and the Holocaust*. Spec. issue of *Israel Studies* 8.3 (Fall, 2003): 65–99. Print.

Claremont, Chris. Interview by Pablo Rodriguez. *Freakytown entrevista a Chris Claremont*. *Freakytown* (Dec. 1, 2011): Web. 2013.

Claremont, Chris (w) and Dave Cockrum (a). "Gold Rush." *The Uncanny X-Men* #161 (Sep. 1982). New York: Marvel Comics.

_____ and _____. "X-Men VS Magneto!" *The Uncanny X-Men* #150 (Oct. 1981). New York: Marvel Comics.

Claremont, Chris (w) and John Romita, Jr. (a). "The Spiral Path." *The Uncanny X-Men* #199 (Nov. 1985). New York: Marvel Comics.

_____ and _____. "The Trial of Magneto!" *The Uncanny X-Men* #200 (Dec. 1985). New York: Marvel Comics.

_____ and _____. "What Was That?!!" *The Uncanny X-Men* #196 (Aug. 1985). New York: Marvel Comics.

Irving, Christopher, and Seth Kushner. *Leaping Tall Buildings: The Origins of American Comics*. Brooklyn: PowerHouse Books, 2012. Print.

Kaplan, Arie. *From Krakow to Krypton: Jews and Comic Books*. Philadelphia: Jewish Publication Society, 2008. Print.

Marrus, Michael R. "Ghetto Fighter: Yitzhak Zuckerman and the Jewish Underground in Warsaw." *The American Scholar* 64.2 (Spring 1995): 277–284. Print.

Spiegelman, Art. *Metamaus: A Look Inside A Modern Classic, Maus*. New York: Pantheon Books, 2011. Print.

Strömberg, Fredrik. *Jewish Images in the Comics: A Visual History*. Fantagraphics Books, 2012. Print.

Sweeney, Marvin. *Reading the Hebrew Bible After the Shoah: Engaging Holocaust Theology.* Minneapolis: Fortress Press, 2008. Print.

Wiesel, Elie. *Night.* New York: Bantam Books, 1960. Print.

Wistrich, Robert S. "Israel and the Holocaust Trauma." *Jewish History* 11.2 (Fall, 1997): 13–20. Print.

Yablonka, Hanna, and Moshe Tlamim. "The Development of Holocaust Consciousness in Israel: The Nuremberg, Kapos, Kastner, and Eichmann Trials." *Israel and the Holocaust.* Spec. issue of *Israel Studies* 8.3 (Fall, 2003): 1–24. Print.

Sexy Art, Speculative Commerce: The X-Men #1 Launch Extravaganza

TIMOTHY ELLIOTT *and* ROBERT DENNIS WATKINS

From about 1998 to 2000, as one of the authors of this piece perused comic book store back issue bins, three issues always seemed to be present: *X-Force* #1 (Aug. 1991) in its poly-bag, *Batman* #500 (Oct. 1993) featuring the downfall of Bane, and copies of writer Chris Claremont and artist Jim Lee's *X-Men* #1 (Oct. 1991). *X-Men* #1 was the most omnipresent comic in this holy triumvirate of over-produced 1990s comics.

In the late 1980s and early 1990s and the X-Men series was arguably enjoying its highest level of commercial success thus far, shipping the flagship *Uncanny X-Men* title twice a month and maintaining several successful spinoffs including *New Mutants* (soon to become *X-Force*), *Excalibur* and *X-Factor*. Yet, the 1991 launch of *X-Men*, a second core X-book, is seen by many as one of the precursors to the comics market crash of the mid–90s. Jonathan Last argues that this inevitable burst was built on a speculative market run rampant to the point that a comic could fetch some 1000 percent its initial cover price some 20–30 years later. Though aspects of how the 1990s comics-collecting hysteria led to the near-destruction of the industry have been well documented, *X-Men* #1's failure to attain a place as an iconic collector's item has not received sufficient attention.

X-Men #1's revamping of the X-franchise entailed spinning off an entirely new series, streamlining characters and continuity, and employing several then-ground breaking marketing strategies—all designed to cater to the consumer-driven comic book collecting hysteria of the early 1990s. Following the collecting boom of the late 1980s, it seemed like a good time to create the next highly collectable (and profitable) comic milestone, and what better way than through modernizing Marvel's X-Men property, a sales juggernaut with a strong popular culture presence. In their quest for omnipresence, Marvel succeeded. *X-Men* #1 set the Guinness world record for most single issues sold, but many of those issues ended up as bargain bin fodder just five years later—indicating an oversaturation of the market (Marvel.com). The profound gap between issues sold and issues kept can partly be explained by the politics of the speculator's market, as will be discussed, but first, the comic itself had to be worth buying in 1991. This reader-friendly #1 issue used the twin tactics of simplified characterization and exaggerated sex-appeal to lure in a diverse enough demographic of new readers and longtime fans to the tune of a reported sales total of 8 million copies.

A Motley Crew of Mutants

X-Men #1 features a number of callbacks to past characters as it slowly introduces new characters that had been part of the core team since Claremont began writing the book in the wake of *Giant Size X-Men* #1, the property's first major relaunch. First, Claremont and Lee emphasize the stakes by introducing a rejuvenated and resplendent Magneto, the X-Men's primary nemesis. The same portrait of Magneto appears on the cover of 2 of the 5 variants as he stands with his palm open and stirring with magnetic energy, eyes narrowed, teeth clenched. When the self-styled Master of Magnetism shows up on the second and third page of the comic, he states his name in a bold purple font and puffs out his chiseled chest as magnetic power swells from both his hands. Lee couples this dramatic pose with Magneto's powerful disruption of a group of warring space-farers to showcase the character's majestic powers, while Claremont's dialogue about Magneto's present state of indifference towards humanity nods to the evolution of the character in *Uncanny* from villain to X-Men leader to mildly neutral recluse ripe for a return to villainy.

The primary threat of the issue in place, co-plotters Claremont and Lee introduce the newly minted *X-Men* team via a splash page on pages 6 and 7. This X-team features a veritable who's who of X-characters from Claremont's lengthy run with the team. *X-Men* #1 team features all five of the original team members who had spent most the 1980s in Louise Simonson's *X-Factor* spin off. Staple characters from Claremont's 1970s and 1980s work including Colossus, Banshee, Storm, and Wolverine, join the five original X-Men.

In terms of the character's appearances, Lee focused on presenting the most familiar, classic versions of most of these core characters. Beast and Iceman's costumes are rather self-explanatory—blue fur, icy body, respectively—and so the pair's appearance was not noticeably updated. Jean Grey and Storm have been outfitted with period-common tight fitting spandex. Colossus and Wolverine's costumes' have changed colors but retain the same basic designs from 1975.

Due to a combination of events, Angel (now Archangel) and Cyclops have both undergone major changes in appearance. Archangel's transformation into a metal-winged, blue-skinned warrior receives no formal explanation, but neither does Cyclops's decisions to bulk up like Arnold Schwarzenegger and ditch his hood/visor combo in favor of a visor that exposes the character's hair for the first time. These major design changes in Archangel and Cyclops's appearance, dictated by events from *X-Factor* and Lee's desire to modernize the X-leader respectively, are minimized simply as the characters interact, seemingly oblivious to these changes.

Rogue's new-found confidence and very 90s leather jacket can easily be attributed to Lee's artistic and narrative preferences, a paring of self-confidence with a character's body and sexuality, best shown in Lee's depiction of the character as a beautiful, principled match for Magneto in *Uncanny X-Men 269* (Oct. 1990) and *274* (March 1991). Rogue's pose on page 8 suggests the character is now an empowered, majestic do-gooder, while Forge's presence alongside Beast and Banshee in the trenches of the X-Men's war room suggests that he is the group's resident techie, long past his dubious past actions and confusing romantic entanglements with Storm.

Relative X-newbies Gambit and Psylocke (especially the Asian ninja version of the character) appear on page 11 with Wolverine in the sewers. Gambit's trench coat and Psylocke's purple hair help the pair stand out even amongst the various metal bodied, optic-blasting X-folks. Psylocke's martial arts strikes and stealthy (if revealing) attire help contextualize this ninja character in American popular culture.

Once the creative team establishes its cast of heroes and villains, the next step was to create an enticing 1990's sheen for the X-universe, one that built off of the grimy/gritty comic book revolution of 1988 spurred by the release of *Watchmen* and *The Dark Knight Returns*. Lee obliged by putting militaristic style X-uniforms and leather jackets on some of the characters. Similarly, Magneto's newly minted goons, the Acolytes, certainly look the part of a 1990's character—high boots, arm guards, flowing capes, and questionable hair styles. Despite Lee's attempts to put as many pockets as possible on Cyclops's utility belt, or to play up Wolverine's vicious nature, the X-Men are not a fundamentally gritty franchise. Even Magneto, as harrowed a villain as one might find— pushed to acts of nuclear terrorism and isolationist threats by a mix of exhaustion and perceived persecution—does not kill the Beast when the furry hero dives for Magneto's head. Gambit even makes a point about charging his cards to stun rather than to kill, a nod to the violence and carnage the X-Men consciously avoid. With a revitalized Magneto threatening the world, the stakes are high in *X-Men* #1, but a favorable resolution is rarely in doubt. Instead of deadly violence and potentially continuity-shaking conflicts, Lee focused on making the book more adult through a mix of sexualized women and classic superhero adventure.

Jim Lee's X-Pool Party

Where collector's items create something memorable or valuable—a new character, a fluke success, or a rare comic with limited mint copies—*X-Men* #1 was more of a mass-market cash grab. This comic, when dissected in 2013, is neither memorable nor rare; instead it's more like the comics' equivalent of Michael Bay film—fun, attractive, sexy, bombastic, and ultimately hollow. Seen as a comic blockbuster, *X-Men* #1 was an enormous success, selling a reported 8 million copies (Marvel.com). When viewed as a collector's item it becomes apparent that trying to create both a blockbuster and a collector's item in the X-Men reboot was an impractical and confusing misstep. The disposable nature of the comic book is felt strongest in the bizarre X-Men Pool Party pin-up included alongside several other pin-up posters and sketches in the back matter of *X-Men* #1.

Cyriaque Lamar, columnist for *i09*, wrote on the ridiculousness of this pin-up, which he calls the X-Men pool party. While Lamar uses the pin-up as a metaphor for the state of the X-Men franchise circa 2010, our analysis will look at the blockbuster fodder of *X-Men* #1, best seen in the issue's amped-up sex appeal, a case of content without depth, pretty packaging with no lasting content. Essentially, the pin-up is a superfluous image of superheroes dressed in sexed-up bathing suits, chilling around the swimming pool. First and foremost, the reader will notice a set of sensual, bare legs—slightly crossed and flirtatious—cover the majority of image's front. These legs are attached to a monokini-clad Psylocke. Direct in center and behind Psylocke is either a dejected or coquettish Rogue. And in the back, a giant Beast, jumps into the pool. We will dissect each of these three images below.

On top Beast—in loose swim trunks and an oversized snorkel—cannonballs into the water with a terrified Trish Tilby clinging onto his shoulders. Tilby's outfit, a black one-piece swimsuit and an oversized hat, seems to be the most conservative in the whole pin-up; however, the angle eclipses the details of her swimwear and all the reader sees is her shoulders, head, and legs. Still, compared to her traditional, human reporter clothes, this outfit seems a bit more playful. But the view of a playful Beast and a terrified Tilby, is a visual metaphor for the whole blockbuster issue: a fully grown boy wearing exaggerated clothing and accessories pays no attention to an objectified woman. While Tilby is a bit hidden behind her blue-furred paramour, the objectification of Rogue is front and center.

This issue introduced Rogue's new costume, "the green and yellow suit, along with the leather jacket, [that] kind of became Rogue's trademark look" (Luzifer, Monolith, and Jay). Although this trademark outfit is more skintight than past costumes, it still shows no real skin. In the pin-up, by contrast, Rogue wears a French-cut, one-piece swimsuit—a common style from the late 1980s and early 90s (and a callback to the common French-cut look of swimsuits in classic pin-ups). In a recurring theme of the pin-up, Rogue's suit reveals that there is an extreme temperature difference between the men and women— while all the men are nippleless, Jim Lee seems to go out of his way to hint at the underlying shape in many of the women's suits. This invitation to the male gaze is most apparent in revealing swimwear worn by Rogue and Jean Grey (pictured to the viewer's left of Rogue). While Psylocke doesn't suffer quite this same indignity, the purposeful placement of her legs more than makes up for any lack of sheer swimwear.

The strange thing about this placement isn't just the visual emphasis of Psylocke (which focuses on her far more than her supporting-role on the team demands) but also on her swimsuit. While many of the characters in the pin-up are wearing swimsuits that reflect their costume themes (Rogue's is green and yellow for example), Psylocke seems to be wearing her costume. As Lamar (quoting his sister) puts it, "'I never knew if Psylocke was wearing a bathing suit or her normal costume ... they were pretty much interchangeable'" (Lamar). On closer observation, the viewer will notice that while similar to her regular outfit, the bathing suit is actually skimpier. Instead of the full, one-piece ninja suit she wore in this issue with many different wrist and leg straps, she's wearing a mix between a monokini and cut-out swimwear, a wardrobe change that suggests that this comic isn't about art, content, or collection— it's about money, sensation, and sex.

The message the pin-up seems to give is especially disconcerting because the X-Men are one of a scant few superhero groups that prominently feature women. As Lamar laments, "here is *the* superteam in which the majority of the interesting, powerful characters are female, and more often than not they simply stand around looking skimpy and/or dying" (Lamar). *X-Men* #1 offers a chance to reinvent the franchise while literally grabbing millions of readers and the audience is given an issue with a sexed-up pin-up as a coda instead.

The rest of the characters don't fare much better in the pin-up. Storm stands at the perfect angle as to be able to show the side of her bikini-clad breast while focusing on her near-thong bikini bottom. Charlotte Jones, a minor human character, gets off easy wearing a traditional bikini while Jean

Grey wears a one-piece swimsuit that also features a French-cut bottom, some sideboob, clear nipple lines, and plenty of skin. While the boys aren't objectified in precisely the same way, they offer a beefcake look to match. Cyclops wears a thong, Wolverine wears cut-off jean shorts (with the top-button undone), and the remaining X-males wear similar suits and sport similarly exaggerated muscles.

One thing to consider is that in this setting they should be dressed like this—they're at a swimming pool. Or maybe the authors and artists were just having fun while introducing new characters to the masses. While this explanation seems plausible at first, it falters because the swimming pool has no relation to the plot and there are no character names with the images to assist in character identification. This is a reward for the long-time fans who already know the characters and budding 14-year old boys who want to stare at penciled women. This pin-up functions as an extension of the sexual undercurrents of Jim Lee's X-Men art (and the upcoming 1990s in general). Michael Lavin points out that "the trend toward super-heroines as sex objects reached an interesting peak in the early 1990s when both Marvel and Image published a series of annual swimsuit issues. These annuals, clearly capitalizing on the yearly Sports Illustrated phenomenon, contained poster-type drawings or paintings of popular female comic book characters posing in revealing swimsuits" (Lavin). The pool party not only cements the issue as popcorn entertainment but also illustrates a troubling trend of objectification of women in comics.

The positions and depictions of the X-women match up with many feminist critiques of media that, descending from Mulvey's groundbreaking 1975 essay "Visual Pleasure and Narrative Cinema," focus on representations of women as objects catering to the male gaze. The pool party shouts to its readers that, although this story is going to show powerful women engaging in typical superhero violence and breaking misogynist stereotypes, the X-Women are going to do so wearing as little clothes as possible and in the most sexualized manner allowable without crossing the PG-13 line. Sheri Klein suggests that such exposition of the female body has been part of the tradition of art and comics. She writes, paraphrasing R. Betterton, that "comics and painting traditions both have produced particular ways of presenting the feminine body with the male viewer in mind. The spectator is always assumed to be male, and the ideal woman is always assumed to be there to flatter him" (Klein 61). She goes on to mention that they are presented in a way to become objects, or objectified. Charlie Anders writes about the problem of the representation of Supergirl and how she often was portrayed "flaunting ass instead of kicking it" (Anders 72). Although X-Men #1 issue shows women kicking plenty of ass, it still likes to have them showing it while they kick it. Anders argues that it's problematic to have heroines dressed as if they are only there to visually stimulate the male readers. The X-Woman create a contradiction of sex symbol and role model.

This tension between sex object and assertive heroine plays on the idea that women superheroes in the 1990s were breaking traditional roles and challenging the misogyny of old comic strips where, as Jehanzeb writes, the woman's place was either in the home or in distress all while being a sex object. Mark Voger points out "Dark Age" (i.e. 1990s era) comic book clichés, including several that apply to *X-Men* #1. One of these Dark Age clichés is the cheesecake trend, industry slang for hypersexualized depictions of women. Voger quotes Trina Robbins on this trend, "if you look at today's super-heroines and the way they're drawn, they are very insulting to women.... They're pushing it like it's some kind of feminist thing, with this strong woman. But then the art ... is insulting" (141). This objectification is troubling and prominent. Lavin points out, "many of the comics which do portray strong, interesting heroines nevertheless still pander to young male readers. Despite all of their admirable qualities, [they] are still drawn in skimpy outfits and sexy poses" (Lavin). Lavin mentions "it remains clear that without gratuitous pinups, such books would have far fewer male readers" (Lavin). Claremont and Lee created strong women, but these women, as penciled in this pin-up and throughout the issue, were meant to be ogled by boys.

Still, the pin-up is kind of a throwaway piece of fluff in the issue. The reality is that *X-Men* #1 tells a story in its first thirty-some odd pages where the characters' costumes might possibly serve some purpose such as empowerment or functionality. Throughout the issue, we presume the characters are wearing costumes for a reason, whether that's comfort or for light armor protect; skin-tight spandex costumes seems to have been the order of the day in 1990 for both genders. Although they are sexual in nature and often accentuate the feminine form catered to a male gaze, the X-women's costumes aren't outright peep shows. This particular pin-up, as well as the issues as a whole, is what it is: a popcorn piece that, while not void of story, is primarily made to entice readers with its flashy character designs and sensual drawings. This is what leads to mega-selling blockbusters, but it also makes the content become the opposite of collectible; instead it becomes cheap, disposable—like all of the literal throwaway copies in bargain bins.

Speculation Politics and *X-Men* #1's Omnipresence in Bargain Bins Nationwide

Troy Brownfield points out a pattern in Marvel's strategy for creating a sales/speculation juggernaut circa 1991, namely to team an all-star creator with a new #1 book, as seen in Todd McFarlane's *Spider-Man* #1 (Aug. 1990) and Rob Liefeld's *X-Force* #1. Voger includes these sort of "#1 and #0 Issues" among his Top 10 Dark Age Clichés (145). These #1 or #0 issues, were jumping on points intended to entice new readers, or, as Voger suggests, remind readers of the this franchise or character's cool-factor by establishing a new title, a spin-off, or a solo book for an unheralded team member, "whatever it took to get #1 issues out there" (145). In contrast to Jack Teiwes's discussion of DC Comics's 1980s reboot of Superman born out of a response to low sales and situated in a desire to "create a 'new' version of Superman more suited to a 1980's audience" and that audience's pocket books, *X-Men* #1 was a greedier expansion/revision of an existing product (125). According to the comics sales aggregator Comichron, the number one selling book in March of 1988 was *Uncanny X-Men* #231 (March 1988), a signpost of sales success that suggests that Marvel's relaunching of the property into two separate books was spurred on by a desire for additional profit.

Sean J. Jordan discusses the major industry shift from perceiving comics as "newsstand items to [perceiving them as] collectibles," a seismic shift that changed the way comics were produced, marketed, and consumed. Eckert discusses the 1990's mentality of buying comics with the hopes that a pristine comic would net an exponential amount of money twenty or thirty years later. The Baby Boomers had certainly created this market for comics, but as Eckert argues, the "their rarity is what drives the prices up, not necessarily their age," and so sitting on some one hundred copies of a pristine book while other comics speculators or dealers did the same was counterproductive to increasing a collectible's worth. Eckert's research is reflected in Phill Hall's stipulation that, while some 8.5 million issues of X-Men #1 were pre-ordered, only about 3 million of those issues were sold to the public—the rest were kept by dealers and speculators in the hopes that they would have 5.5 million mint copies of *Action Comics* #1 (June 1938) on their hands. The inherent contradiction of a commodity based on rarity maintaining its value in the face of a seemingly irrational number of people owning this rare first issue odds did not dawn on comic collectors and speculators at the time. Chuck Rozanski, owner of the popular Denver comic shop chain Mile High Comics, places the blame on comic book distributors who made it far too easy to (at least temporarily) maintain a comic shop with nothing but enthusiasm and a low level of capital. Once these fledgling shops opened, they began speculating and so Rozanski argues that most of the printed but unsold copies of *X-Men* #1 and other "overprinted books from 1989–1995" were presented to him with the following narrative: "My ____ had a comics shop for X years, and finally closed in 199X. These are the comics they had left over when they closed."

Hall further discusses that the retailers have to decide how many copies to order of a number 1 issue sight unseen. Instead, publishers rely on brief plot synopses and hype from the publishers. Given the sheer amount of guestimation that Hall argues goes into ordering the right number of books, it's no surprise that Rozanski's fledgling comic store owners over-ordered and eventually found themselves out of business. The collectibles market is infamous for its boom and bust cycles. According to Rozanski, publishers

> actually thought all the comics they were printing were selling to eager fans, when in fact, I estimate that at least 30% of all the comics being published from 1990–1994 ended up as overstock in comics dealers inventories. When the weight of these unsold books finally collapsed the retail end of the business, the publishers saw their numbers decline drastically.

With all of this comic book industry background in mind, *X-Men* #1 remains very emblematic of comics-as-speculation era, aka the Dark Age of Comics, a time when publishers were excited to create new properties that would cater to a new breed of fans/collectors who were invested in core characters but also in each individual spin-off. The over-flooding of the market happened largely due to publisher's abilities to stoke demands for characters with eagerly anticipated creative teams, with covers designed to encourage readers to buy more than one copy of the book, and with the aforementioned lack of useful ordering information for retailers, such that store owners were taking gambles with the number of copies to pre-order. Hall argues that this process makes it so comic companies can use the direct market system to "factor out most of the risk."

    X-Men #1 seemed like a safe bet based on 1990's comic book logic. The title features a vetted, if fading, comics scribe writing the characters that made him famous, accompanied by a rising star artist with a history of successful collaboration with said scribe on a number of issues of *Uncanny X-Men* (some 16 issues between *Uncanny X-Men* #248 [Sept. 1989] and *277* [June 1991]). The characters were popular enough that Marvel could publish 5 different covers (one a full gatefold and the other 4 covers featured segments of the gatefold). Numerous other Marvel recent #1 titles had sold well, including Liefeld's *X-Force* #1, an X-spinoff featuring portions of the cast of *New Mutants*. The formula seemed foolproof, and the book certainly moved a number of books out of stores and into consumers' hands; however, some twenty-two years later we're most concerned with the book's shabby omnipresence. Perhaps the retailer's over-ordering and fans' massive under-consumption say far more about the 1990's speculative market than the forty-eight pages that comprise *X-Men* #1.

    There's certainly some cultural, critical, and even commercial force behind the argument that *X-Men* #1 isn't totally emblematic of the Dark Age and the speculation bubble. Superman's death in *Superman* #75 (Jan. 1993) was more memorable to the general public, and McFarlane's *Spawn* or *Spider-*

Man titles were probably more influential, yet *X-Men* #1 retains a certain derelict omnipresence in all its five alternate cover glory. This issue holds the title of the world's most sold comic book. *X-Men* #1 continues to haunt bargain bins partly because, as Rozanski claims, there are so many copies of it that it will be some 30 years before the issue's value has increased to anything close to even its cover price. This issue is a blockbuster made to introduce new and old audiences to the premiere X-team of the 1990s, and it serves this primary purpose with aplomb. Marvel used its late 1980s/early 1990s formula of pairing up all-star creators with new titles to spike a wave of interest and speculation around its X-titles that produced an excessive number of copies of a single issue. This particular artifact from the Dark Age of comics functions then, not as an enduring collector's item—a rare item increasing in value from behind a sealed polybag, but rather as a prominent piece of pop culture jetsam, floating through almost every comic shop's quarter or dollar bin.

Works Cited

Anders, Charlie. "Supergirls Gone Wild." *Mother Jones*. 32.4 (Jul/Aug 2007): 71–73. Print.
"Archetypes, Commercialism, and Hollywood: A History of the Comic Book." *Random History.com*. RandomHistory.com, 18 March 2008. Web. 22 April 2013.
Brownfield, Troy. "Friday Flashback: *X-Men* #1 (1991)." *Newsarama.com*. TechMedia Network.com, 01 July 2010. Web. 20 April 2013.
Claremont, Chris (w, p) and Jim Lee (a, p). "Rubicon." *X-Men* #1 (Oct. 1991). New York: Marvel Comics
Claremont, Christ (w) and Jim Lee (a). "The Cradle Will Fall." *Uncanny X-Men* #248 (Sept. 1989). New York: Marvel Comics.
_____ and _____. "Crossroads "*Uncanny X-Men* 274 (March 1991) New York: Marvel Comics.
_____ and _____. "Free Charley." *Uncanny X-Men* #277 (June 1991). New York: Marvel Comics.
_____ and _____. "Rogue Redux "*Uncanny X-Men* 269 (Oct. 1990) New York: Marvel Comics
Claremont, Chris (w) and Rick Leonardi (a). "...Dressed for Dinner!" *Uncanny X-Men* #231 (March 1988). New York: Marvel Comics.
Claremont, Chris (s, p) and John Byrne (a, p). "The Fate of the Phoenix."*Uncanny X-Men* #137 (Sept. 1980). New York: Marvel Comics.
Claremont, Chris (w) and Walt Simonson (a). "Rogue." *Uncanny X-Men* #171 (July 1983). New York: Marvel Comics.
Comichron. John Jackson Miller, 2013. Web. 28 April 2013.
Eckert, Chris. "Why Superhero Comics Sucked and the Industry Tanked, Pt. I." *Contempt of Comics* (8 August 2006). Web. 24 April 2013.
Ginocchio, Mark. "Gimmick or Good-X-Men #1" *Comics Should Be Good*. Comic Book Resources (7 April 2013). Web. 26 April 2013.
Hall, Phill. "My Monthly Curse #9: Taking Apart a Guinness World Record." *Bleeding Cool.com*. Avatar Press, 9 May 2011. Web. 20 April 2013.

Jehanzeb. "The Objectification of Women in Comic Books." *Fantasy Magazine*. August 2008. Web. April 29 2013.

Jordan, Sean J. "Why Comic Books Are Almost Dead." *The Research and Planning Blog*. The Research and Planning Group. 16 April 2010. Web. 27 April 2013.

Jurgens, Dan (w) and Brett Breeding (a). "The Death of Superman Part 7: Doomsday." *Superman* #75 (Jan. 1993). New York: DC Comics.

Klein, Sheri. "Breaking the Mold with Humor: Images of Women in the Visual Media." *Art Education*, 46.5 (Sept. 1993): 60–65. Print.

Lamar, Cyriaque. "The X-Men's 1991 Pool Party = Everything That's Wrong with X-Men in 2010." *i09*. Gawker Media. 16 January 2010. Web. 26 April 2013.

Last, Jonathan V. "The Crash of 1993." *The Weekly Standard* (16.37). The Weekly Standard LLC, 13 June 2011. Web. 25 March 2013.

Lavin, Michael R. "Women in Comic Books." *Serials Review* 24.2 (1998): 93. *Academic Search Premier*. Web. 29 Apr. 2013.

Liefeld, Rob (a, p) and Fabian Nicieza (s). "A Force to Be Reckoned With." *X-Force* #1 (Aug. 1991). New York: Marvel Comics

Luxifer, Peter, Monolith, and Homer Jay. "Rogue: Costume Gallery." *Uncanny X-Men.net*. 26 July 2005. Web. 26 April 2013.

McFarlane, Todd (a, w). "Torment Part I." *Spider-Man* #1 (Aug. 1991). New York: Marvel Comics.

Moench, Doug (w) and Jim Aparo (a). "Dark Angel I: The Fall [Knightfall 19]." *Batman* #500 (October 1993). New York: DC Comics

Mulvey, Laura. "Visual Pleasure and Narrative Cinema." *Screen*. 16.3 (Autumn 1975): 6–18. Print.

Rozanski, Chuck. "The Vicious Downward Spiral of the 1990's." *Tales from the Database*. Mile High Comics, Inc, August 2002. Web. 10 March 2013.

"SDCC 2010: Marvel Breaks into Guinness." *Marvel.com*. Marvel Entertainment LLC, 24 July 2010. Web. 15 April 2013.

Teiwes, Jack. "The New 'Man of Steel' Is a Quiche-Eating Wimp! Media Reactions to the Reimagining of Superman in the Reagan Era." In *The Ages of Superman: Essays on the Man of Steel in Changing Times*. Ed. Joseph J. Darowski. Jefferson: McFarland, 2012. Print.

Voger, Mark. *The Dark Age*. Raleigh, N.C.: TwoMorrows, 2006.

Fatal Attractions: Wolverine, the Hegemonic Male and the Crisis of Masculinity in the 1990s

GERRI MAHN

Branded

Because of the social pressure to conform to normative behavior, it is difficult to be a man; much less an X-Man. Men are expected to be fathers, husbands, sons, and brothers. They are expected not only to provide for their families but protect them as well. These traits were passed down from father to son over the course of generations. Men worked the fields. Men went to war. But what happened to men when those old roles changed? Today, both men and women vie for the same jobs, fight side by side on the battlefield, and share the responsibility of providing for the family. The code of honor once considered chivalric, has become obsolete. The traditional ways men would show respect to women are now considered oppressive. Hegemonic masculinity has been distilled down into the shape of the hero and dispersed through books, films, and television. Writers, actors, and artists became the vanguards of masculinity who breathed life into those inert clay forms. They weaved the fabric that told the history of hegemony; regulated and managed gender regimes; articulated experiences, fantasies, and perspectives; reflected on and interpreted gender relations (Donaldson 646).

Gender was a driving force for comic book narrative since the medium was specifically innovated in 1933 for a male demographic. The format, once derided for its youthful readership, is now recognized in the postmodern conversation of pop culture relevancy as a social mirror. Within those brightly colored pages, the idealized man took shape in the form of the superhero. Even with the strong economy of the 1990s the U.S. was experiencing its share of cultural anxieties. We were engaged in the Gulf War, anxiety rose regarding a possible Y2K event which might decimate American infrastructure, and the AIDs epidemic was no longer being conveniently ignored. Despite their youth, Marvel readers were aware of the changing, conflicted, world around them. The 1993–1994 story arc titled "Fatal Attractions," which ran through *The Uncanny X-Men* and its spinoff series *X-Men*, *X-Factor*, *X-Force*, *Excalibur*, and *Wolverine*, focused on themes of war, perceived technological threat, and disease which were overt social issues relevant to their generation; as were the discursive narratives eroding traditional gender roles and the resulting crisis of masculinity. "In a post-modern world lacking clear-cut borders and distinctions, it became hard to know what it meant to be a man and even harder to feel good about being one" (Reichardt and Sielke 564).

The 1970s saw a rise in the academic recognition of masculinity as a social construct and of a power dynamic differentiating "normative" from "non-normative" types of behavior theories which began to take hold in the 1990s (Bird 120). It would have been easy to dismiss the crisis of masculinity as an effort to revive patriarchal systems of dominance. But that would have ignored the impact heterosocial paradigms of behavior had on the hegemonic male.

Masculinity was typified by what it was not: "feminine" (Brown 26). The historically accepted narrative of the hegemonic male had been the lynch pin for most gender theories; used to evoke privileged or overtly biased behavior. One of the lasting legacies the three successive waves of feminist movements had was to transform the hegemonic male into an example of oppressive behavior.

"Fatal Attractions" reflected overt themes of violence and ideological fear present in the 1990s, as well as a gender conflicted, trying to rediscover its purpose in the postmodern world. When women started the conversation about gender oppression, there had to be an antagonist and that antagonist had to be men. Early feminists were not necessarily wrong to make that assertion; there was no denying the rich and extensive history the patriarchal system of dominance enjoyed—globally. Yet, while women had experienced increased equality, little consideration was given to the generation of men who had inherited an almost exclusively destructive narrative of identity. The irony of it was that gender interaction for the hegemonic male was not about controlling women; it was about the influence men had over other men (Donaldson 655).

The hegemonic male, by definition, was the apex of masculinity. This figure was not

> ...assumed to be normal in the statistical sense; as only a minority of men might enact it. But it was certainly normative. It embodied the currently most honored way of being a man, it required all other men to position themselves in relation

to it, and it ideologically legitimated the global subordination of women to men" [Connell and Messerschmidt 832].

When males gathered in social groups, studies showed they created hierarchical ranking systems which resulted in an alpha, beta, and so on down. The hierarchical male groups were distinct from the social clusters created by females, which could fragment and reform dependent upon a more democratic decision making process instead of outright ranking (McGuffey and Rich). The super intended male set the standard for behavior and defined the parameters of both acceptance and social bonding within the gendered group. Leadership was assumed through prominent physical presence, athleticism, and successful interactions with females along the socially accepted delineation of frequently oppressive gender lines. The term heteronormative behavior indicated male to male or male to female interaction that was strictly heterosexual in nature and therefore exclusionary. While we will refer to some of the dynamics previously identified in the so-called heteronormative paradigm, normative constructs already ensured groups that experienced bias occupied a position within society (Gaffney and Beverly 139). Gender defiance and gender correction was applied to all members and focused on behaviors which were denied legitimation as masculine, marginalized, or suppressed entirely (Bird 121).

The representation of the idealized man in Marvel comics could best be described as the reflection seen in a carnival mirror; it distorted the image of known constructs. The soldier became Wolverine. The scientist became Beast. The X-Men were representative of the best male traits, be they moral, emotional, or physical. "The superhero body represented, in vividly graphic detail, the muscularity, the confidence, the power that personified the ideal of phallic masculinity, the alter-ego the identity that must be kept a secret depicted the softness, the powerlessness, the insecurity associated with the feminized man" (Brown 31). X-Men comics provided a robust example of masculinity for young boys, which clearly separated right from wrong, good from evil, normative from non-normative hypermasculine behavior (Brown, 32). Any confusion experienced by the characters acted as a point of reference for their readers who were struggling to reclaim their own identity. "Within the cultural context of denaturalized and decentered masculinity, was an abyss at the heart of subjectivity concealed in the traditional coherent male ego" (Fernbach 241).

Can't Go Around Him

In many ways, Wolverine was the idealized male. He overcame any weakness he experienced as a child, either in character or in physicality. He experienced personal tragedy and emotional trauma, yet continued to thrive. He was a warrior; who could fight with a brutal, animalistic, skill or comport himself with the Zen-like control of a trained samurai. Yet it was that animalistic, nearly feral, side to his personality which linked his identity to the hypermasculinity of the uncultured and uncivilized (Brown 30). The more bestial he became the more unbound and pronounced his manhood. Wolverine dominated his environment, it did not dominate him.

The dichotomy between rank and social grouping was expressed in interpersonal relationships. Take the dynamic between Cyclops and Wolverine; both had the capacity to function as alpha males but the X-Men accepted Cyclops as their leader and his power of authority was validated by Professor X, who assumed the ultimate role of patriarchal dominance. Rather than compete, Wolverine put himself at the fringe of the group. As a functioning hegemonic male in his own right, he could recalculate perceived gender norms within the paradigm of the hierarchy; a behavior which would not be possible for lower ranked members of the X-Men. Whether that behavior was accepted or deemed transgressive by Professor X, was another matter entirely.

In X-Factor, differences in masculinity were accentuated by contrasting the higher (Havok) and lower (Multiple Man) ranked males. Like Cyclops, most of Havok's subordinates were closer to his level in the hierarchy, such as Quicksilver, or to a lesser degree, Guido. They displayed fundamental traits of the hegemonic male by suppressing expressions of physical and emotional weakness, rarely showing signs of indecision or fear, and their virility was readily apparent in their physicality. Those traits differed from Multiple Man, who was physically slight, required specific direction, and expressed a predilection for being in the company of others to the point that isolation resulted in anxiety (*X-Factor* #87, Feb. 1993). Having a low rank was within the parameters of normative male behavior, so long as the individual acknowledged that rank in the paradigm was absolute. Despite the fact that Cyclops was an alpha male he would revert to the role of beta in the presence of Professor X, no matter how long the Professor had been apart from the team.

Since the X-Men were idealized, their displays of extreme physical abilities were coupled with equally extreme environments. In *X-Men Unlimited* #1 (June 1993), Cyclops, Storm, and Professor X survived a jet crash in the Antarctic. The narrative opened with Cyclops wandering around a snow storm with his eyes squeezed shut since the loss of his visor would prevent him from controlling his optic blasts. He was suffering from cracked ribs, a collapsed lung, and wearing nothing but his torn blue and yellow X-Men uniform (which one imagines was made from a non-insulating lycra blend). He reacted to the environment and his injuries with a grimace; what would kill a normal man was merely a tough day for Cyclops. His condition was in stark contrast to his female counterpart, Storm, who survived the same crash virtually unharmed, yet succumbed to pain caused by a massive electro-magnetic discharge administered by another mutant that "tore and shred at the very womb of mother earth" (*X-Men Unlimited* #1, June 1993). Cyclops, despite his injuries, carried Professor X to safety, and then rescued Storm emotionally and physically. Within the gendered narrative it was acceptable for Storm, despite her own role as a leader with formidable power, to be overcome. The same behavior would not be acceptable for Cyclops or Professor X.

In contrast to the robust physicality of his subordinates Professor X suffered from acute symbolic castration (paralysis) and symbolic compensation (extraordinarily strong telepathy). Any lack of physicality demanded augmentation; an extension of the phallus, and thereby virility which typically stemmed from the use of technology. In modern parlance this could be viewed as a techno-fetish, or technological augmentation used to lessen individuation, a feeling of dissolution, or castration anxiety (Fernbach 243). In combat narratives that symbolism was typified through the use of enormous weaponry; guns, rocket launchers, swords, and knives. Augmentation could be bionic; Colossus could transform his body into metal and use it to shield himself from emotional and physical trauma. Cable relied on weaponry and techno-organic physical embellishments. Cyclops needed his visor to keep his optic force blast from erupting unchecked and Wolverine could unsheathe metal claws. Professor X's wheelchair paled in comparison to Cerebro, a powerful computer which enhanced his innate psychic abilities, or the Shi'Ar exoskeleton which allowed him to walk during the final battle in "Fatal Attractions" with Magneto.

Despite having the appearance of normative behavior, an extreme display of overt virility could be just as damaging to gendered rank as feminized behavior, which was rare in "Fatal Attractions." Even female characters who engaged in emotional outbursts exhibited feats of strength and athleticism; both masculine displays. The behavior correlated with studies of female athletes who performed as well or better than their male counterparts and then were described as manly. The designation of masculine attributes was meant to be complimentary; it was difficult for their male teammates to view them as women who achieved in their own right (Anderson). Within the context of a changing narrative, the lines of discursive gender definition became blurred and tolerance increased. Studies of male cheerleaders indicated that their initial views of women as sexual objects diminished after continued interaction with the female athletes. The women became individuals and the men built relationships with them based on a foundation of mutual respect and understanding (Anderson 272). The same behavior became normalized in X-Men comics over time, evidence of which was present in "Fatal Attractions."

The hegemonic male also corrected gender transgression for expressions of fear, an emotion displayed by humans, not heroes. Humans automatically ranked as inferior in the gender hierarchy to superheroes. For example, the human President of the United States expressed personal fear and was still perceived as normal whereas X-Men only expressed fear for others or the possibility of failure. Within the same, strict, paradigm, poor physical performance or emotional weakness was considered feminine and therefore not tolerated. Yet Magneto, Professor X, and Wolverine were frequently given to dialog which contained poignant emotional depth. They were examples of a phenomena which allowed alpha males to create their own pattern of acceptable behavior, once defined as feminine, then abruptly de-feminized.

De-feminization did not occur arbitrarily in comics; a study of gendered behavior in children observed that a girls' hand clapping game was initially shunned by boys, having been classified as feminine. Yet when the alpha male participated in the game, and achieved some degree of proficiency he soon began teaching the game to other boys in his social cluster without fear of remediation. The game was de-feminized. The language, which made up a chant accompanying the game, was altered to convey male interests and provided the boys a sense of ownership over the activity (McGuffey and Rich).

The ability to randomly de-feminize behavior begs the question, what is the point of all this figurative chest pounding if masculinity exists purely as a social construct? At their core human beings, regardless of gender, have certain biological urges; a primal self that must be recognized as contributing to the psychology of how we relate. Masculinity is a dichotomization of biological versus cultural, and thus marginalizes or naturalizes the body (Connell and Messerschmidt 836). The hegemonic male, at the pinnacle of his social group, had the assurance of social support and therefore enjoyed a higher likelihood of survival. He would have greater access to supplies, surplus of food, and would therefore be more likely to thrive than his lower ranked counterparts. As a result, the hegemonic male became the most viable mate. In practice, this is a gross oversimplification; the hegemonic male is no less idealized than an X-Man. Masculinity perceived as a construct does not correspond to the lives of actual men; it is a set of widespread ideals, fantasies, and desires (Connell and Messerschmidt 838).

The biology of those desires inform the gender narrative. In a recent study, groups of women were shown images of naked men (the study was corrected for known preferences in height and musculature) the majority of whom indicated a preference for longer penises with greater girth (Mautz, et al). The study also noted that the women polled spent additional time lingering over images of men with larger penises.

Did Len Wein compensate for Wolverine's short stature by giving the character a large phallus? No one except his many female liaisons knows for sure. Since it would not be socially acceptable to assert his masculinity by walking around naked, he conveyed his virility through displays of physical prowess. In that sense, Wolverine was no different from the other male members of his team, and this behavior was why his female counterparts could express emotional weakness. They did not have to convince their peers of the strength of an unseen phallus, or reinforce their rank in the male paradigm.

Women of the X-Men validated the super idealized male. In "Fatal Attractions," a woman's role as a viable member of the team was emphasized by her gender differences. Females were not concerned just with the Acolytes or the Legacy Virus, they focused on mother/daughter/sister or romantic relationships with the other team members. Storm identified a mother/daughter relationship between herself and the planet (and Kitty Pryde). Moira McTaggert, though just a human ally, was typically ranked at the same level as Professor X for her intelligence, authority, and self-sufficiency. Her insufficient maternal attitude toward her adopted daughter, Wolfsbane, could be construed as masculine. Likewise, Storm engaged in emotional outbursts (feminized behavior), yet stood up to Professor X when he asked her to steal; a behavior contrary to her moral code (masculine assertion). Moira and Storm both acted in the nebulous area outside of prescribed gender paradigms, but remained women and therefore could expect to receive fewer, if any, sanctions on gender deviations (McGuffey and Rich 617). Despite those occasions of gender autonomy Moira and Storm often required saving by a male member of the team. Compartmentalization supported the hegemonic paradigm instead of disrupting it; the hegemonic male rarely required rescue and when he did, he was saved by another hegemonic male.

Colossus Unleashed

Wolverine's initial role in "Fatal Attractions" was marginal until the third act, when he took center stage. As he had done for decades, Wolverine embodied all the positive traits of the super idealized man. He was a capable protector with a high degree of physical prowess and self-sufficiency who dealt with significant emotional trauma quietly. He did not call attention to his personal problems, nor was he given to unnecessary complaining since, "Expressing emotions signifies weakness and is devalued, whereas emotional detachment signifies strength and is valued" (Bird 125).

As a hero, Wolverine was a role model for the youth who struggled to find a place within their own social hierarchy. Boys who fell short within the hierarchy imagined themselves in his place and gained a symbolic rank by proxy. Boys who achieved alpha and beta status used the stories as blue prints for appropriate morality, and as examples of gender remediation. Magneto, Professor X, Colossus, Cable, and Exodus all exiled teammates considered weak or disobedient, as do high status boys in order to maximize their influence and minimize deviants by identifying and labeling them as outcasts (McGuffey and Rich 618).

Complex consequences which came directly on the heels of gender remediation predicted the outcome of "Fatal Attractions." The two groups fought, attempted to maintain tight control over the behavior of their members, and both patriarchal dominants confronted each other for the final battle in Magneto's orbiting fortress, Avalon. The clash between the two distinct groups was where Wolverine's highly gendered identity became a major factor (*X-Men* #25 [Oct. 1994]).

Earlier in the story, Magneto had exploded the metal in Cable's body and essentially neutered him (*X-Force* #25 [Aug. 1993]). The appendages were replaced, Cable survived and reemerged whole. Later, Professor X retrieved Colossus from his self-imposed exile in Avalon, but only after Magneto had been defeated, and while his followers lacked a functioning alpha who could challenge the Professor's authority. Professor X forced Colossus to relinquish his metal body and become his weaker self. That body, which did not have the required amount of mental or physical toughness (Donaldson, 644) was made to re-experience physical and emotional trauma which stemmed from his inability to save his sister's life. His perceived failure as a man to protect his family resulted in his desire to cut off his weaker self. Professor X made the decision to be transgressive and made Colossus relive the ordeal and submit to his grief before allowing him to go back into self-imposed exile (*Uncanny X-Men* #315, Aug. 1994).

When Wolverine and Magneto finally faced off, the confrontation was deeply intimate. Wolverine had penetrated Magneto with his claws and in return, Magneto ripped all of the adamantium out of Wolverine's body. It did not come in a single stream, but in long arcs, erupting from dozens of points on Wolverine's body, ravaging him as it flowed upward toward Magneto like a boiling liquid. He sprawled, mostly naked, across the cover of *Wolverine* #75 (Nov. 1994) while spikes of adamantium peaked all over his body. Wolverine was not just castrated once, but over and over again; the metal was not something that had supplemented his virility so much as it was an integral part of his physicality. Without it, he was permanently diminished.

After the battle, when the X-Men returned to Earth, their jet began to break up as it reentered the atmosphere. Inside, Jean Grey and Professor X tried to keep Wolverine alive. From a vantage point inside his mind, Professor X (and therefore the reader) could see that Wolverine actually chose to die. Dying meant freedom from pain; it also meant giving up. This was an imperative and defining moment in terms of his masculine identity. Even death was made to submit to the super idealized male's authority. He had control over his own fate, right up to and including mortality. At the exact same time, Jean Grey was almost swept out of the jet. On the brink of death, Wolverine was cognizant of what was going on around him, he intuitively understood the peril that Jean Grey faced, and leapt from his deathbed to save her. The only thing that could revive the diminished hegemonic male was a necessary act of chivalry.

At the end of the 20th century, men entrenched in the hegemonic paradigm found themselves adrift. Their role at home and in society had slowly capsized. The entire gender found itself in crisis, and like Wolverine, the damage to their identity could not be ignored. The hegemonic male would have to change.

Out of the Light and Into thy Father's Shadow

Comic book heroes who were known for their dual identities had clearly delineated masculine and feminine traits. Superman and Clark Kent. Batman and Bruce Wayne. The Incredible Hulk and Bruce Banner. One was strong, the other weak. One emerged in times of crisis and the other disappeared. One would succumb to emotion, the other put that emotion aside to accomplish his goals. The benefit of duality was that the two sides never really needed to reconcile with each other. Both could remain safely compartmentalized, safely separate, and thereby support the socially accepted gender narrative.

Wolverine did not have the benefit of duality. He was one man, with a single personality, which had to reconcile itself to a weaker physicality. His need to prove himself and reclaim his role in the masculine hierarchy happened immediately. Having returned safely home to Professor X's school, he allowed himself two weeks of recuperation. After which time he attempted to join his teammates, as they were training with non-lethal, interactive, hologram combat simulations in the Danger Room. In a stunning display of gender correction the X-Men abandoned him as Professor X proceeded to pit Wolverine against battle droids, which were more formidable than the holograms. His teammates watched him struggle and remarked on his apparent fear. While Moira expressed concern for his safety, Professor X responded that "Logan has to learn this about himself" (*Wolverine* #75 [Nov. 1994]). He was teaching his subordinate a lesson. The curriculum for that lesson included public shaming, ostracizing, and physical pain.

Even in his diminished capacity, Wolverine still believed himself to be the hegemonic male. Frustrated, afraid, he was driven to his knees. He threw his head back, screamed in pain, and managed to unsheathe his claws, which were now only bone. Blood poured from his wounds and despite the situation, Wolverine had partially achieved his goal, having proved his continued virility. Like Cable and Colossus, he refused to accept his symbolic castration as permanent.

It was his fear that set him apart from the other X-Men, who were above fear, who had the moral superiority, physical prowess, and natural confidence to render them beyond its grasp. The emotion feminized him according to the historically prescribed definition of the hegemonic male. His new and shattered masculinity, despite the existent virility, was an expression of agony. Later, as if to illustrate this point, when Wolverine shows Jubilee his diminished claws, a butterfly lands on them. By the close of the issue Wolverine has rejected his loss of rank and status. Like Colossus, Wolverine chooses a self-imposed exile, unlike Colossus, he does not subordinate himself to an alternate group. Wolverine will make his own way; redefine his own sense of gender identity.

If gender delineations are a social construct, then who can say that any one type of behavior is wrong? Despite the inclusive nature of the male social cluster, men do not exist in a vacuum. They cannot wed themselves to outmoded forms of behavior, regardless of historical precedent, and the opportunity to define male identity through feats of strength are rapidly disappearing (Large 26). The crisis of masculinity was a direct result of the lopsided argument which sought to demonize one gender in order to elevate another. Crisis recovery will depend on new identity formation, new behavior models, which come from a holistic approach to gender constructs. There needs to be room for change and acceptance without the automatic assumption that change in itself is another form of feminization. Men could cherry pick the best attributes in the historic narrative of their identities and model themselves off feminists who rewrote the book on what it meant to adhere to normative, gendered, behavior. No longer would they have to define masculinity with the unacceptable aspects of fighting. Instead this behavior would become the subordinate term, characteristic of the weakling or the coward rather than the hero, while emphasizing modes of masculinity based on self-control and moral courage (Large 27). De-feminization of behavior can be initiated by any hegemonic male, granting them a unique level of autonomy within the bounds of gendered behavior, which is where real change and the survival of the male identity would be precipitated.

A difficult aspect of rebuilding gender identity could come from language i.e. "masculine behavior" and "feminized behavior." Studies linked lower rates of depression in adolescence, with regards to gender orientation, in individuals who experienced the development of more masculine traits. According to the study, girls were normalized by their peers as feminine while they were prepared for subordinate roles (mother, wife), while boys were normalized for roles that would trade in leadership and therefore certain personal freedoms (Barrett and White 453). Boys who believed they did not possess the so called traits of masculinity were more likely to develop mental health issues (Barrett and White 464). What surprised the researchers was that the girls with the least amount of masculine traits also suffered increased depression.

The reason is obvious: personal freedom and accomplishment is preferable to subordination no matter the gender. "Manhood, as displayed and negotiated in contemporary culture and cultural criticism, has ceased to refer to a universal, though unmarked and concealed state of being Nor is masculinity, as feminism has insisted for a long time, a supposedly stable and homogenous entity identical with power and patriarchal dominance" (Reichardt and Sielke 564). Perhaps when the hierarchy is rewritten, and the conversation of postmodern gender identity concerns itself with individual merit, the crisis of masculinity will evaporate. In a postmodern/postfeminist world full of political and economic upheaval, the fictional narrative of the idealized gender driven male identity can be built from a broader scope of traits, both physical and emotional. That new expression of virility can be defined by the courage it took to attain individuality outside the parameters of crumbling and archaic social constructs, "reworking pervasive and popular conceptions of gender by incorporating previously disassociated concepts of softness with hardness, of mind with body" (Brown 41). Like Wolverine, the real hegemonic male will make his own way, play by his own rules, and reject the handicaps which would be applied to him by others.

REFERENCES

Anderson, Eric. "'I Used to Think Women Were Weak': Orthodox Masculinity, Gender Segregation, and Sport." *Sociological Forum* 23.2 (2008): 257–280. Print.
Barrett, Anne and Helene Raskin White. "Trajectories of Gender Role Orientations in Adolescence and Early Adulthood: A Prospective Study of the Mental Health Effects of Masculinity and Femininity." *Journal of Health and Social Behavior* 43 (2002): 451–468. Print.
Bird, Shannon. "Welcome to the Men's Club: Homosociality and the Maintenance of Hegemonic Masculinity." *Gender & Society* 10.2 (1996): 120–132. Print.
Brown, Jeffrey A. "Comic Book Masculinity and the New Black Superhero." *African American Review* 33.1 (1999): 25–42. Print.
Connell, Robert W. "A Whole New World: Remaking Masculinity in the Context of the Environmental Movement." *Gender and Society* 4.4 (1990): 452–478. Print.
Connell, Robert. W. and James Messerschmidt. "Hegemonic Masculinity: Rethinking the Concept." *Gender & Society* 19.6 (2005): 829–859. Print.

Demetriou, Demetrakis Z. "Connell's Concept of Hegemonic Masculinity: A Critique." *Theory and Society* 30.3 (2001): 337–361. Print.

Donaldson, Michael. "What Is Hegemonic Masculinity?" *Theory and Society* 22 (1993): 643–657. Print.

Fernbach, Amanda. "The Fetishization of Masculinity in Science Fiction: The Cyborg and the Console Cowboy." *Science Fiction Studies* 27.2 (2000): 234–255. Print.

Gaffney, Justin and Kate Beverley. "Contextualizing the Construction and Social Organization of the Commercial Male Sex Industry in London at the Beginning of the Twenty-First Century." *Feminist Review* 67 (2001): 133–141. Print.

Grunberg, Isabelle. "Exploring the "Myth" of Hegemonic Stability." *International Organization* 44.4 (1990): 431–477. Print.

Jackson, Peter. "The Cultural Politics of Masculinity: Towards a Social Geography." *Transactions of the Institute of British Geographers* 16.2 (1991): 199–213. Print.

Large, Judith. "Disintegration conflicts and the restructuring of masculinity." *Gender and Development* 5.2 (1997): 23–30. Print.

Lobdell, Scott (w), Peter David (w), J.M. DeMatteis (w), Larry Hama (w), Joe Quesada (a), Brandon Peterson (a), John Romita (a), Chris Bachalo (a). *The Uncanny X-Men: Fatal Attractions*. New York: Marvel Worldwide Inc., 2012. Print.

McGuffey, Shawn and B. Lindsay Rich. "Playing in the Gender Transgression Zone: Race, Class, and Hegemonic Masculinity in Middle Childhood." *Gender & Society* 13.5 (1999): 608–627. Print.

Mautz, Brian, Bob Wong, Richard Peters, Michael Jennions. Penis size interacts with body shape and height to influence male attractiveness. *Proceedings of the National Academy of Sciences of the United States*, April 2013. Web. 13 April 2013.

Maynard, Steven. "Rough Work and Rugged Men: The Social Construction of Masculinity in Working-Class History." *Labour/Le Travail* 23 (1989): 159–169. Print.

Reichardt, Ulf. and Sabine Sielke. "What Does Man Want? The Recent Debates on Manhood and Masculinities." *Amerikastudien/American Studies* 43.4 (1998): 563–575. Print.

Traister, Bryce. "Academic Viagra: The Rise of American Masculinity Studies." *American Quarterly* 52.2 (2000): 274–304. Print.

Generation X:
Mutants Made to Order

DAVID ALLAN DUNCAN

In the early 1990s superhero comic books in America reached a significant level of popularity evidenced by the success of the Teenage Mutant Ninja Turtles, the Batman movie franchise, *Wizard Magazine*, and the speculation market. At Marvel Comics, the early 1990s belonged to mutants; *X-Men* #1 (Oct. 1991) sold a record amount of copies, a wildly popular *X-Men* animated series (1992–1997) appeared on TV, and the comics market was saturated with an array of X-men spin-off titles numbering in the double digits. In 1994, high on this success, Marvel released *Generation X*—a new monthly comic series created by writer Scott Lobdell and penciler Chris Bachalo. It is a title that stood, initially, in notable contrast to the other superhero books of the decade. *Generation X* was unique in mainstream superhero comics, clearly a product of and for its namesake age group.

In the decades since the 1960s, The X-Men had slowly built a fan base as it reacted to the social culture of each era. Each generation of X-Men grew up and moved on to various more adult life-paths, creating a recurring need to reiterate the original directive of Xavier's School for Gifted Youngsters: educating young mutants to control their abilities—a dynamic established in the first issue. Over the course of 30-plus years the X-Men eventually exemplified (though not expressly) the natural course of a school system including elements such as the graduation of older students, the induction of new learners, professor rotation, and even alumni-driven endeavors. In the 1980s this manifested in the publication of *The New Mutants* (March 1983), featuring a new class of young students.

It was inevitable that these recruits would mature and move on. "The teenage intake of New Mutants was transformed from students to warriors under the tutelage of Cable (debut #87: May 1990)" (Trushell 158). By the

128

end of the decade these new mutants were more of a militia than a class of pupils and made the transition from *New Mutants* to *X-Force*—written and drawn by 1990s superstar Rob Liefeld. The void left by the title was eventually addressed by Marvel. Writer Scott Lobdell explained, "Bob [Harras, X-title editor] had originally told me that he wanted to bring back the New Mutants book…. I decided I didn't want to put the kids back in the X-Mansion because they had done it before and it just didn't seem to work" (DeFalco 196).

Whether intentionally or not, Lobdell's trepidation about repeating *New Mutants* would lead to a series that closely—perhaps even ironically—matches the generation for which it was created and after which it was named. The series overwhelmingly reflects the trends, social views, cultural concerns, as well as the narrative tendencies of the 1990s.

The monthly *Generation X* series focuses on a group of mostly new teenage mutant characters being trained not by Professor Xavier, but Sean "Banshee" Cassidy and Emma "White Queen" Frost; and the school was set at the Massachusetts Academy (former home of the Hellions, rivals of the New Mutants) instead of the School For Gifted Youngsters in New York. Educated by a super-powered loudmouth and a telepathic aristocrat, the popular ex–X-Man Jubilee (who can create plasma light blasts from her hands) is joined by other teen mutants: previously established Husk (who can shed her skin, revealing alternate forms), Chamber (whose own powers blew a hole in his chest and jaw), Synch (who can emulate the powers of nearby mutants), Skin (who has several feet of extra skin that he can control), Mondo (who can absorb the texture of the objects he touches), M (a powerful telepath who can fly), and Penance (with red, razor sharp skin and long claws). These were powerful mutants, but they were also young, lost, and cynical—just like the intended audience.

The readers of *Generation X* embraced the bleak worldview that came with growing up during the sociopolitical turbulence of the decades leading up to the impending new millennium. Growing up through the 1980s gave Gen-Xers a particularly jaded and fractured world-view. Given such phenomenon as the continued dismantling of the family-model, the office of the president being held by a film star, the perpetual rise in poverty, the tragedy of the Challenger space shuttle explosion, and the Exxon Valdez oil spill eco-disaster, it is no surprise that the high anxiety, self-obsession, and social turmoil of the 1980s gave way to an apathetic and increasingly ambivalent generation of slackers in the 1990s. Everything great or significant for the country and the culture had seemingly either already happened or already failed, "so all Gen-Xers grew up in the aftermath of a beautiful but unrealized dream, and this sad fact informs their sensibility" (Hanson 11). Even the label of Generation X is appropriately vague, and is most often used to identify the generation born post–World War II baby boom, anywhere around 1960–1980.

This wide classification provides much of the ambiguity associated with this generation. *Generation X* creators Scott Lobdell (b. 1963) and Chris Bachalo (b. 1967) were born on the early end of this spectrum, and are most likely reaching a readership that was born closer to the end of this span. As cultural theorist Scott Bukatman notes, "superhero comics remain a largely subcultural phenomenon, produced largely by young males for somewhat younger males" (95), so the gap between creators and readers for this title is not truly significant enough to delineate a generational break. Lobdell and Bachalo were essentially making work for themselves—a common adage of contemporary authors. There is an apparent catharsis and irony in the role reversal of generational responsibility in *Generation X*. The authors create a group of young mutants who are charged with learning how to safeguard the mostly older generations, although Lobdell and Bachalo's age group usually harbors resentment toward their elders, who failed to provide a stable society.

The dichotomy of protecting a society whose majority despises them has been a driving thematic element in the X-Men franchise for decades. For the generation of mutants showcased in *Generation X*, reaching for that altruistic moral compass is not a priority. This perfectly mirrors the apathetic disconnect of Gen-Xers. "[T]hese 'slackers' are the Gen-X equivalent of hippies: They withdraw from the rat race as a half-assed rebellion against dehumanizing cultural forces. Yet slackers seek no revolutionary means for overturning or even healing the culture that appalls them" (Hanson 15).

The culture of Generation X does not seek to destroy, rebel, or replace the culture of the previous generation. Rather, the tendency is to respond with indifference, resignation. The often-lackadaisical attitude toward the social norms of the past is a result of the defeat of those that came before. There is no direct pride associated with one's own success or hard work. We can see these ideals manifested in the *Generation X* comic series. There is rarely a lament for actual family, or real home. Michael Tueth, talking about television shows of this generation, notes, "the gang in the office or the friends who hang around the apartment have become the family. The few shows that are not primarily work-centered are usually not set in traditional home environments" (102). Even so, there is a sense of ennui associated with the family dynamic within *Generation X*. Characters are not simply resigned to their classmates as family, nor do they outright reject the notion of family. The hard-boiled loner-type is more often associated with the rebel-characters of the previous generation. The family dynamic is passive and even flippant at times. Jubilee's obsession with her former role in the X-Men, as well as her quasi-father/daughter relationship with Logan makes her unique in caring about family, albeit her surrogate family. Paige's brother is New Mutant Cannonball. The only acknowledgement of this is in issue 18, where she writes him a childish and self-indulgent letter. Most of the students seem homeless or parentless—a common trait of X-Men characters. The team-as-family motif is present, but is not presented as particularly charming or even desired by the team. Several narrative elements in the series establish the importance of family to the generation before the Generation X students. Professor Banshee's family castle, Cassidy Keep in Ireland, warranted a story that lasted a few issues. The subplot reinforces Banshee's dedication to family and his loyalty to his students. But for the students, the solace and support of family is not diligently sought after. Lobdell says, "Now we're living in a society where, for lack of a better word, we're the walking wounded. How many peoples' parents are still together?" (Sodaro 34).

The family and medical back-story surrounding the character Monet "M" St. Croix is a particularly complex one—an intention of the original creators though it plays out differently given the shifting creative staffs over the seven year run (DeFalco 215). Lobdell and Bachalo originally intended M to be twins sharing a single body. Bachalo even notes that her age was around 16 years old because the twins were 8 years old (DeFalco 216). Lobdell and Bachalo left the series, so their intention was never made manifest in the subsequent stories. Eventually, the Monet in the early issues of *Generation X* is revealed to be the combination of twins Nicole and Claudette St. Croix, merged to replicate their missing sister Monet. Claudette is autistic, while Nicole is rather talkative. The team's archenemy, Emplate, is revealed to be the brother of the twins and the killer of their parents. Penance is the actual Monet; her brother Emplate turned her into the mute, red, spiked creature. Unresolved original creator intentions—like the fate of M—are indicative of the system of rotating creative staff members so common in mainstream superhero comics.

Worth noting is the explanation of M's frequent trances, which due to her strength leave her completely immovable by her faculty or classmates. These trances initially happen without explanation or even regularity—sometimes while taking a written test administered by Beast, sometimes during a fight or mission. These trances were designed to be a product of M's autism—a condition later diagnosed by Beast. Autism is neurological disorder characterized by problematic or absent social skills; it is often accounted for by genetic mutation. The number of reported cases of autism rose in the 1990s, giving it a substantial connection to this generation, either by awareness or development. Early symptoms of this disease are often perceived as the child's rejection of or indifference to their own family. Jeff Gordinier points out that characters in Gen-X narratives are usually "so stuck that they don't even know they're stuck, and only drastic action will dislodge them from their trance" (40). In issue #21 (Nov. 1996) rather than answering the questions on the written test, M constructs an elaborate origami building.

M's potential for direct minority reader-connection extends beyond her less-than-common neurological disorder; she is also Muslim—a rarity in mainstream comics. Multiculturalism has been a major aspect of the X-Men since the new team in 1975, which plays well into the struggle-for-acceptance theme that dominates many X-Men storylines. In *Generation X* there is a seeminglly obsessive sense of diversity.

The characters are as varied as possible; Chamber is from England, Monet is Algerian, Mondo is Samoan, Skin is Mexican-American, Penance was (originally intended to be) Yugoslavian, Husk is from Kentucky, Synch is from Missouri, and Jubilee is Chinese-American. The characters are rarely played as stereotypes, and Lobdell acknowledged this: "We are going to try to do something really radical and introduce a young, black character into comics who isn't angry," Lobdell says, "Synch is the most likely candidate for leadership..." (Sodaro 33).

Ideally, leadership is one of the skills taught and modeled for adolescents in schools, and the school setting is very important in *Generation X*. Lobdell and Bachalo take it as a great opportunity to mirror the likely audience of the series—high school students. The series explores the dynamics of the various relationships: student/teacher, student/student, teacher/teacher, teacher/parent. The school is seen as a relatively positive environment for most of the new students, though the multifaceted nature of adolescence shines through. In *Generation X* #2 (Dec. 1994) we see Skin and Husk playing scrabble, spelling out derogatory names toward each other—"hick" and "loser." Other students are considerably proactive: "Jubilee volunteers to attend the school, because she wants to better serve the X-Men by developing her powers, which up to now have been pretty useless," says Lobdell (Bittner 36). Others exhibit the stereotypical Gen-X resignation to the situation, being neither upset nor excited about the school.

The series also explores the individual motives of the teachers early on—each having a different point of view. Compared to the clear command held by parental figures to the previous generation, these surrogate parents hold only a damaged measure of authority, which they struggle to hold. Instead of the strength and stability of the original depiction of Professor Xavier, these teachers carry their own problems and often guide their pupils toward trouble rather than away. Prof. Cassidy seems focused on survival and maintaining a normal life. His role to the students is in contrast to his tumultuous relationship with his mutant daughter (Siryn of X-Force). Prof. Frost is a more complex instructor. She joins the faculty as a sort of curriculum concession after the death of her previous students (the Hellions, which she formed as adolescent competition to Xavier's New Mutants). Lobdell notes that, "her way didn't work. Ten teenage kids were killed specifically because she didn't teach them well enough " (Sodaro 32). Constantly reminding her of this failing, the buildings used for *Generation X* is the previous home of her school.

Just like early Uncanny X-Men and early New Mutants, the school is the central binding element of the *Generation X* series—after all, the absence of the learning environment in the other X-Men titles is what led to the creation of the series. The character relationships are all established with in the context of academic study. Yet, true to the Gen-X tendency of disarming important matters via flippant reverence or cynical banter, the scholastic elements are often displayed in a jocular light. On a mission to Maine in issue #4 (Feb. 1995) the class tries to pass through a police check point by claiming to be on a field trip. "We're so excited, Officer," says Jubilee.

In *Generation X* #5 (July 1995) Banshee is seen trying to reach out to Penance by using difference languages, hoping one will click with her. It is played like a teacher trying to help a troubled student—eventually, in a strange act of role reversal, the teacher gives an apple to the student. In *Generation X* #17 (Jul. 1996), Skin is practicing a new way of using his powers (a sort of skin slingshot), and thinks to himself about how Banshee taught him the move. Of course, it is still new to him, so he does not quite pull it off perfectly; but the implication is that he is learning from his professor. *Generation X* #21 (Nov. 1996) brings Beast, a visiting professor, into the classroom to administer a midterm exam. The behavior of the students in this setting is humorous and indicative of their attitudes. Penance climbs into the classroom, seeming to know her role as a student, but is only able to shred the paper. Jubilee mostly just doodles sketches of her classmates in the margins—even drawing Penance along side the phrase, "'nuff said." Sometimes the drama outweighs the humor—in *Generation X* #17 (July 1996) we see Synch's parents accosting Banshee about his teaching and what they expected their son to get out of the program: "You claimed you could help our son—teach him to use his powers.... You broke that promise!"

The social connection that the X-Men have to the age group of their readership is a well-established point of discussion. "The superhero origin is a metaphor for adolescence.... The X-Men are ready metaphors for adolescent alienation and also for bigotry, standing in for any 'other'" (Coogan 15). But this generation is more complex than the pimple-popping losers that the Stridex ads in comics seem to reach out to. Ennui, anger, cynicism—attitudes most often associated with adolescence—seem to permeate the psyche of this age group to a more enduring degree. The issues they face are heightened well beyond an inconvenient and embarrassing zit. "There's an issue where [Penance] passes out, ... Banshee goes to lift her up and almost slices his hands off. This is a character who needs to learn how to function in society" (Sodaro 33).

During interviews, the creators and editors on this series emphasized their use of non-pretty mutants: the less socially viable students whose mutant abilities were disfiguring, and thus devoid of the freedom to wander society undetected—a capability of normal looking mutants. "We're going in different directions with this title," said Bob Harras to *Wizard Magazine*. "This new group of students aren't poster-child mutants. Some of them are disfigured" (Sodaro 33).

Chamber's chest and jaw were destroyed as a result of the initial manifestation of his powers, "All that remains is a cascade of vile energy pouring from the cavity. As one might expect, he's not a particularly happy mutant" (Sodaro 34). This constant visual and physical reminder of this curse forces him to wrap his face and neck whenever venturing into public. Skin's grotesquely exaggerated extra skin and Penance's razor sharp red exterior are also difficult to hide.

Lobdell experienced his own teenage body trauma: His lungs developed blisters, which put him into the hospital for a length of time during his late teens as he underwent surgery and recovery. His illness was not a result of some error that he made, but rather was produced by his own body. Lobdell—a Gen-Xer himself—also mentioned his personal affinity to the X-Men characters of Beast and (in particular) Nightcrawler—especially because of their outward disfigurement. "Nightcrawler is a mutant twenty-four hours a day, seven days a week, in a way that most of the other characters aren't. He probably had the right to be the most bitter because he's the type of mutant most likely to be feared and hated by a world he was sworn to protect" (DeFalco 194). This type of outward representation of bodily damage is certainly in tune with Gen-X society's obsession with body modification art (tattoos, piercings). Bukatman notes, "[it] fetishizes the body as a spectacle of marginality, not to mention the body in pain..." (Bukatman 120). The visual damage of one's body correlates to the damaged culture.

This representation of a damaged persona also extends beyond the body to the attire of the character. The importance of costuming within mainstream superheroes is intrinsically linked to the fashion of the era. The mindset of adopting and sporting popular trends in the form of clothing is not altogether unlike putting on a costume. The sleek design of most Silver Age heroes (particularly revamps like Infantino's Flash for DC) is certainly a product of the 1950's space age optimism, just as the X-Men's Dazzler is an obvious product of the 1970's disco era.

The *Generation X* comic series sought to represent—and surely connect with—a readership whose fashion ideology is less celebratory than those generations before. Flare and formality are all but destroyed in the grunge aesthetic. This taste can certainly be connected to the prevailing temperament.

Clare and Adam Hibbert note that fashion design of the 1990s articulates a "mood of chaos and disintegration. Many young people adopted anti-fashion 'grunge' styles, wearing clothes that deliberately looked dirty and scruffy. ... Fashion-conscious teens, meanwhile, turned to secondhand stores to build their own retro styles" (48). The ragged look of plaid flannel shirts and awkward-sized clothing stands in stark contrast to the formal clothing donned by most of the older X-Men.

Fashion and body art—though cultural trends—still represent a personal decision in the life of the audience, though the student mutants in *Generation X* have little choice over their own powers and school uniforms. The shared experience that affected this generation's connection to the shifting culture is the shift from an analog culture to one that is increasingly digital. This generation stands on a bridge between two worlds, being able to see in both directions; though growing up reading children's books that came with 45 rpm records, they now store their music in a digital cloud. This onslaught of technology (and the transition) has been embraced by Gen-Xers; notably it baffles the previous generation (rejecting the transition) and is already the norm for the subsequent millennial generation (no need to transition) (Chamberlain 7). "They were creating—from scratch—new routes with which to navigate the world, and they were overthrowing all the old ways of watching and selling and sharing things" (Gordinier 53). This view of technology manifests itself both in and out of the *Generation X* comic series; from the very beginning we see the importance of technology to this title.

In the 1994 X-title crossover event "Phalanx Covenant" (which served as a precursor to *Generation X*), many of the soon-to-be-students are attacked by hive-minded techo-organic mutant haters seeking to assimilate young mutants. The use of technology to deliver comics was barely on the horizon, yet Marvel held an on-line press conference on August 25, 1994 on CompuServe. The entire first issue was available digitally on services such as AOL and other Internet Service Providers several weeks before the print release ("Today's Superheroes"). It took about 90 minutes to download the issue with a fast connection. The event itself was news to the industry, since nothing like it had really happened before. In addition to the digital release, fans type-chatted with Lobdell and Bachalo—discussing the story, art, and characters— live via the online event ("Marvel to Promote").

This new generation of comic creators saw the trajectory of the medium, the industry, and the creator's role in it all. Jack Kirby had fought publicly for his artwork and lost, the Comics Code was losing its authority, Speedy got hooked on drugs, Batman readers voted to kill Robin, Frank Miller and Alan Moore dismantled superheroes, self-publishing became significantly viable, comics were winning non-comic awards, creators rights were a hot topic, and graphic novels were taking hold outside of fandom. The creators responsible for *Generation X* had not participated in any of the revolutionary events that created the post-*Watchmen* dark days of comics. Though at first it may seem like their predecessors set them up for success, the effects of these events mostly lead to a speculation market and an eventually embarrassing era of mainstream superhero gimmickry, flashy-style derivation, and vapid narratives. *Generation X* hoped to reach beyond its contemporaries, by being something different both in story and art.

By this time comics fandom was increasingly fractured. The growing alternative comics market was really striking a chord with older high school students. Books like DC Vertigo's *Sandman* were casual reading fare at many lunchroom tables. In many ways the collective developments of the cult of the artist (via Marvel) and the cult of the writer (via Vertigo) had instilled Gen-Xers with a heightened appreciation for the comics auteur. Douglas Wolk discusses the mainstream/indy schools of thought regarding comics of merit: "The best ones are usually by writer/artist teams who plan the look and feel of their collaborations" (28). *Generation X* was clearly conceived within this ethos. Lobdell and Bachalo were often co-credited as creators, not writer and penciler. Lobdell recalls establishing this collaboration in conversation with Bachalo: "We're going to come up with the characters together. This isn't going to be my team, drawn by you. This is our book!" (DeFalco 197). Lobdell would purposefully write the most bizarre stuff he could imagine only having Bachalo make "it look even more bizarre than [he] thought it could" (Bittner 38).

In the early 1990s Chris Bachalo had risen to prominence not as a mainstream superhero artist, but as an alternative comics artist on the Vertigo title *Shade the Changing Man*, a particularly psychedelic and abrasive series. His work was strikingly unique. The *Comics Journal*'s Rich Kreiner says his artwork on *Shade*, "gives the madness its full measure with a lush, convincing, novel, and consistently interesting visual presence," taking care to point out his daringly graphic page design: "the adventurous games he plays with panel borders, running margins in defiance of right angles and page edges, setting gutters to roam irrespective of scenes, focal objects, or cropping considerations" (44).

In part due to Bachalo's pencils, non-superhero readers and creators were gravitating towards *Generation X*. In an interview with *The Comics Journal*, *Usagi Yojimbo* creator Stan Sakai said, "I buy Generation X, just because I kind of like the artwork.... I've been buying it ever since the first issue just because the artwork is different" (Thompson 61).

Not only were readers and fans excited about Bachalo's art, so was the industry. Harras says, "as soon as I saw the character sketches, I wanted Bachalo for the book" (DeFalco 181). His work set him apart from what had become a downward spiral of style-derivation within mainstream superhero comics in the 1990s. "One big difference between art comics and superhero comics is what their readers look for in them. What matters most in art comics is the way the cartoonist communicates his or her content—the creator is always an almost-tangible presence" (Wolk 110). The involvement of Bachalo and Lobdell seemed as intrinsically linked to the success of this book as *Sandman's* success depended on Neil Gaiman writing it.

At its onset, *Generation X* looked nothing like the other X-books. Lobdell says:

> [Bachalo] had previously done a two-page sequence where the people just sat and talked, doing all the things that we do when we're having an intimate conversation. His editor on that book made him redraw it to add a little more action. I said, "Chris, I want you to be different, if you give me two pages of knees, I'll write two pages of knees. You don't have to ape Jim Lee or Whilce Portacio on this book" [DeFalco 197].

Bachalo's panel layout and compositions are dynamic in a way that distorts and toys with the perception of space and page. It seems a natural course of analysis to connect Bachalo's work with that of *New Mutants* artist Bill Sienkiewicz. The comparison of reader responses is worth noting. Sienkiewicz's artwork proved to be difficult for many readers at the time, this is mostly credited to the work on the title that Bob McLeod and Sal Buscema had done; perhaps it was a little ahead of its time. Bachalo defined the look and feel of *Generation X*, and that preliminary artwork and character designs were used extensively in advertising and press releases. This fed perfectly into the Gen-X obsession with behind-the-scenes material. The irony would be that the effort to associate Bachalo's art with this title would ultimately be in vain because he would leave the book for long stretches and other artists were left to hold the line—most falling short of those initial aesthetics.

In addition to his stylized characters and complex page construction, Bachalo also embraces the use of repetitive pattern in all of his work—so much so that it becomes a defining characteristic of his work. The checks are evident in *Shade, Death*, and *Generation X*. The check pattern has been associated with the alternative/punk scene since the late 1970s when British ska musician Jerry Dammers created the iconic Walt Jabsco character for the 2-Tone record label (Missreverie). In that context the pattern emblemized the merging of musical styles and racial equality. In addition to its link to alternative music, the checkerboard pattern is also associated with Lewis Caroll's *Through the Looking Glass* and the artwork of M.C. Escher—explorers of dual realities and distorted perceptions. After a hiatus on the series, Bachalo's return is announced in *Generation X* #16 (June 1996) with a checkerboard pattern behind his name.

Another visual trait in Bachalo's comics is the repetitive use of distorted photocopied panels—most often a character's face. Bachalo seems to take a previous panel and enlarge it on a photocopier for use in subsequent panels; he embraces the distortion of the drawing, engorged line weights, and any dust or pockmarks evident in the transfer. *Generation Next* #4 (June 1995) begins with the use of this photocopy method. The panels pull back on an enlarged smiley-face watch to reveal its wearer, a likely homage to *Watchmen's* smiley-face zoom. In *Generation X* #20 (Oct. 1996), Bachalo uses the photocopy trick at the beginning as the supervillain Bastion examines Chamber on a video monitor, and later as he looks at Chamber's former, undamaged face.

This graphic device immediately brings to mind the DIY punk and grunge aesthetic associated with band flyers and zines (like that of Jamie Reid). This DIY zine culture is often considered a forerunner, or at least a parent, to the alternative comics movement of the 1980s. It also seems to reference the industry practice of photocopying similar panels during art production as a time saver (often viewed as a cheat). Rather than trying to hide the practice— as many artists do by making subtle changes to the facsimile—Bachalo embraces it as a stylistic motif.

About his own work Bachalo defers to comics creator Jeff Loeb: "[He] once said to me that I look at the world through a different set of eyeglasses to everyone else. I liked that" (DeFalco 225). Bachalo and Lobdell—like the rest of their generation—see the world through pop-culture saturated eyes. The Generation X age group grew up in a media-saturated culture. They have been raised by the television, film, and music of their own age and those generations before. Television sitcoms run in seemingly endless syndication, films rise to cult status (warranting repeated viewing), and portable cassette and CD players allow for listeners to soundtrack their whole day. Lobdell tells Tom Defalco, "as a result of my childhood, I have a vast knowledge of television prior to 1980..." (DeFalco 189).

Using pop culture references in new narratives is a major trend within Generation X storytelling. Using character dialog that discusses or debated topics from popular culture further connects the reality of the audience with the fiction of the story; "it's a conversation in which Gen-X audience members could easily participate. [...] it's a simple matter of speaking to viewers in their own idiom" (Hanson 14).

The students meet villain M-Plate in the first issue (Nov. 1994). When confronted with who would be the mortal enemy of Generation X, Jubilee calls him Snuffleupagus—a *Sesame Street* character that, for a long time, only Big Bird could see. This is an appropriate reference given that only a few pages before M-Plate passed through the airport crowd unnoticed.

The pop culture references continue, showing up in almost every issue.

In *Generation X* #18 (Aug. 1996) we see Skin behave like Spider-Man, using his extra skin to snatch groceries and swing around. A character in the same issue is cursing the weather and takes on the dialect of *Looney Tunes* character Yosemite Sam: "Rassum Frassum... Wind... Rassum frassum." And *Generation X* #28 (June 1997) features creative credits that reference *Gilligan's Island's* opening; Lobdell as Gilligan and Bachalo as the Skipper.

In the story introducing readers to the characters who would become Generation X, before the characters were in their own title, Jubilee makes a reference to Superman in *X-Men* #30 (Mar. 1994) when Paige changes her form—which involves the shedding of her skin:

> JUBILEE (as Paige husks): "Can't you, like, find a phone booth if yer gonna change like that?"
> HUSK: "I don't understand the reference. "
> JUBILEE: "I forgot you don't read comics."

Of course, Marvel has made constant self-references, often working the creators and bullpen staff into the narratives—understanding Marvel in-jokes was a badge of honor for fans, but these often reach out beyond the Marvel Universe into an larger context. "The combination of pop-culture references, unconventional narrative structures, and the cynical, know-it-all posture that many Gen-Xers wear as a status symbol produces a peculiar brand of reflective postmodernism" (Hanson 15).

Gen-Xers are used to having their reality and fiction blended. When Bachalo returns to the series after a hiatus, he incorporates Stan Lee as a host character to the issue. Regarding *Generation X* #17 (July 1996), Bachalo says, "I thought, well, you know, 'Stan Lee Presents,' why not have Stan Lee present the issue? Host it, like Rod Serling in the Twilight Zone? I figured I'd throw him in and see what happens" (DeFalco 217). The presence of Lee as a host was not a new spectacle to Marvel Comics. Lee's self-image as a showman found its way into several story openings. So even the use of the pop-culture icon in a comic based on things he created decades before is a reference in and of itself. Stan Lee even scripted his own dialog for the *Generation X* cameo. Jokingly breaking the fourth wall is common in Marvel comics. In *Generation X* #19 (Sept. 1996) a frog tell a few of the other characters, "I have to go boys, I'm needed on page four." There is a frog on the counter in page four.

The series was humorous and cynical, and the success of the book seemed to be a sure thing; but alas there were troubles from the start. Marvel was not the only purveyor of superheroes looking to exploit the grunge culture. As Marvel began announcing *Generation X,* Image Comics was concurrently advertising a forthcoming comic book series called *Gen X* that would feature teenage heroes. Eventually Image changes the name of their title to *Gen 13*—

a reference to the 1993 book *13th Gen: Abort, Retry, Ignore, Fail?*, by William Strauss and Neil Howe that explored the same age group. *Gen 13* even featured a character named Grunge—if the connection was not obvious enough.

Problems unrelated to the quality of the series itself began to swell up around *Generation X*. The speculation market was bursting; X-Men titles seem to be too numerous to count. "When asked how many more X-titles the comic market could bear, Harras says that as long as people keep buying them, Marvel will keep publishing them" (Sodaro 36). The intricate narratives weaving between multiple titles over multiple decades rivaled soap operas and alienated new readers (Trushell 160). The Marvelution meetings set up for retailers were not well received; and Marvel's acquisition of Heroes World Distribution became a business fiasco. Comic orders were tanking at a devastating rate across the entire industry. Eventually Marvel filed for bankruptcy.

From a creative standpoint, *Generation X* was never able to get a toehold on the readership. Editorial involvement forced the young book into a massive, world altering convoluted crossover called "The Age of Apocalypse" in 1995. The massive event took over nine monthly or bi-monthly titles for a total of 34 issues. Each book was renamed and all characters and storylines were thrown out and redesigned. Generation X becomes *Generation Next* for four issues (Mar.–June 1995). Bachalo, who was initially opposed to *Generation X*'s mandated involvement the crossover, was swayed by editor Bob Harras who allowed him to include ideas in *Generation Next* that were not approved for *Generation X* (DeFalco 216). The result may ultimately be that the four-issue alternate reality story for *Generation Next* is a more stable and cohesive comic narrative than the main series, which struggled to find its place—just like its namesake.

Before leaving *Shade the Changing Man* at Vertigo, Bachalo had told DC editor Karen Berger than he would return for a sequel to the *Death: The High Cost of Living* mini-series (March–May 1993) he had worked on with Neil Gaiman (DeFalco 216). When that call came, he vacated *Generation X* skipping issues 7 through 16 to work on *Death: The Time of Your Life* (April–July 1996), a series he did not finish because of its slow schedule.

Marvel even sought to push the series out to other media. Before the monthly book was grounded as a long-running popular series, Marvel attempted to turn the series into a TV movie debuting on Fox Television in February of 1996. It was written and produced by Eric Blakeney, who was used to writing drama for strong young characters, having worked on the teenage police procedural *21 Jump Street* (Allstetter 58).

This preemptive capitalization seems misguided given that it started production less than one year after the comic series began. They were unable to pull off the more gruesome mutants; among others, Chamber was just too difficult to depict with a television budget. The cast seems ironically pretty in the light of the comic series' initial advocacy for ugly mutants. The group of attractive young actors seem more akin to the charming teens on *Saved by the Bell*—the most successful Saturday morning show in the early 1990s—than to the visibly damaged students in the monthly comic.

These efforts by Marvel seem like the workings of a corporation desperate for money. All of these factors—creative interruptions, "The Age of Apocalypse," Bachalo's departure, the TV movie—make the ultimate unraveling of this series inevitable. Bachalo returned for a few years, but the opportunity had already seemed to pass—the new readership simply lost. The bridge between alternative comics and superheroes crumbled and would have to be built elsewhere. The last few years of the *Generation X* series were created under several different creative teams each trying to deal with the efforts of the previous team while attempting to maintain the only readership left— X-Men fans.

Generation X failed to consistently reach either the alternative market or the established x-fans. It jumped between the two, while never planting firmly enough in either to ensure the measure of success needed for any Marvel title to survive. The series mirrored the stereotype of its namesake generation in its unfocused path and disheveled vision.

In some ways the character Paige "Husk" Guthrie serves as a light metaphor for the *Generation X*/Gen-X correlation. She's an odd character even to her creators. Regarding Lobdell's work on Husk, Bachalo says, "I thought he was working for the wrong company. He should be over at Vertigo, land of the really strange characters" (DeFalco 214). She is a child without her own personal heritage—her brother came first. As the younger sister of New Mutants' Sam "Cannonball" Guthrie, she is the second child in her immediate family to get involved with the X-Men. She sees herself in the light of Sam's reputation and dissent, placing her into a context defined by her predecessor.

Excluding Jubilee (because of her former lead-character status), Husk was a peripheral character in the other x-books the longest. She manifests the dichotomy of the beauty and ugliness. She sheds her skin, revealing an alternate form underneath—but she cannot necessarily control it completely, but the more that she learns about materials, the more varied her options. The symbolism of these elements themselves (stone, glass, etc.) could each warrant analysis. Just like the other students, just like Gen-Xers, she is still learning about her own abilities. In *Generation X* #3 (Jan. 1995) after Husk is scratched deeply by Penance, Banshee ask what will happen to her wounds when she returns to her original form. She replies, "Honestly? I don't know. I suppose we'll have to find out together."

Early on in the series we see Husk falter in issue #5 (July 1995). There is a scene where she gets drunk. Lobdell made a point to show the negative results in issue #6 (Aug. 1995). She feels bad and throws up; she even loses the respect of her classmates. Lobdell says, "I don't think the consequences came from the writer's or editorial point of view, but rather, they came from the character. If you stay true to the characters, they'll provide their own sense of morality" (Brady 43).

Just as Generation X made the transition from an analog era to the digital age, Paige is a hayseed Kentucky girl who, toward the end of the series becomes particularly savvy with computers—to the benefit of her classmates. She would eventually cultivate an affinity to issues involving the environment—which at once mirrors the popular trend of going green As well as the generational importance of finding place and position. The only thing about Husk that does not chime with Gen-Xers is her reputation as a hard worker; she was never seen as the slacker.

Paige—like most of the other *Generation X* characters—found a place in the continuing X-Men titles, with less subversive narrative and visual styles. There was no place for alt-comics in the 1990's Marvel Universe. *Generation X* had shown the immediate potential to connect with an audience not usually associated with mainstream Marvel superhero comics; but the early absence of Bachalo crushed any esteem the series might have garnered from the high-brow readers.

The failure of *Generation X* over time (even a short time) to live up to its early creative potential was thematically inevitable. Just as Gen-Xers struggle with social position, stumble over responsibility, and revel in their own culture, an ongoing monthly comic book series that too totally embraces the ideology, tendencies, and culture of that generation will certainly end up so stuck that it cannot recognize its own stuckness.

WORKS CITED

Allstetter, Roy. "Mutant '90210'" *Wizard Magazine* 54 (1996): 56–61. Print.
Bedford, Mark. "Smells Like 1990s Spirit: The Dazzling Deception of Fight Club's Grunge-aesthetic." *New Cinemas: Journal of Contemporary Film* 9.1 (2011): 49–63. Print.
Bittner, Drew. "Freshmen Class." *Comics Scene* 2.47 (1994): 34–39. Print.
Brady, Matthew. "Sonic Youth." *Wizard Magazine* 56 (1996): 40–43. Print.
Bukatman, Scott. "X-Bodies (the Torment of the Mutant Superhero)." In *Uncontrollable Bodies: Testimonies of Identity and Culture*. Ed. Rodney Sappington and Tyler Stallings. Seattle: Bay, 1994. 93–129. Print.
Chamberlain, Lisa. *Slackonomics: Generation X in the Age of Creative Destruction*. Cambridge, MA: Da Capo, 2008. Print.
Claremont, Chris (w) and Brent Anderson (a). "Chutes and Ladders." *Uncanny X-Men* #160 (Aug. 1982). New York: Marvel Comics. Print.

Coogan, Peter M., and Dennis O'Neil. *Superhero: The Secret Origin of a Genre*. Austin, TX: MonkeyBrain, 2006. Print.

DeFalco, Tom. *Comics Creators on the X-Men*. London: Titan Book, 2006. Print.

Gordinier, Jeff. *X Saves the World: How Generation X Got the Shaft but Can Still Keep Everything from Sucking*. New York: Viking, 2008. Print.

Hanson, Peter. *The Cinema of Generation X: A Critical Study of Films and Directors*. McFarland &, 2002. Print.

Hibbert, Clare, and Adam Hibbert. A History of Fashion and Costume. Vol. 8, The Twentieth Century. New York: Facts On File, 2005. Print.

Howe, Neil, and William Strauss. *13th Gen: Abort, Retry, Ignore, Fail?* New York: Vintage, 1993. Print.

Kreiner, Rich. "Vertiginous Heroes." *The Comics Journal* 163 (1993): 41–44. Print.

Lobdell, Scott (w) and Chris Bachalo (a). "Third Genesis." *Generation X* #1 (Nov. 1994). New York: Marvel Comics. Print.

_____ and _____. "Searching." *Generation X* #2 (Dec. 1994). New York: Marvel Comics. Print.

_____ and _____. "Dead Silence." *Generation X* #3 (Jan. 1995). New York: Marvel Comics. Print.

_____ and _____. "Between the Cracks." *Generation X* #4 (Feb. 1995). New York: Marvel Comics. Print.

_____ and _____. "Bye." *Generation Next* #4 (June 1995). New York: Marvel Comics. Print.

_____ and _____. "Don't Touch That Dial!" *Generation X* #5 (July 1995). New York: Marvel Comics. Print.

_____ and _____. "Notes from the Underground." *Generation X* #6 (Aug. 1995). New York: Marvel Comics. Print.

_____ and _____. "The Teeth of Our Skin." *Generation X* #17 (July 1996). New York: Marvel Comics. Print.

_____ and _____. "For the Sake of the Children." *Generation X* #18 (Aug. 1996). New York: Marvel Comics. Print.

_____ and _____. "Don't Wait Up." *Generation X* #19 (Sept. 1996). New York: Marvel Comics. Print.

_____ and _____. "Bodies in Motion." *Generation X* #20 (Oct. 1996). New York: Marvel Comics. Print.

_____ and _____. "To Live and Die and Molt in L.A." *Generation X* #21 (Nov. 1996). New York: Marvel Comics. Print.

_____ and _____. "Oh, Now I Get It...." *Generation X* #28 (June 1997). New York: Marvel Comics. Print.

Lobdell, Scott (w) and Tom Grummett (a). "Out of Sync!" *Generation X* #16 (June 1996). New York: Marvel Comics. Print.

"Marvel to Promote New Comic Book with Electronic Distribution." *AP News Archive*. The Associated Press, 24 Aug. 1994. Web. 30 Apr. 2013.

Missreverie. "The Checkered Pattern Checks Right in Fashion." *Fashionista NOW*. Fame Cherry, 15 Oct. 2010. Web. 30 Apr. 2013.

Nicieza, Fabian (w) and Andy Kubert (a). "The Tie That Binds." *X-Men* #30 (March 1994). New York: Marvel Comics. Print.

Sodaro, Robert J. "I Was a Teenage Mutant!" *Wizard Magazine* 34 (1994): 30–36. Print.

Thompson, Kim. "Stan Sakai." *The Comics Journal* 192 (1996): 52–70. Print.
"Today's Superheroes Are Surfing the Info Highway." *Businessweek Archives*. Ed. Paul M. Eng. Businessweek, 4 Sept. 1994. Web. 30 Apr. 2013.
Trushell, John M. "American Dreams of Mutants: The X-Men-"Pulp" Fiction, Science Fiction, and Superheroes." *The Journal of Popular Culture* 38.1 (2004): 149–68. Print.
Tueth, Michael. "Fun City: TV's Urban Situation Comedies of the 1990s." *Journal of Popular Film and Television* 28.3 (2000): 98–107. Print.
Wolk, Douglas. *Reading Comics: How Graphic Novels Work and What They Mean*. Cambridge, MA: Da Capo, 2007. Print.

What Happens "After Xavier"?
Millennial Fears and
the Age of Apocalypse

JEFF GEERS

During the comic book boom of the early 1990s, the X-Men saw a level of popularity that dwarfed all other superhero books. Claremont and Lee's 1991 launch of the new *X-Men* title, with a gimmick of four different cover images, still holds the record for the best-selling single issue of all time. The Saturday morning *X-Men* cartoon had been a massively popular success, bringing new readers to comics. In 1994, 20th Century–Fox bought the movie rights, a precursor to the recent wave of big-budget blockbuster adaptations. By 1995, the original *Uncanny X-Men* had branched out into 8 different monthly titles.

Unbelievably, it all ended in a flash... a flash of polychrome crystal!

Beginning in February 1995, all of the X-titles were renamed and restarted at issue #1, with a one-shot, *X-Men: Alpha*, explaining the new setting, history, and team rosters. For the next four months, familiar characters and storylines that had been continuing for nearly 30 years were totally replaced with familiar names in new and unfamiliar settings and stories. Due to a time traveler visiting the past and altering the timeline, Professor X was long dead, and the world had been conquered by the arch-villain Apocalypse. The X-Men were now resistance fighters led by Magneto, their greatest adversary, while several of the original team members were now positioned as villains.

While this "Age of Apocalypse" was far from the first time X-Men comic books had visited a dystopian alternate reality, it marked a key quality of rhetoric in American popular culture: a focus on the apocalyptic possibilities presented by the dawning of a new Millennium. Apocalyptic narratives gained a central role in 1990's American culture, in news coverage of doomsday cults, in the rise of rapture-focused evangelical Christian literature, in a focus on Y2K, and even in the ideological shift within the Hollywood action blockbuster. "The Age of Apocalypse" reflects the dominant themes of American Millennial rhetoric, as its bleak alternate reality mutually reinforces themes of fear and hope, ultimately upholding the fictional status quo of the X-Men universe.

"The Age of Apocalypse" actually began several months earlier, during the events of the previous crossover, "Legion Quest"; as a secondary story in several of the different X-books, Professor Xavier's multi-personality-ridden mutant son, nicknamed "Legion," attempted to travel back in time before the founding of the X-Men and kill Magneto, believing this would actually help realize his father's dream of peaceful mutant/human co-existence. Several X-Men also travel back in history to stop him, but they fail when Legion's lethal attack accidentally hits Professor X, who jumps in the way to protect his then-friend Magneto. As the killing blow strikes Xavier, a flash erases Legion and the time-hopping X-Men, rewriting fictional history and beginning the Age of Apocalypse.

The next month's issues returned to the "present day," several decades after Xavier's death. The supervillain Apocalypse has conquered North America and devastated the rest of the globe with nuclear war. It is revealed that, having witnessed the attack on Xavier and Magneto, Apocalypse chose that moment to launch his conquest, much earlier than in the "real" X-Men history. His attacks came before the X-teams had been fully formed and prepared, and he was able to sweep nearly unopposed across the country. Apocalypse's mutant army ruled with an iron fist, while human "flatscans" were rounded up in work camps.

Although the character had only been created and introduced to the X-Men universe relatively recently (as a shadowy threat in the spinoff book *X-Factor* in 1985), Apocalypse's significance and popularity among readers made the villain a perfect world conqueror. As a 5000-year-old "first mutant," he presented a sharp inversion of Professor X's dream of equality—all beings, mutant or human, were equally inferior to the darwinian Apocalypse, the truly strong would survive and triumph, while the weak would be crushed underfoot. Traditional X-Men villains, including Magneto, were presented as honorable foes who could be made to see the errors of their ways (even if they eventually turned evil again in the next issue); Apocalypse, on the other hand, was an uncaring force of nature, the nihilistic power of evolution personified.

However, even without their mentor Professor X, the X-Men still exist in this reality; Magneto has chosen to honor his late friend's philosophy of peaceful coexistence (instead of Magneto's traditional philosophy of mutant superiority through force) and has gathered a band of mutants to fight back against Apocalypse and protect "innocent humans" (a phrase that seems incredibly incongruous coming from early–90s Magneto, who often ranted about "all humans being guilty as a species"). In this reality, Magneto still wears the familiar bucket helmet and cape, but is a family man who cares foremost for his wife, the X-Man Rogue, and their infant son Charles.

Rogue is not the only familiar face on the X-Men's roster: Nightcrawler, Storm, Banshee, Dazzler, and Iceman (now a disembodied being of solid ice) were all regular members of "normal" X-titles. However, the team was now lead by Quicksilver, the son of Magneto who had been everything from evil mutant to Avenger in regular Marvel continuity, and included Sunfire and Morph, secondary characters last seen in the early 1970s, as well as Blink, a minor character killed "off-panel" in her first (unnamed) appearance a year earlier. The biggest shock was the presence of Exodus and Sabretooth, who were known to loyal *X-Men* readers as nefarious villains.

Elsewhere in "The Age of Apocalypse," the former X-Men Colossus and Shadowcat, now married, ran a brutal training camp for Magneto's youngest recruits, a twisted parallel of the *New Mutants* and *Generation X* series. Gambit was a "mutant Robin Hood," stealing supplies from Apocalypse and giving them to starving humans. The time-traveling futuristic soldier Cable no longer existed; instead, "Nate Grey" was a clone with incredible psychic powers (a far cry from Cable's physicality and fondness for massive armaments). The Beast, normally the X-Men's jovial, blue-furred scientist, was now an evil, twisted geneticist conducting horrific experimentation. While only the X-books were replaced, the entire Marvel Universe was decimated; non-mutant characters like Ben Grimm, Tony Stark, and even Gwen Stacy were shown as leaders of the human resistance.

Perhaps the biggest shock was the reversal of a long-running love triangle—Jean Grey was no longer married to Scott Summers (a recent high-profile event in X-Men continuity), but was part of an independent strike force with her lover, Weapon X (a Wolverine missing most of his left arm). Scott Summers, not only an original X-Man, but the longstanding team leader, was now a Lieutenant to Apocalypse's "Four Hoursemen" (with a recent fight with Wolverine leaving him with only one eye he is literally a cyclops).

All eight of the titles involved in "The Age of Apocalypse" featured an overarching story of Magneto's final push against Apocalypse, with the hope of using the alien M'Kraan crystal to travel back in time and reset history. While in many ways a typical crossover story involving several smaller quests and twists, it was much darker and bleaker than usual X-Men stories. These characters had a high mortality rate (even for X-Men), and even small victories were pyrrhic—in *Generation Next*, for example, the "teacher" Colossus sacrifices all five of his young "students" in order to rescue his missing sister from Apocalypse's work pits. Eventually, Magneto and his X-Men are able to assault Apocalypse's stronghold, use the M'Kraan crystal to travel back in time and stop legion, and even destroy Apocalypse himself in single combat. "The Age of Apocalypse" does not end with a return to normalcy, however (at least not until the next month's issue)—the surviving X-Men simply stand and watch as they are annihilated, first by falling nuclear bombs, then as reality itself is swallowed by the encroaching M'Kraan crystal.

This was far from the first time the X-Men books had visited a dystopian alternate reality. In 1981, Claremont and Byrne's "Days of Future Past" storyline, future versions of the X-Men traveled back to the "present" to prevent a future of mutant-hunting sentinels and internment camps. The popularity of this story arc led to several other "alternative future" plots incorporated into the larger X-Men mythology. These visions of a terrible future emphasized the X-Men's utopian goals by demonstrating the horrible results of a failed mission. Xavier's vision of a peaceful coexistence between mutants and homo sapiens had always seemed just out of reach—"ordinary" humans reacted to the X-Men with fear and distrust—but the consequences had never been so fully realized. This dark vision of the future, in fact, reinforced the claims of Magneto, who connected mutant persecution with his childhood escape from Nazi concentration camps; in the potential future of the X-Men, prison camps were the final fate of all mutants.

In many ways, "The Age of Apocalypse" derives inspiration from "Days of Future Past"—the few surviving X-Men are a mix of changed familiar faces, like an aged Wolverine and adult Kitty Pryde, and new characters such as Rachel Summers (the future daughter of Scott Summers and Jean Grey); as in the Age of Apocalypse, supervillain Magneto has taken Professor Xavier's position as leader of the X-Men (and is seen confined to a wheelchair, just like Professor X). The mutant prison camps in "Future Past" are mirrored by the genetic breeding pens where Apocalypse's scientists engineered "flatscan" (nonmutant) DNA from captured humans into an artificial army. "Future Past" also set the precedent of introducing new characters into X-Men continuity, as Rachel Summers would later become a regular member of several X-teams after her initial brief introduction.

While "Days of Future Past" was one of the most well-known and revisited (it has been featured in dozens of comics and several television and film depictions) stories in the narrative history of the X-Men, it was at its core a limited vision of the future, initially contained within only two issues; the alternate future is only part of these, as a significant portion of the storyline is focused on the events resolving in the "present," as Kitty Pryde prevents this future from occurring. "The Age of Apocalypse" event represents the evolution of this dystopian vision, giving more time and detailed development to exploring the entire changed world, with events taking place across not only a war-ravaged former United States, but illustrating the global destruction in a refuge-filled Eurasia, an atomically devastated South America, and the potential sanctuary in Antarctica. This was made possible through the takeover of multiple X-titles for four months, plus additional supplementary titles. Finally, rather than glimpsing a possible future, "The Age of Apocalypse" is a horribly altered *present*—the massive annihilation is not just what might happen, but is happening "now," reinforcing the overall sense of fatalism.

The "Age of Apocalypse" storyline marked the first steps in a series of popular publications in the mid–1990s (from both Marvel and DC) focusing on apocalyptic themes and depictions of dark, dystopian superhero narratives. A year after Marvel's X-Men crossover, DC published *Kingdom Come*, a miniseries by Mark Waid and Alex Ross that heavily quoted the Biblical Book of Revelation to tell the story of a world-shattering conflict between "classic" DC superheroes and their grimmer, futuristic descendants. While *Kingdom Come* was originally just a 4-issue miniseries, its story was later expanded by several follow-up arcs and was incorporated into DC continuity a decade later. Its success actually inspired Marvel to develop the similar *Earth X* "maxiseries" (encompassing nearly 50 issues over 5 years) beginning in 1999. Both of these series adhered much more closely to the traditions of classical literary apocalyptic texts, with "prophet" figures guiding readers through highly symbolic visions of destruction and rebirth. What makes "The Age of Apocalypse" event significant is not simply that it was the first of the 1990's apocalyptic crossovers, but it occurred within the established continuity of the X-Men's fictional universe. *Kingdom Come* and *Earth X* were both "imaginary stories" that exist separately from the dominant narrative continuity (a longstanding tradition in superhero comic books); no matter how shocking the events in these stories are, readers know that there is no threat to the status quo. "The Age of Apocalypse" storyline, however, was by its very existence a threat to three decades of X-Men stories—readers had a dedicated interest in seeing things returned to "normal."

Apocalyptic film and literature from contemporary American popular culture differs significantly from Biblical and Medieval texts; John Walliss writes that they are "characterized by a fundamental desacralization—if not inversion—of the apocalypse" (85). In contemporary accounts, the destructive or cataclysmic event is not only natural or human-made (rather than supernatural or divine action); therefore, these modern apocalypses might be avoided or undone in a way that is not possible with divinely fated end times.

The focus of a contemporary apocalypse is not the new world that follows the cataclysm, but an elegy for the world that was destroyed—an "explicit valorization of the contemporary social order" (Walliss 85). Like many "imaginary stories" and other alternative futures in superhero comics, the strange setting and characters in "The Age of Apocalypse" serve to remind us of the primacy and importance of the normal continuity; it presents an a reminder of the "naturalness" of continuity, reinforcing the "real" characters and setting through comparison.

Like most religious texts, apocalyptic narratives also clearly distinguish between believers and non-believers, with the use of heavily symbolic rhetoric reinforcing this exclusivity with the desired audience. This separation is superficially criticized in the "Age of Apocalypse" books, as the archvillain Apocalypse himself maintains a list of "the chosen" and "the forgotten," claiming to know who will be strong enough to survive the world he has made. Like most comic book villains, he and his henchmen are eventually laid low by those who he has labeled weak. However, the books themselves rely on subtle references to the distant, often-forgotten past of X-Men comics. Characters who were only minor references in decades-old stories return as major players in this alternate world. For example, the first soldier of Apocalypse the new X-Men fight (and defeat) is a re-envisioned "Unus the Untouchable," a character that had first appeared in *The X-Men* #8 as a foe for the original team in 1964; Unus had not made an appearance in over a decade, and his last cameo wasn't even in an X-book, but in a Spider-Man spin-off title. Along with the revival of forgotten past characters, "The Age of Apocalypse" emphasized minor differences to well-known characters that only dedicated fans would notice.

In many ways, the cataclysmic rhetoric in the Age of Apocalypse parallels larger trends of Millennial concerns in 1990's America. Disaster films like *Armageddon* and *Deep Impact* depicted global destruction; the *Left Behind* series examined the possible rapture in clinical detail. While these cultural trends have been found in the years approaching the ends of many previous centuries, the contemporary trend of Millennialism was exacerbated by the recent end of the Cold War, where global devastation was a frighteningly real possibility. As folklorist Daniel Wojcik noted in 1997:

> Beliefs and narratives about the end of the world have fascinated people throughout human history. [...] During the last half of the twentieth century, however, widespread beliefs about a meaningless apocalypse have emerged and now compete with traditional religious apocalyptic worldviews. In view of such [fatalistic] attitudes, and the numerous potential disasters that threaten humanity, it is no surprise that with the approach of the year 2000, apocalyptic anxieties have intensified and doomsday speculation flourishes. At the end of the second millennium, ancient apocalyptic traditions converge with recent secular predictions of catastrophe and inflame the popular imagination [1–2].

This new kind of millennialism blended traditional cultural anxieties and religious belief with a practical understanding of the destructive power available to world powers in the 20th century, especially during the Cold War threat of nuclear annihilation. In his 1990 study of the final years of each century since 999, historian Hillel Schwartz suggested that "we have been preparing for the end of our century further in advance than people of any other century" (11).

While much of the concern for the world's end can be linked to the pervasive threat of the Cold War, the prominence of apocalyptic texts in 1990s popular culture is also connected to larger trends in American religion; religious rhetorician Stephen O'Leary notes that the "popularity [of apocalyptic prophecy] has undergone a remarkable resurgence in the latter half of the twentieth century" (7). Hal Lindsey's popular Revelation texts and the televangelism of Jimmy Swaggart and Jerry Falwell in the 1970s and 80s led to a rise in fundamentalist concern for realizing Biblical prophecy. In 1991, a Gallup poll found that 15 percent of Americans thought the Persian Gulf War fulfilled prophecies of Armageddon, while a 1994 U.S. News and World Report survey estimated that between 30 and 44 percent of Americans embraced beliefs about the Rapture (Wojcik, 8, 42). These concerns are also evidenced by popular best-sellers like *Left Behind* (1995), and *The Bible Code* (1997), a numerological reading of scripture that presumed to foretell nuclear war.

Perhaps the most prominent reflection of American millennial concerns took place in April 1993, when nearly 100 people were killed after a 51-day-long standoff between federal agents and Branch Davidians, an apocalyptic sect. The Branch Davidians, "who believed they lived in the end days," writes historian Eugen Weber, "regarded themselves as the righteous destined to play a part in the grand scenario of Armageddon" (215–216).

In an examination of different forms of apocalyptic narratives in popular culture, Douglas Cowan suggests that such texts reveal three common fundamental aspects to our visions of the future: "we understand that human life is *fragile* [,] we understand that human technology is *fickle*[,] we believe that the human spirit is *strong*" (625).

In her book *Apocalypse and Post-Politics: The Romance of the End*, Mary Manjikian suggests that "Apocalyptic literature [...] provides an 'eternal' perspective which allows us to see the finiteness of the American [...] experience in grand, totalizing terms" (27). "The Age of Apocalypse" event, as an apocalyptic text of the X-universe, similarly provided a new perspective, independent of three decades of complicated, convoluted soap-opera continuity. These short, contained stories represent the fundamental mythos of the X-Men distilled into brutal simplicity—a team of misfits, fighting an impossible battle for people who hate and fear them.

WORKS CITED

Cowan, Douglas. "Millennialism, Apocalypse, and American Popular Culture." *The Oxford Handbook of Millennialism*. Catherine Wessinger, ed. New York: Oxford University Press, 2011. 611–627.

Manjikian, Mary. *Apocalypse and Post-Politics: The Romance of the End*. Lanham, Md.: Lexington Books, 2012.

O'Leary, Stephen D. *Arguing the Apocalypse: A Theory of Millennial Rhetoric*. New York: Oxford University Press, 1994.

Schwartz, Hillel. *Century's End: A Cultural History of the Fin de Siecle from the 990s Through the 1990s*. New York: Doubleday, 1990.

Walliss, John. "Apocalypse at the Millennium." *The End All Around Us: Apocalyptic Texts and Popular Culture*. London: Equinox, 2009. 71–95.

Weber, Eugen. *Apocalypse: Prophesies, Cults, and Millennial Beliefs through the Ages*. Cambridge: Harvard University Press, 1999.

Woljcik, Daniel. *The End of the World as We Know It: Faith, Fatalism, and Apocalypse in America*. New York: New York University Press, 1997.

Race and Violence from the "Clear Line School": Bodies and the Celebrity Satire of X-Statix

ADAM CAPITANIO

In July 2001, Marvel Comics published *X-Force* #116, debuting a brand new team of superhero mutants. The cover illustration featured this new team bursting forth seemingly from a cloud of energy, rushing directly at the reader and recalling the famous cover to *Giant-Size X-Men* #1 (May 1975), which similarly introduced a new group of mutant heroes. By the end of *Giant-Size X-Men* #1, soon-to-be fan favorites Wolverine, Colossus, Storm, and Nightcrawler had saved the original X-Men from certain doom and become regular X-Men characters. At the conclusion of *X-Force* #116, two-thirds of the newly introduced team was dead, punctuated by gruesome full-page spread at the very end of the issue.

The finale of *X-Force* #116 offers a good sense of writer Peter Milligan and artist Mike Allred's sensibilities and their goals with *X-Force* and later *X-Statix*. Neither creator had worked for Marvel comics before *X-Force*. Milligan came from a subversive tradition of comics writing, beginning at the satirical British comics magazine *2000 A.D.*, and he later wrote for DC's mature audience Vertigo line, mostly on the mind-bending *Shade, the Changing Man*. Allred is best known as the creator of the indie comic *Madman*, which combined the superhero genre with narrative and artistic experimentation. As their first issue of *X-Force* demonstrated, Milligan and Allred brought their decidedly non-mainstream sensibility to the X-Men family of comics. For the next three years, in the pages of *X-Force* and then *X-Statix*, the writer/artist pair satirized the superhero genre, especially the interpersonal and social melodrama of the X-Men. However, their main focus was drawing attention to issues of the body—especially race and violence—that often lay underexplored in superhero comics, and placing them within a context that connected super-heroic bodies to a larger critique of the visual culture of fame and celebrity.

X-Force/X-Statix featured a team of super-powered mutants who, rather than being hated and feared by humanity like the X-Men, were idolized as celebrities. Instead of battling evil out of a sense of responsibility or justice, X-Statix intervened in criminal or wartime affairs for the media attention. In other words, the mutants of *X-Statix* do not fly off to war-torn countries to stop violence or rescue innocents as positive ends in themselves, but rather as the centerpiece entertainments for a synergistic merchandising empire. The group is followed into action by Doop, a floating green blob armed with a camera and speaking a language that only members of X-Statix seem to understand. Doop takes footage of the team's violent exploits, capturing images of them frying, melting, maiming, and murdering terrorists, enemy soldiers, and criminals. X-Statix's adventures then become feature television, and the group holds press conferences and sells official branded products. Meanwhile, in a parody of storytelling in the X-Men comics, characters both fall in love and fight with one another—although most of the in-fighting is planned with a ratings boost in mind.

The superhero genre has long been an important ground in popular culture for thinking about and representing violence and the human body. Scott Bukatman writes that in superhero comics "[t]he body is obsessively centered upon [...] what superheroes embody are ambivalent and shifting attitudes toward flesh, self, and society" (49, 51). Superheroic bodies take great volumes of punishment, as the genre repeatedly and continually demonstrates; heroes are "armored [... and] rigid against the chaos of surrounding disorder" and can therefore be "permitted the narcissistic luxury of self doubt, [because] their power and ultimate triumph are guaranteed" (56). In other words, because superheroic bodies are nigh invulnerable, it becomes necessary to generate interior conflicts to drive characters. The first inkling of this was the "revolution" in superhero storytelling that 1960s Marvel titles like *Fantastic Four, Spider-Man,* and *The Incredible Hulk* are usually credited with. The only real exception to this formula of hard bodies and vulnerable souls, Bukatman points out, are the mutant heroes of the X-Men. The X-Men have "traumatized, eruptive bodies" whose "internal powers are uncontrolled; where once superheroes guaranteed social stability, they now threaten to disrupt it" (68–70). In other words, X-Men like Cyclops, who cannot control his powers, or Storm and Wolverine, whose emotions spill out into bodily expressions through their deadly powers, do not have the same bodily mastery as the traditional superhero. They defy a division between body and psychology common in other superheroes.

The mutants of *X-Statix* follow this focus on bodies that are uncontrollable and crippling. Guy Smith, aka Mister Sensitive, has grey skin covered with scaly bumps and a pair of tiny tentacle-like protrusions jutting from his forehead, and requires a special suit, provided by Professor X, to prevent his super-senses from being completely overloaded. Vivesector undergoes a werewolf-like transformation from bookish academic to hairy, clawed monster whenever he recalls the emotional abuse of his father. Even the more "normal" members of the team suffer some physical effect from their powers: U-Go-Girl gets exhausted and sleepy after teleporting, and becomes dependent on drugs to stay awake, while the Anarchist's very sweat is a kinetically charged explosive.

In the X-Men comics, the transformed or uncontrollable body is the focus of prejudice and bigotry—because mutants are either "inhuman" or dangerous, as Bukatman says, they "threaten to disrupt" stable social categories. For example, consider the indictment of faith-based bigotry in the graphic novel *God Loves, Man Kills*, where the villainous preacher William Stryker claims that "whatever a man's color or beliefs, he is still human. Those children—and you X-Men—are not!" To "prove" his point, Stryker singles out Nightcrawler, the mutant teleporter who resembles an elfin devil, and bursts out, "Human?! You dare call that ... thing—human?!?"

In the typical X-Men narrative, suspicion over the superheroic body functions as a metaphor for racial bigotry. Sean Howe rhetorically asks, "[w]as it a coincidence that the nonviolence-preaching Professor Xavier and his arch-enemy, the by-any-means-necessary warrior Magneto, lined up so neatly as metaphors for Martin Luther King and Malcolm X?" while Bradford Wright notes that "Marvel attacked intolerance and bigotry without making explicit reference to segregation or the struggles of African Americans" in *The Uncanny X-Men*, who "found themselves persecuted by bigots who were opposed to mutants" (Howe 48; Wright 219).

As Wright suggests, X-Men comics avoided the thornier aspects of exploring racial bigotry by displacing it onto anti-mutant bigotry. Part of the problem was that even at its most multicultural, the characters of *The Uncanny X-Men* were largely white. Many of the multicultural characters introduced in *Giant-Size X-Men*, such as the Japanese Sunfire and the Native American Thunderbird, were gone from the regular comic within months. In other words, *The Uncanny X-Men* was problematic in that it homogenized a set of concerns related to racism and displaced them onto a set of largely white characters, removing the ability of minority characters to take part in their own struggles.

I think *The Uncanny X-Men* probably deserves a more charitable interpretation than that, but it's problematic nonetheless. *X-Statix* addresses that problem by placing issues of race and the body front and center. In *X-Force*

#121, the team needs to choose new members to replace the deceased Bloke and Saint Anna, both killed in their previous mission. The front-runner is the Spike, an African-American mutant who can generate and fire sharp spikes from his skin. Tike Alicar, aka the Anarchist, is opposed to the Spike's membership. Even though both are black, Tike calls the Spike a "glorified spear-chucker," making use of a racist, pop-linguistic term related to the image of an African savage.

The Spike returns the favor later, dubbing Alicar "Captain Coconut" at a press conference "because he's black on the outside. And white on the inside." Spike appears at the press conference dressed like a stereotypical image of the "dangerous black man": jacket open, revealing a chest tattoo, cornrows, gold chains, and flanked by two bodyguards who evoke pop-cultural images of the Black Panthers and the Nation of Islam. In both Tike's disparaging reference and in the Spike's assertion of his own authentic blackness over Tike's, *X-Statix* refers to the history of the visual signs of race: not just related to color, but to a host of other associations that visually "read" as racial, including hair style and fashion. In other words, Spike's appearance is easily "legible" as "black" for a culture that often relies on visual shorthand to understand and position others.

In the next issue, we learn why Tike is so sensitive to the Spike's accusations of "not being black enough." Opening with the images reminiscent of Ezra Jack Keats's classic children's book *The Snowy Day*, Tike's narration reads "so there was this little kid who lived way up north where the winters were long and very very white. And I mean white." "White" carries a double meaning, referring to both the snow and the racial milieu Tike grew up in, where the other children made fun of his color. This overwhelming whiteness leads to his OCD: "washing his hands real hard—until they're raw—to see whether he can wash his color away. Maybe underneath he was snow white, like every other damn thing up here." The last two panels of this flashback make the point visually, as we see Tike and his white, adoptive parents ice-skating on a pure white surface. The next panel takes place after Tike's explosive sweat manifests itself for the first time, and shows him collapsed in a puddle, surrounded by the brown earth beneath the white ice. In juxtaposition, the two panels flip Tike's childhood expectation of finding whiteness underneath his blackness. Underneath the whiteness that fills the first panel, the second panel reveals brown earth, with Tike squarely in the middle.

The two panels also present an image of family togetherness destroyed by Tike's mutant difference, and explicitly conflates race and mutant-ness. In the first panel, Tike and his family are happy, and the narration reads "his parents didn't care that their adopted son was different than the other kids. Maybe they even loved him more because of it." But the second, where Tike sits in the earth, separated from his parents on the other side of the panel, reads "when his sweat-thing started kicking in, well, that was a whole other ball game. I guess it was one difference too many for them." There is a slippage in these panels, and in the narration, between two kinds of difference: racial and mutant. It is the sort of slippage that X-Men comics have relied on for years as their central metaphor, and which *X-Statix* brings it to the fore, perhaps losing some subtlety in the process. But at the same time it enables Milligan and Allred to ground notions of difference and bigotry in the body, demonstrating how forms of Othering are based on bodily appearance, whether it be skin color or the body transformed by mutation.

In other words, both race and mutation can be "read" on the body explicitly in *X-Statix*. However, if the mutant body, uncontrollable and a threat to social stability, is equated with the racialized body, than that too must be similarly threatening. If the history of superhero narratives is anything to go by, then that threat must somehow be neutralized. The Spike is recognizably "black" because he easily fits within a larger matrix of cultural imagery surrounding race. His racialized body is containable because it fits within preconceived visual representations—in other words, it is explicable and categorizable. However, Tike is "visible" both as black and a mutant, such that his white parents can no longer take his difference—in other words, his body becomes "excessive."

X-Statix's attention to race in this manner suggests a critique of bodily representation in superhero narratives and in visual culture more broadly. Milligan and Allred parody the visual signs of race used to slot the Spike into an understandable "type"—"a glorified spear-chucker"—that even a fellow black man utilizes. Meanwhile, the Spike's insulting term for Tike—"Captain Coconut"—indicates a disconnect between the surface visual and underlying meaning. The ways that Tike is depicted in "excessive" terms, with an ambiguous dimension to his body and the panels surrounding him, and indeed his very identity, indicates a way of showing the racialized body beyond visually stereotypes.

In addition to the racialized body, *X-Statix* also investigated the body destroyed by physical violence. Before Milligan and Allred took over the book, *X-Force* was a symbol of the "extreme" era of 1990s comics, which focused on violence, overly grim and serious characters, and shock and excess as narrative devices. This sort of extreme storytelling even afflicted relatively benign characters like Spider-Man.[1] Milligan and Allred took the tactics of the extreme '90s and demonstrated that the violence and narratives those comics engaged in had real consequences, thereby suggesting that superhero narratives specifically, and media and visual culture more broadly, downplay the significance of large-scale violence.

One could easily critique the superhero genre for its depiction of the consequences, or lack thereof, of violence. As Bukatman discusses, in most superhero narratives bodies are portrayed as armored and impenetrable. Thus, for a narrative genre that relies so heavily on violent confrontations, there is still remarkably little death, dismemberment, and trauma. This is particularly galling in the case of characters like Wolverine, whose adamantium claws cleave through metal, flesh, and bone with ease. Yet it is rare to see the bloody carnage the Wolverine should, logically, leave in his wake. The focus on the bodily violence of superhero combat in *X-Statix* signals a critique of the genre, produced at a time when that violence was becoming more common and acceptable in mainstream comics publishing.

Around the same time as Marvel began publishing *X-Statix*, they also launched the Marvel MAX line, featuring the company's less fantastic characters—the Punisher and Nick Fury chief among them—in gruesomely violent storylines. While some of these comics were critically acclaimed, in particular Garth Ennis' writing on *The Punisher*, none of them suggested an overt interest in social commentary or satire. In other words, they offered violence as spectacle and entertainment. Milligan and Allred's *X-Force* was itself violent enough that the Comics Code Authority, the longstanding body that self-regulated the content of the mainstream comics industry, returned *X-Force* #116 to Marvel and demanded significant changes.[2] In response, Marvel simply ceased submitting their comics to the CCA, leading to its demise a few years later (Allred).

Despite playing a central role in the end of the CCA, thus paving the way for an increase in violent content in mainstream comics, *X-Statix* signaled that nothing within its pages should be taken seriously, including that violence. The issue of *X-Force* that the CCA criticized and returned gleefully pointed out the lack of the traditional seal on its cover (Howe 411). However, it was the visual quality of *X-Force/X-Statix* that carried much of the satiric force. As Sean Howe notes, the "Kirbyish primitiveness of Mike Allred's art, and the primary-color palette, only accentuated the ironic corruption of old-fashioned Marvel innocence" (411). Allred himself said that "[s]upposedly I'm from the 'clear line school' that holds a certain innocence that by contrast gives violence an extra jolt when it presents itself. Violence is a horrific thing, and I don't like the idea of someone becoming numb to it" (Allred). Meanwhile, by contrast, the artwork by Laurence Campbell in Ennis' *The Punisher* aimed at a naturalistic feel. Part of the reason *X-Statix* may have angered the CCA was because it criticized superhero violence through its aesthetic: Allred's bright, blocky artwork, which recalled Silver Age pop-art rather than gritty realism, made the gruesome violence in the book all the more disconcerting.

What was the narrative context for the violence of *X-Statix*? In *X-Force*

#116 (Jul. 2001), Zeitgeist, the team leader (at least until his death at the issue's end), sits in his apartment with two lingerie-clad women, reviewing tapes of the team in "North Africa" stopping a "nasty little coup by fanatical tribesmen." As he evaluates the team's tactics in the narration, the women tempt him to bed, and one tells him "we think that watching your exploits, all this blood and death and heroism and stuff it gets you, well ... you know." As Zeitgeist and the women embrace in silhouette, the big screen television behind them displays one of Zeitgeist's victims being skeletonized by his acidic vomit. This moment, appearing at the very beginning of Milligan and Allred's run on *X-Force/X-Statix*, forms the basis on their critique of violence in popular visual culture. The horrific bodily violence being perpetrated by these mutants is meant as entertainment, to be viewed as Zeitgeist does—both dispassionately (as in his tactical review) and as an incitement to pleasure. This becomes a pattern of representation in *X-Statix*—Allred's artwork depicts the gruesome consequences of superheroic violence, while the characters see it as either a job, or as the audience does, something to be enjoyed. Violence is the explicit means by which X-Statix's disruptive bodies in turn disrupt the social.

In addition to Allred's artwork, which both evokes and corrupts traditional depictions of superheroes, Milligan and Allred signaled that *X-Statix* was an explicit commentary on previous modes of graphic storytelling through many allusions to prior comics and illustration. Of course, the cover of *X-Force* #116 (Jul. 2001), as discussed above, referred back to that of *Giant-Size X-Men* #1, and Allred made overt reference to that famous cover yet again with *X-Statix* #1. These covers suggested that *X-Statix* should be taken as a rejection of prior X-Men comics, much like *Giant-Size X-Men* #1 (May 1975) did in relation to earlier issues of *The Uncanny X-Men* through its introduction of a new cast of characters. In this case, however, *X-Statix* can be taken as a denunciation of prior modes of comic book depictions of violence. *X-Force* #123 (Feb. 2002) takes us inside the head of the group's cameraman (woman? thing?) Doop, with panels that explicitly allude to paintings by Hieronymous Bosch and Salvador Dali. In *X-Force* #128 (Jul. 2002), Allred included as the background to one of his panels the famous line drawing of a man and woman which accompanied the deep space probe Pioneer 11 on its trip into outer space, intended to provide anyone who found it an idea of what beings from Earth look like. Finally, one of the final splash panels of *X-Statix* #26 (Oct. 2004), in which Milligan and Allred killed off the entire team, features Guy and Tike in an image that mimics the final still frame of *Butch Cassidy and the Sundance Kid*. This is to say nothing of the comic book covers, film posters, and screen print backgrounds that find their way into the panels of the comic.

The purpose of these references is to tie *X-Statix* to a longer history of visual culture, in particular visual culture that deals with the body as a reference point. For example, Bosch's *The Garden of Earthly Delights* depicts human beings in various states of bodily mutilation and transformation while suffering the torments of hell. The Pioneer 11 drawing of a man and a woman establishes the human body as a key reference point for understanding the Earth. By layering such images over, under, and within his drawings, Allred integrates *X-Statix* into a longer history of representations of the body as transformed and "Othered"—a history that both racialized and violently mutilated bodies have been a part of.

These somewhat disparate strands of *X-Statix*—its explicit rather than sublimated attention to race, critique of superhero violence, and frequent allusions to the history of visual culture—can be united by taking a closer look at the key theme of *X-Statix*: its focus on celebrity culture. Here is where *X-Statix* introduces its biggest wrinkle to the X-Men formula: rather than being hated and feared for their unusual bodies and extraordinary powers, X-Statix are rich and famous for them, part of a media machine that presents them and their violent adventures as fodder for consumption.

Many scholars of celebrity culture have argued that the contemporary period has seen an "intensification" of both the number of famous people and the public interest in their private lives and careers. Chris Rojek notes that "seven out of ten workers in the advanced economies gain their livelihood from the service sector, [such that] culture in king ... [s]ervice labour revolves around being adept in symbols, ideas and communication" (14). Moreover, over the course of the 20th and into the 21st centuries the generation of celebrity has been aided by the mass media and the "invention of public relations and the growth of the promotions and publicity industries" (Turner 10). Of course, the presence of the mass media in our daily lives has exponentially increased in the last century, as we moved from print media and film, to the near ubiquity of radio and television broadcasting, to the ability to call up various forms of media instantly with the internet and on-demand, streaming video and downloads.

The violent footage taken by Doop of X-Statix's adventures anchors a media empire, with X-Statix toys, restaurants, farm teams, and movies. The team members spend more time at press conferences, on talk shows, and at premieres than "fighting evil." In the aforementioned issues where Tike is taunted about his racial identity, Phat and Vivesector are convinced by Spike Freeman, the team's owner and manager, to increase their visibility in the media by deliberately picking fights with their teammates. Freeman also convinces Guy Smith to recruit the Spike to avoid "X-Force [being] seen as a racist institution" arguing that "the days when a big corporation could put a few black people on reception and claim they were working for a [sic] egalitarian society are long gone." In other words, the substance of X-Statix's adventures matters very little: what matters is how they are seen (not as a "racist institution") and what they can sell (themselves, as celebrities).

Graeme Turner argues that reality television has also contributed to the "intensification" of celebrity culture mentioned earlier. Television networks, he writes, have "decided that rather than being merely the end-user of celebrity, they can produce it themselves ... [the] celebrity [of reality TV stars] is produced out of nothing, bypassing what we might think of as the conventional conditions of entry" (53). While X-Statix do exhibit the "conventional conditions of entry" to fame—they have extraordinary abilities and undertake extraordinary actions—their celebrity is primarily a construct, built from the drama of their press conferences, where the Spike and Tike argue over authentic blackness, or the manufactured conflicts within the group, explicitly designed as a media show.

Furthermore, because of their status as mutants, what X-Statix have to sell is primarily their bodies and the extraordinary abilities therein, somewhat akin to models or professional athletes. In his book *Heavenly Bodies*, Richard Dyer analyzes how the images and meanings of movie stars are constructed and interpreted by audiences. His insights are equally valid for other kinds of celebrities, and the process he describes is depicted in *X-Statix*. "Stars," Dyer writes, "are made for profit ... [and] are involved in making themselves into commodities" (5). The "raw material of the person" plays a significant role, but it can be altered through "make-up, coiffure, clothing, dieting and bodybuilding" (5). According to Dyer's formulation, the star transforms his or her body into a sellable commodity, manipulating the "raw material" into a palatable and desirable public image—which would, of course, include any racial or "mutant" qualities in the case of the superheroic body.

So what the characters of *X-Statix* are selling are their bodies, or, more specifically, the image of their bodies. This is why the question of race is so significant to Tike and the Spike; to sell themselves, they must conform to a popularly commodified image of their racialized bodies. In *X-Force* #129, Guy is furious at Freeman's insistence that the team not yet acknowledge the death of Edie Sawyer, aka U-Go-Girl. In a splash page outside X-Force headquarters, a TV journalist reports on the outpouring of concern for Edie. Behind the journalist, we can see the crowd grieving, but also clad in U-Go-Girl t-shirts, holding aloft posters, and burning official X-Force candles. This echoes Tyler Cowen's idea that celebrities often function as a way of generating group identity, but a group identity focused around consumption (3). Meanwhile, inside the headquarters, a figure of Edie, depicted in close-up, is juxtaposed with a word balloon saying "X-Statix," Edie's idea for a new team name and her last words. The action figure demonstrates the degree to which Edie's body has been reduced to a commodity object; she is gone, but the action figure remains, replacing and "speaking" for her after her death renders her silent. The crowd outside, with its t-shirts and other commodities, fully embraces that process.

X-Statix #9 (Apr. 2003) brings together the various strands of the comic together, and we can use it to observe how they operate synchronously. The team once again finds itself fighting in Africa. While the panels depict soldiers getting cut in two by Tike's blasts, their eyes gouged out by Dead Girl, and their necks snapped by Guy Smith, Tike's narration worries about what media professionals would call the "optics" of the event: "Notice something? That's right. The bad guys are all black ... in the X-Statix movie, we'd better have a more ethnically diverse enemy than the one we've got today." The main plot of the issue revolves around the making of an X-Statix movie, and the manipulation of events to make the superheroic team even more palatable to a mass audience. In other words, it involves the star making process that Dyer talks about, the production of the celebrity image through "not just his or her films, but the promotion of those films and of the star through pin-ups, public appearances, studio hand-outs and so on, as well as interviews, biographies and coverage in the press" (2). The X-Statix film generates images of the super team for broad consumption. For the purposes of the film, Edie is brought back to life because, as the director tells Guy, "our research suggests that the public is more interested in seeing Edie than Venus" [another, current team member]. Moreover, a mutant named El Guapo is added to the team because "some of our investors wanted a Latin presence." In other words, in this simulacrum, X-Statix become even more manufactured and subjected to media commoditization than they are already.

Sharon Ginsburg, a gargoyle-like mutant lawyer who blames X-Statix for the loss of her wings, attacks the set of the film and mistakes the actors for the actual superheroes. When the real Guy Smith confronts her, he has to be rescued by El Guapo, the "false" member of the team. In other words, the "image" of the team gets mistaken for the real thing, and even after a correction is made, the "real thing" is saved by the image. The real and the imitation X-Statix are interchangeable, as both are reducible to the status of mere images by a celebrity obsessed, visually oriented culture.

At the end of the issue, X-Statix hold a press conference to screen footage from their most recent battle—the one in Africa, seen at the start of the issue. However, the footage has been manipulated. Tike narrates: "we massage it a little first, using the wonders of modern technology. Computer-generated images, that kinda thing." In the two panels accompanying this narration, an image slowly comes into focus—it is the same panel as the very first of the issue, only now the faces of the enemy soldiers are white, having been transformed into members of a "dissident Mormon group." The enemy soldiers have literally been whitewashed, and the journalists covering the event believe the manipulation completely. Moreover, the racial transformation of the enemy suggests that race is interchangeable, and that the "clear" signs of race are dependent on other visual cues, such as those used by the Spike. Race is as manufactured as stardom, and thus as much a part of a system that commodifies the body.

Let me summarize the larger point. *X-Statix* can be best understood as a critique of comic book representations of the human body, particularly the human body marked as racially "different" and the human body subjected to violence, as these representations have been central to the history of superhero narratives. However, it extends that critique to the larger field of contemporary visual media, presenting that media as dedicated to the presentation of bodies for consumption, interested in digestible surface stereotypes and failing to interrogate the violence that typically passes as entertainment. *X-Statix* depicts that violence as the root of our visual media system, and the largest concern is how violence can be integrated into larger narratives of pleasure, personal tragedy, or political correctness. However, although violence is central to the representations of the visual media, the media profits by the transformation of bodies into celebrity commodities. The many references to the history of visual culture helps to indict that history in this process; very little, Milligan and Allred seem to say, has seriously challenged the idea that human bodies should be subject to the consumptive logic of celebrity. Just as racialized bodies are made palatable through their integration into a recognizable system of representation, the capacity of mutant bodies to do violence, thus disrupting the social, are controlled by integrating that violence into a larger entertainment system.

The final issue of *X-Statix* is a testament to the success of Milligan and Allred's storytelling abilities. Echoing the first issue, where the members of X-Force all died violently, the X-Statix are killed off. Milligan and Allred take one final swipe at the superhero genre: rather than the standard resurrection, belying the consequences of violence and muting the narrative impact of a character's death, the members of X-Statix are truly dead. However, unlike the introductory issue of *X-Force*, instead of feeling shock due to the "clear line school" depiction of violence, we feel a sense of loss for these characters who, because of their flaws as greedy, fame-obsessed poseurs, were more recognizably human than their oft-revived, nigh-invulnerable cousins.

Notes

1. Todd McFarlane, whose name is often synonymous with the extreme '90s, wrote and penciled *Spider-Man* in the early '90s, which saw "Your Friendly Neighborhood Spider-Man" confront villains guilty of child abuse and rape. The same decade saw Spider-Man face Carnage, an unrepentant serial killer.

2. For more on the development of the Comics Code Authority in response to violence and horror in comics, see Wright, chapter 6, and David Hajdu, *The Ten Cent Plague: The Great Comic Book Scare and How It Changed America.*

WORKS CITED

Allred, Mike. "Looking Back on X-FORCE and X-STATIX with Mike Allred." Interview with Albert Ching. *Newsarama.com*, 18 Jan 2012. Web. 31 May 2012.
Bukatman, Scott. "X-Bodies: The Torment of the Mutant Superhero (1994)." *Matters of Gravity: Special Effects and Supermen in the 20th Century.* Durham: Duke University Press, 2003: 48–80.
Claremont, Chris (w) and Brent Anderson (a). "God Loves, Man Kills." *Marvel Graphic Novel* #5 (1982). New York: Marvel Comics.
Cowan, Tyler. *What Price Fame?* Cambridge: Harvard University Press, 2000.
Dyer, Richard. *Heavenly Bodies: Film Stars and Society.* Second Edition. New York: Routledge, 2004 (1986).
Hajdu, David. *The Ten-Cent Plague: The Great Comic-Book Scare and How It Changed America.* New York: Picador, 2008.
Howe, Sean. *Marvel Comics: The Untold Story.* New York: Harper Collins, 2012.
Milligan, Peter (w) and Mike Allred (a). "Exit Wounds." *X-Force* #116 (May 2001). New York: Marvel Comics.
_____ and _____. "Lacuna: Part One: Captain Coconut." *X-Force* #121 (December 2001). New York: Marvel Comics.
_____ and _____. "Lacuna: Part Two: Larry King Has the Flu." *X-Force* #122 (January 2002). New York: Marvel Comics.
_____ and _____. "Tick Tock." *X-Force* #123 (May 2001). New York: Marvel Comics.
_____ and _____. "Someone Dies." *X-Force* #128 (July 2002). New York: Marvel Comics.
_____ and _____. "Good Omens Part One: Edie Sawyer Saved My Life." *X-Statix* #1 (September 2002). New York: Marvel Comics.
_____ and _____. "X-Statix: The Movie." *X-Statix* #9 (May 2003). New York: Marvel Comics.
_____ and _____. "Are You Ready?." *X-Statix* #26 (October 2004). New York: Marvel Comics.
Milligan, Peter (w) and Duncan Fegredo (a). "X-Storm." *X-Force* #129 (August 2002). New York: Marvel Comics.
Rojek, Chris. *Fame Attack: The Inflation of Celebrity and its Consequences.* London: Bloomsbury Academic, 2012.
Turner, Graeme. *Understanding Celebrity.* London: Sage, 2004.
Wein, Len (w) and Dave Cockrum. *Giant-Size X-Men* #1 (1975). New York: Marvel Comics.
Wright, Bradford W. *Comic Book Nation: The Transformation of Youth Culture in America.* Baltimore: The Johns Hopkins University Press, 2001.

Mutating Metaphors: Addressing the Limits of Biological Narratives of Sexuality

CHRISTIAN NORMAN

Writers of the X-Men have long used their characters and storylines as metaphors for real-world bigotry. Humankind's fear and hatred of mutants initially served as a representation of racial tensions, but more recent stories have shifted the focus to discrimination based on sexuality. In this piece, I argue that shifting the metaphor of mutants from race to sexuality necessarily positions sexual orientation as biologically predetermined, a move that proves problematic for the long-term acceptance of LGBTQ identity. To make this argument, I examine the mutant metaphor from the perspective of queer theory to establish why this portrayal is troublesome. Specifically, I focus on two storylines from the 1990s to the early 2000s, the Legacy Virus and the mutant cure, both of which illustrate the problems and possibilities of using mutants as a metaphor for sexuality.

The X-Men occupy a unique place in the Marvel Universe. Whereas the Fantastic Four and the Avengers can revel in the spotlight and are adored by the masses, the X-Men have always been outsiders. Many X-Men comics begin with a variation on the theme of "mutant heroes fighting to protect a world that hates and fears them" as a way to bring readers into the story. One of the most prevalent and resounding themes in X-Men comics is mutants metaphorically representing those who experience real-world hatred and bigotry. While several Marvel heroes are feared and/or reviled by the public, take, for example the Hulk or Spider-Man, mutants are unique in that they are feared and hated not as individuals, but as a group. As a result, writers, fans, and critics often compare the hate and discrimination faced by mutants to the real world hate and discrimination faced by humans labeled different or "other." Long-time

Uncanny X-Men writer Chris Claremont stated in 1982 that, "The X-Men are hated, feared, and despised collectively by humanity for no other reason than that they are mutants. So what we have here, intended or not, is a book that is about racism, bigotry and prejudice" (qtd. in Lyubansky 76). Much of the scholarship about X-Men comics has focused on precisely this metaphor, arguing that mutants stand in for racial discrimination. Authors have focused on how the racially charged atmosphere of the mid 1960s heavily influenced the original X-Men comic books (Trushell 154), with many writers paying special attention to the duo of Professor X and Magneto as representations of Martin Luther King, Jr. and Malcolm X respectively (Lyubansky 86, Trushell 154–155, Skir 22).

While early X-Men comics used mutants to represent racism, recent stories have largely shifted the mutant metaphor, focusing instead on discrimination based on sexuality. Again, the scholarship has followed suit, as authors direct their attention to the possibility that mutants are now more indicative of a queer metaphor. For example, William Earnest examined the first three major motion pictures based on the X-Men by replacing the term "mutant" with "gay" to argue that the films do "important social and political work on contemporary controversies such as the treatment of gay and lesbian Americans" (221). While Earnest's work focuses on the films, the same metaphorical shift had already occurred in the X-Men comics, and persists to this day. Recent stories mirror the bigotry aimed at the LGBTQ community. In *New X-Men* #117 (Oct. 2001), Xavier's school is picketed with signs that say "God Hates Mutants," which conjures images of anti-gay protests staged by religious groups such as the Westboro Baptist Church headed by Fred Phelps, and their signs emblazoned with the slogan "God Hates Fags." During the time the X-Men are temporarily relocated to San Francisco, *Uncanny X-Men* #509 (June 2009) introduces legislation, named Proposition X, that would restrict the marriage and reproductive rights of mutants. This fictitious legislation is clearly aimed at real-world legislation Proposition 8 in California. I could go on to name more stories that help establish the link between hatred of mutants and anti-gay bigotry, but will stop here to consider the ramifications of "queering" the mutant metaphor.

As a rhetorical device, shifting the metaphor from race to sexuality helps comic creators to keep a title relevant as time progresses. And in many ways, mutants as a metaphor for sexual orientation make a lot of sense. Some mutants are born with obvious physical difference from "baseline," or normal humans, but the vast majority of X-Men characters' mutations are not visible. So, just as gays and lesbians might "pass" for straight, many of the mutants in the X-Men comics might pass for human, as mutant powers are often noticeable only when used. The decision for characters in the comics to reveal their status as a mutant publicly or to attempt to blend in with humans mirrors the process of "coming out of, or staying in, the closet." Further, mutants are usually depicted as manifesting their powers during puberty, which is commonly seen as the time in which sexual attractions would begin to manifest and project outwardly (Calzo et al. 1658). Mutants may also be born to two "baseline humans," just as a straight couple can have a gay child. In these respects, mutants work better as a metaphor for sexual orientation than for race. Within the world of the X-Men comics, mutants are born with a genetic difference, an "X-Gene" that marks them as biologically different from "normal" humans.

However, the mutant as queer metaphor is problematic because, like all metaphors, it conceals even as it reveals (Lakoff and Johnson 10). These problems are particularly evident if considered from the perspective of queer theory and recent work on gender and identity. While metaphorically casting sexual orientation clearly fits within the mainstream LGBTQ political and legal strategies (Weber 680), many queer theorists and scholars have argued that using a strategy that casts one's sexual orientation as biologically determined is short-sighted in its goals and may well lead to further problems in the future for the movement. This rhetorical move may position queer identity as "natural," but it also runs the risk of reinforcing the assumption of heterosexuality's normality.

Biological Determinism

Claims that sexual orientation is innate, that one does not choose to be gay, are extremely pervasive in pro-LGBTQ rights discourse. The overwhelming popular consensus among pro-gay groups and individuals is that "same-sex desire is biologically inherent" (Weber 679–680). Even President Obama, in a 2004 debate with Alan Keyes stated that he believes homosexuality is innate and is not a choice, despite not openly endorsing gay marriage until years later. In fact, within much of the popular discourse surrounding issues of LGBTQ rights, denying that sexual orientation is anything but biologically determined is seen as an indicator that one must be anti-gay. With the majority of popular pro-gay discourse supporting the idea that sexual orientation is biologically determined, it may come as a surprise that this argument is actually a major point of contention within queer theory and scholarship. To get a better idea of why this debate within pro-gay advocates is largely ignored in much of the public/popular discourse, I will first outline the biological determinist view as well as the scientific and political rationales for its usage in LGBTQ rights discourse.

The biological determinist strategy that dominates LGBTQ rights discourse emerged largely in the 1980s as a way to legitimize non-heterosexual orientation as "natural." Weber ties the move toward determinist arguments to various events in the eighties, including the rise of the Christian Right, the increased visibility of the LGBTQ community and the rise of HIV/AIDS in the gay male population (682). Weber argues that these events, combined with an upsurge in conservative politics, helped push pro-gay individuals and institutions to focus on civil rights over sexual liberation (682). The push for LGBTQ rights, including same-sex marriage, repealing "Don't Ask Don't Tell," and eliminating bans on donating blood, took precedence in the LGBTQ community. The narrative that sexual orientation is biologically determined helped strengthen claim that gays should be a protected group. LGBTQ advocates have often bolstered their political strategies by turning to scientific studies in an attempt to prove the "natural" origins of sexual orientation in biology.

Where advocates of LGBTQ rights often use biology to support their arguments, the Religious Right often mobilizes arguments that claim sexual orientation is a matter of individual choice. Wilcox notes that "the idea that sexual orientation is a choice is a prominent part of the political agenda of the religious right" (242). Social conservatives use choice-affirming arguments in order to cast homosexuality as a negative and/or sinful lifestyle. Further, religious organizations have attempted to use such arguments as a basis for often dangerous so-called "reparative therapy" measures aimed at converting LGBTQ individuals to a straight lifestyle (Bennett 331). The connection between choice-affirming options and anti-gay religious, social, and political movements leads many to associate non-biological arguments about sexual identity with anti-gay motives. However, scholarship on queer theory and gender identity complicates the easy distinction of "biology good, choice bad" and requires us to take a more nuanced look at the issue. Many queer theorists actually argue that biological determinist arguments may be useful in the short term, possibly leading to some policy goals, but that they are potentially dangerous for the long-term acceptance of LGBTQ individuals

While many LGBTQ individuals have come forward expressing that they have "always been" gay and had no choice in the matter, the truth is that not all LGBTQ individuals share that experience and the biological determinist argument only serves to ignore and/or silence their stories. Those that believe they made a conscious decision to be queer and/or those who feel their sexuality is more fluid are often pushed aside by those in the LGBTQ community who wish to advance the biological determinist narrative of sexual orientation (Weber 684; Pickhardt 951). By ostracizing and silencing those individuals whose sexual identity does not fit the dominant paradigm of the biological determinist narrative, the LGBTQ community mirrors heterosexist bigotry by promoting discrimination against those who deviate from the norm.

Queer theorists who eschew the biological determinism model seek instead what they call a "social constructivist" model of sexual orientation (Kitzinger 137). Social constructivism posits that sexual orientation is molded by the social world one inhabits rather than predetermined by biology/genetics. This does not necessarily mean that one makes a conscious and deliberate "choice" to be gay at a particular point in life, or that there is no genetic component to sexuality, but that one nonetheless "becomes" gay as he/she acts out their gender/sexuality in a process Judith Butler calls "performativity" (43). This process includes a person's performances of gender and sexuality and the ways in which social and cultural forces influence and encourage certain aspects of those performances. By situating real, performing bodies within a discursive network or social context that makes those performances intelligible, Butler's conception of performativity accounts for those who feel that they have "chosen" their sexuality as well as those who feel they have "always been" that way.

Thus far I have outlined the biological determinist model of sexual orientation and complicated the notion that it is the only viable "pro-gay" stance. In order to more fully illustrate the dangers of the biological determinist model, I turn to specific storylines in X-Men comics that metaphorically portray sexual orientation as predetermined at birth through genetics. In my analysis, I will show how these stories corroborate queer theorists' fears that biological determinism depicts queer identity in a negative light, normalizes heterosexuality, silences certain queer identities, and runs the risk of pathologizing homosexuality.

The Legacy Virus

In *X-Force* #18 (Jan. 1993), mutant villain Stryfe releases a plague called the Legacy Virus, which ravages the mutant community. Over the next eight years of publication, the Legacy Virus claimed the lives of many relatively high profile mutant characters, including Illyana Rasputin, AKA Magik, in *Uncanny X-Men* #303 (Aug. 1993). The virus attacked X-genes like a cancer and progressed to cause the infected mutant to lose control of his/her powers and eventually to die. The time the virus took to kill the infected mutant varied greatly. Some mutants were revealed to have contracted the virus, but never showed the dire physical signs of other mutants that were close to death. Throughout the story, scientists including the X-Men's own Beast and ally Moira MacTaggert attempted to find a cure and were consistently frustrated in their attempts.

It is almost impossible to see the Legacy Virus as anything other than a metaphorical representation of HIV/AIDS. Both viruses affect the cells of the infected person's body and may ultimately result in death. Both the Legacy Virus and HIV may take years before the infected person fully feels the effects of the disease. Most importantly for my analysis, both viruses were initially associated with a specific minority group. Initially, the Legacy Virus was believed to only affect mutants. However, in *Excalibur* #80 (Aug. 1990) Moira MacTaggert revealed that she was infected with the virus, the first (and only) case of a human contracting the disease. The Legacy Virus narrative thus mirrors the HIV/AIDS narrative, as it was initially identified with a disenfranchised population and led to the group's further alienation, in part because it was also understood to be communicable to the general population.

X-Men comics depicted human responses to the Legacy Virus in a way that mirrored the homophobic response to HIV/AIDS in the real world. In the one-shot issue *X-Men Prime* (July 1995), Trish Tilby, reporter and ex-girlfriend of Beast, breaks the news of the Legacy Virus on air. The issue depicts Tilby before the report being asked by a colleague if she can go through with the story, warning her that the hatred of mutants will only increase if she does so. Ultimately, Tilby breaks the story and public displays of hatred against mutants follow; one mutant is even beaten to death. In *Uncanny X-Men* #323 (Aug. 1995), Beast, looking tired and disheveled, confronts Tilby in her news studio. After mocking Tilby with a sarcastic round of applause, Beast asks her, "How does it feel to be nominated for a Pulitzer *and* sell out an entire race in one fell swoop?" When Tilby begins to respond, Beast cuts her off, accusing her of "fann[ing] the flames of intolerance even higher—by going public with a bunch of half-rumors about the legacy virus" and intimating that her story "already led to the beating to death of one innocent mutant."

While the Legacy Virus stories are intended to make the reader feel sympathy for the plight of mutants, they prove problematic as a metaphorical representation of sexuality because of their adherence to the biological determinist model. The Legacy Virus story draws a clear distinction between mutants and humans based on genetic difference, a difference the virus exploits. As a metaphor, this story normalizes heterosexuality by casting its metaphorical other (mutants) in a negative light. Many queer theorists note that this is a problem inherent to rhetorical strategies that presume biological determinism; they cast heterosexuality as the norm from which LGBTQ individuals deviate. As Weber argues,

> Biological determinism works as a phenomenon that normalizes same-sex desire while leaving heterosexism in place and disenfranchising certain queer people from fully participating in an accurate articulation of their experiences in political and popular discourse [685].

In short, biological determinist arguments do not question the cultural legitimization of heterosexuality and the basic need to legitimize LGBTQ lifestyles.

By adhering to biological determinism, the LGBTQ community may reach some short-term policy goals, but will still inhabit a world in which non-heterosexual identity is tolerated, rather than truly accepted and culturally valued.

Moreover, biological determinist positions often lead to arguments that stress the negatives of gay identity. For example, LGBTQ advocates commonly make an argument that goes something like this: "Since a rational person given a choice between being gay or straight would choose to be straight, and there are many rational people who are gay, being gay must not be a choice" (Pick-hardt 935). As Weber notes, "'we didn't choose this' has become a common rallying cry for members of the LGBTQ community striving for equal rights under the law" (680). This argument automatically frames being gay as less desirable than being straight. Weber argues that, by taking such a view, "a hole emerges at the center of pro-gay political discourse in which gayness is defined in negative terms rather than its own terms" (683). The argument that a rational person would not choose to be gay still encourages the idea that being gay is somehow inherently negative, since such a choice would so obviously be a bad one.

Because it owes its coherence to a metaphor rooted in biological determinism, the Legacy Virus storyline similarly perpetuates the notion that non-heterosexuality is an inherently negative subject position, and one that no rational person would choose to occupy. The Legacy Virus actually *is* a mutant disease. The virus was designed to target mutant genes. Only one human ever contracted the virus, and she was in direct contact with it for extended periods of time due to her research. By pinning the Legacy Virus to a mutant gene, the storyline perpetuates not only a narrative of biological difference, but of a threatening biological difference. Mutants are dangerous and cannot help but to be dangerous due to their genetics. Adhering to the biological determinist model in this case runs against the logic that AIDS is not actually a "gay disease." Further, focusing on mutant's presumed biological differences from humans (read: gay differences from straight) does not fight the belief that those genetic differences result in a less desirable identity.

At first glance, the Legacy Virus as a metaphorical representation of HIV/AIDS seems to be sympathetic to the LGBTQ community's struggles with respect to HIV/AIDS. However, because the Legacy Virus is predicated upon a genetic difference between humans and mutants, it actually perpetuates the very logic of oppression that made them vulnerable to the scapegoating in the first place. This leads me to the second of my focal stories, which further illustrates the dangers of pathologizing mutancy and, by extension, non-heterosexual orientation.

The Mutant "Cure"

In 2004, Marvel Comics launched a new X-Men title, *Astonishing X-Men*, written by Joss Whedon and penciled by John Cassaday. The series began with a six issue story arc title "Gifted" in which a scientist, Dr. Kavita Rao, announces that she has discovered a way to biologically convert mutants into baseline humans. This "mutant cure," as the media call it, becomes a point of contention for mutants in general and the X-Men in particular as they debate the ethicality of such a measure. Unlike the Legacy Virus stories, which inadvertently reveal the shortcomings of the biological determinist view on sexuality, the mutant cure storyline is a meditation on these shortcomings. Specifically, it stresses that what is considered natural is not necessarily considered good and that what is considered natural but not good is often the target of "cures" developed to restore *social* order in the name of a *natural* order.

On the final page of *Astonishing X-Men* #1 (Jul. 2004) Dr. Rao holds a press conference to announce her findings. Her words are juxtaposed with images of the X-Men leaving to confront an enemy. Dr. Rao states, "Mutants are not the next step in evolution. They are not the end of humankind. The mutant gene is nothing more than a disease. A corruption of healthy cellular activity.... We have found a cure." The issue ends on this dramatic note, the final panel a blank black box. Dr. Rao's assertion that the mutant gene is a disease that can be cured mirrors conservative notions of "curing" homosexuality through "reparative therapy." Even though proponents of reparative therapy insist that sexual orientation is a choice and not a matter of genetics, the basic desire behind reparative therapy is to convert a person to becoming a heterosexual, in the same manner that Dr. Rao's cure is aimed at converting a mutant into a human. Even though the comics frame mutants as being caused by genetics, the desire to convert still holds strong. As a metaphor for sexuality, this story lends support to queer theory arguments that basing support for LGBTQ rights on genetics may actually run the risk of pathologizing homosexuality.

Queer theorists are quick to point out that if a genetic cause of homosexuality is discovered, this may lead to efforts to screen for and eliminate such deviant traits (Dunn 377). McShee argues that "the determinist argument could backfire. Christian fanatics could label deterministic homoerotic desire as a 'malfunction,' ... regarding it as a disease in need of being 'cured.' Or it could be viewed as analogous to a permanent disability" (28). One of the primary reasons LGBTQ rights rhetoric adheres so strongly to biological determinism is the fear of far-right arguments about conversion and reparative therapy. But if the LGBTQ community cannot push for greater acceptance of non-heterosexual orientations as an equal and legitimate option, the genetic causes could become a target for homosexual "cures."

Returning to the world of the X-Men, they learn about the cure in *Astonishing X-Men* #2 (Aug. 2004) and begin to discuss the ramifications of its existence. Kitty Pryde notes that the students in Xavier's school are freaking out. She states that "They're terrified, confused—some of them are ecstatic, they don't know how to deal with this." These comments show the range of emotions that would likely come with being given an option to no longer remain a mutant. During the discussion, Wolverine pops his claws, and angrily exclaims, "Woman called me a disease. You know how that feels to me? I can't even sheathe. My claws won't go back. She said we were a disease." This sequence illustrates the dangers of conceiving sexual identity as natural. After all, diseases are natural, and some even caused by genetics, but they are not celebrated despite their naturalness.

The reactions to the mutant cure vary greatly throughout the story arc. In *Astonishing X-Men* #3 (Sep. 2004), a news report announces that "over sixteen hundred alleged mutants are lined up outside Benetech Labs demanding this 'cure'...." The issue visually depicts a long line of mutants outside the lab, many with visually distinguishable mutations. Later in the issue a young student codenamed Wing expresses to Kitty Pryde his fears that mutants will be forced to take the cure. Others, like Wolverine and Emma Frost take offense at the idea that mutancy is something in need of repair. These reactions reflect the concerns over reparative therapy for homosexuality. While many would argue homosexuality is not in need of "repair," many within the LGBTQ community still feel pressure to conform to society norms of heterosexuality.

As if to illustrate the high emotional and material stakes of the issue, Wolverine and Beast come to blows over their disparate views on the cure. Beast and Wolverine's altercation illustrates the potentially divisive nature of the biological determinist model. At the end of *Astonishing X-Men* #2 (Aug. 2004) Beast breaks into Dr. Rao's workspace at Genetech Labs. Dr. Rao assumes Beast wishes to stop her work. However, Beast tells her, "I'm not here to discuss the ethics of your 'mutant cure.' And I'm not here to destroy it." Then, looking down and averting his eyes from her gaze, Beast says, "I just want to know if it works." In the next issue, *Astonishing X-Men* #3 (Sept. 2004), the team's resident telepath Emma Frost picks up that Beast is considering taking the cure himself and alerts Wolverine, who subsequently confronts Beast in his lab and demands that he destroy the sample. Wolverine taunts Beast, asking "You've had enough? You wanna [sic] see how the other half lives their half-lives." Beast responds that he doesn't know what he wants, and that it is none of Wolverine's business anyway. Beast then laments that he doesn't know who he is anymore, saying, "I used to have fingers. I used to have a mouth you could kiss, I would walk down the street and ..." before faltering and calling attention to the physical, emotional, and mental toll his mutation has taken on him.

Beast's mutation, unlike mutants like Wolverine, Kitty Pryde, and Emma Frost, is visually noticeable. The inability to blend in with normal humans is a large part of his desire to take the cure. Beast represents a segment of the mutant population that is on the fringes. Whereas mutants who "look normal" are more able to blend in with human society, mutants with visible mutations often find it even more difficult to gain acceptance. Similarly, those on the fringes of the LGBTQ community, bisexual and transgender individuals, often have trouble gaining acceptance by society at large and even amongst the gay and lesbian movement.

Some queer theorists argue that biological determinism divides the LGBTQ community by normalizing certain conceptions and experiences of queer identity at the expense of others. Arguing that sexual orientation is genetically predetermined assumes a binary structure of sexuality: one is either gay or straight, which necessarily precludes much of the LGBTQ spectrum. Weiss argues that biological models of sexuality further gay and lesbian causes at the expense of bisexual and transgender individuals and only furthers biphobia and transphobia within gay and lesbian communities (53). Similarly, Dunn argues that the biological model of sexual orientation does not really work for those that don't easily fit such genetic explanations (377). Again, one danger of biological determinism is the further alienation of those in the far margins of the LGBTQ community who do not fit nicely into the genetic paradigm. Beast represents those on the margins of the mutant community, who have more trouble being accepted due to their appearance. Beast considering taking the cure illustrates that the biological determinism model may "naturalize" gay and lesbian identity, but that it also leaves out those who identify as neither gay nor straight.

Returning to the story, Wolverine does not back down from his argument with Beast. Wolverine argues that the X-Men have a special responsibility to the mutant community. He states, "Some weak sister in the freshman dorm wants to drop his powers, I could care less, but an X-Man ... one of us caves and it's all over. It's an endorsement stamp for every single mutant to be lined up and neutered." Wolverine's criticism basically comes down to the idea that the leaders and/or spokespeople for the mutant community should not and cannot publicly show support for the idea that being a mutant is less desirable than being a "normal" human. This assertion is similar to critiques of the common argument that a rational person, given the option, would choose to be straight. When LGBTQ individuals, especially those with a large amount of publicity and/or societal influence, assert that they would not "choose" to be gay, this portrays being gay as a lesser option to being straight. Whedon's dialogue here suggests a valid criticism of the common arguments used in biological determinist rhetoric.

Throughout the mutant cure storyline, Whedon and Cassaday critique relying too much on biology as a means of justifying sexual orientation. They craft a story that exposes the dangers of finding a genetic cause without adequately addressing the societal stigmas against homosexuality. The cure storyline shows that, while the biological nature of mutants may be problematic, smart readers and writers will be able to expose those limits and play with the more complex issues of identity in X-Men stories. This story manages to rise above the biological determinist limitations to show the dangers of pathologizing homosexuality and dividing the LGBTQ community. In the end, this story argues that disenfranchised groups must push for true social acceptance or biological arguments could backfire on them.

Both the Legacy Virus and the mutant cure storylines attempt to use mutants as a metaphorical representation of sexuality. Both stories can be read as what Kenneth Burke famously called "equipment for living" by giving readers ways to understand issues of sexual identity and orientation (304). Both provide some helpful guidance toward tolerance, but both fall somewhat short because both are forced by the metaphor to accept biological determinism as a baseline. The Legacy Virus as a metaphor falls into the familiar trap of normalizing heterosexuality (baseline humans) and casting queer identity (mutants) in a negative light. The mutant cure storyline, on the other hand actively critiques the dangers of justifying sexual orientation through biology alone. Despite the barriers presented by biological determinism in the mutant metaphor, I am hopeful that comic creators can find new and exciting ways to spread a metaphorical message of not just tolerance, but of true acceptance for difference that will promote a greater long-term benefit for the LGBTQ community.

WORKS CITED

Bennett, Jeffrey A. "Love Me Gender: Normative Homosexuality and 'Ex-Gay' Performativity in Reparative Therapy Narratives." *Text & Performance Quarterly* 23.4 (2003): 331–52. *Ebsco*. Web. 24 April 2013.

Burke, Kenneth. *Philosophy of Literary Form: Studies in Symbolic Action*. Baton Rouge: Louisiana State University Press, 1941. Print.

Butler, Judith. *Gender Trouble: Feminism and the Subversion of Identity*. New York: Routledge, 1990. Print.

Calzo, Jerel P., Toni C. Antonucci, Vickie M. Mays, and Susan D. Cochran. "Retrospective Recall of Sexual Orientation Identity Development Among Gay, Lesbian, and Bisexual Adults." *Developmental Psychology* 47.6 (2011): 1658–73. *Ebsco*. Web. 23 April 2013.

Dunn, Kathleen. "Biological Determinism and LGBT Tolerance: A Quantitative Exploration of Biopolitical Beliefs." *Western Journal of Black Studies* 34.3 (2010): 367–79. *Ebsco.* Web. 23 April 2013.

Earnest, William. "Making Gay Sense of the X-Men." *Uncovering Hidden Rhetorics: Social Issues in Disguise.* Ed. Barry Brummett. Los Angeles: Sage Publications, 2008. 215–232. Print.

Fraction, Matt (w) and Greg Land (a). "Untitled." *Uncanny X-Men* #509 (June 2009). New York: Marvel Comics.

Kitzinger, Celia. "Social Constructionism: Implications for Lesbian and Gay Psychology." *Lesbian, Gay, and Bisexual Identities Over the Lifespan: Psychological Perspectives.* Ed. Anthony R. D'Augelli. New York: Oxford University Press, 1995: 136–161. Print.

Lakoff, George, and Mark Johnson. *Metaphors We Live By.* Chicago: University of Chicago Press, 1980. Print.

Lobdell, Scott (w), Chris Cooper (w), and Amanda Conner (a). "Out of Time." *Excalibur* #80 (Aug. 1994): New York: Marvel Comics.

Lobdell, Scott (w) and Bryan Hitch (a). "A Nation Rising." *Uncanny X-Men* #323 (Aug. 1995). New York: Marvel Comics.

Lobdell, Scott (w), Fabian Nicieza (w), Bryan Hitch (a), Jeff Matsuda (a), Gary Frank (a), Mike McKone (a), Terry Dodson (a), Ben Herrera (a), and Paul Pelletier (a). "Racing the Night." *X-Men Prime* (July 1995). New York: Marvel Comics.

Lobdell, Scott (w) and Richard Bennett (a). "Going Through the Motions" *Uncanny X-Men* #303 (Aug. 1993). New York: Marvel Comics.

Lyubansky, Mikhail. "Prejudice Lessons from the Xavier Institute." *The Psychology of Superheroes: An Unauthorized Exploration.* Eds. Robin S. Rosenberg and Jennifer Canzoneri. Dallas: Benbella Books, 2008. 75–90. Print.

McShee, Sean. "Can Biology Vanquish Bigotry?" *Gay & Lesbian Review Worldwide* 15.1 (2008): 27–29. *Ebsco.* Web. 23 April 2013.

Morrison, Grant (w) and Ethan Van Sciver (a)."Danger Rooms." *New X-Men* #117 (Oct. 2001). New York: Marvel Comics.

Nicieza, Fabian (w) and Greg Capullo (a)."Ghosts in the Machine (X-Cutioner's Song, Pt. 12)." *X-Force* #18 (Jan. 1993). New York: Marvel Comics.

Pickhardt, Jonathan. "Choose or Lose: Embracing Theories of Choice in Gay Rights Litigation Strategies." *New York University Law Review* 73 (1998): 921–64. *Hein Online.* Web. 23 April 2013.

Skir, Robert N. "X-ing the Rubicon." *The Unauthorized X-Men: SF and Comic Writers on Mutants, Prejudice and Adamantium.* Ed. Len Wein. Dallas: Benbella Books, 2005. 19–28. Print.

Trushell, John M. "American Dreams of Mutants: The X-Men—'Pulp' Fiction, Science Fiction, and Superheroes." *Journal of Popular Culture* 38.1 (2004): 149–168. *Ebsco.* Web. 23 April 2013.

Weber, Shannon. "What's Wrong with Be(com)ing Queer? Biological Determinism as Discursive Queer Hegemony." *Sexualities* 15.5 (2012): 679–701. *Ebsco.* Web. 23 April 2013.

Weiss, Jillian Todd. "GL vs. BT: The Archeology of Biphobia and Transphobia within the U.S. Gay and Lesbian Community." *Journal of Bisexuality* 3.3 (2003): 25–55. *Ebsco.* Web. 24 April 2013.

Whedon, Joss (w) and John Cassaday (a). "Gifted (Part 1)." *Astonishing X-Men* #1 (July 2004). New York: Marvel Comics.

_____ and _____. "Gifted (Part 2)." *Astonishing X-Men* #2 (Aug. 2004). New York: Marvel Comics.

_____ and _____. "Gifted (Part 3)." *Astonishing X-Men* #3 (Sep. 2004). New York: Marvel Comics.

_____ and _____. "Gifted (Part 5)." *Astonishing X-Men* #5 (Nov. 2004). New York: Marvel Comics.

_____ and _____. "Gifted (Part 6)." *Astonishing X-Men* #6 (Dec. 2004). New York: Marvel Comics.

Wilcox, Sarah A. "Cultural Context and the Conventions of Science Journalism: Drama and Contradiction in Media Coverage of Biological Ideas About Sexuality." *Critical Studies in Media Communication* 20.3 (2003): 225–47. *Ebsco.* Web. 24 April 2013.

Grant Morrison's Mutants and the Post–9/11 Culture of Fear

ERIC GARNEAU *and* MAURA FOLEY

Fear of a Two-Dimensional Other

Since 1963, the overarching narrative of the X-Men franchise has thrived as an allegory for American society's ills. Creators from Stan Lee to Bryan Singer to Joss Whedon time and again have constructed stories in which X-Men characters act as fictionalized, sometimes barely disguised stand-ins for real-world minority groups, hated and feared by a world that doesn't understand them. In the early 21st century, the hatred and fear those characters faced took on challenging new dimensions.

In May 2001, celebrated Scottish comics scribe Grant Morrison began a three-year run writing Marvel's mutants. Unsurprisingly, he utilizes the same mutants-as-minority storytelling technique that proved successful for nearly four decades. However, throughout his run, Morrison taps into an increasingly complex sociopolitical climate. Morrison's work on *X-Men* is less an examination of mutants as superheroes than of mutants as a varied, multifaceted set of subcultures all facing homogenizing and marginalizing treatment from humanity—and from themselves. Moving beyond the dichotomy of "good" and "evil" mutants, the series explores mutant existence with a particular interest in how social groups define their own way of responding to malicious outside forces. And in the real world, those forces were certainly brewing.

The terrorist attacks of September 11, 2001 accelerated and exacerbated an existing trend in American consciousness to which the X-Men could certainly relate: fear of the Other. After the attacks, the U.S. government strengthened or created many domestic and international policy initiatives, especially the wars on crime, drugs, and terror, using these fears. The stated goals of these policies were and continue to be the protection of U.S. citizens and U.S. interests. However, these policies established, through their enforcement, a strict definition of "acceptable" American culture: middle-class, white, and native-born. Many sociologists, economists, and political scientists refer to this mixture of nationalism and cultural anxiety as the "culture of fear."

It is this culture in which Morrison's *X-Men* exists. By portraying mutantkind as a richly diverse culture (with richly diverse opposition), Morrison is able to color the mutants' world with a political reality that seems both incredibly timely and eerily prescient. The complex world Morrison constructs pulls from and sheds a light on the political climate of post–9/11 America, particularly the cultural cost of the War on Terror. It's this tense, volatile climate, and especially how members both outside and within the targeted culture respond to it, that we're interested in here.

The Culture of Fear: A Background

Before we discuss how Morrison's mutants react to being the homogenized, Othered object of terror, it behooves us to look a bit at the history of such a concept. President Richard Nixon could be called the father of declaring "war" on nonpolitical entities to this end, and his choice of the word "war" was no accident. In a post–World War II America, war represented more than battle—it symbolized an era in which political and cultural unity reached a perceived apex (Simon 260). During this time, America also enjoyed incredible racial homogeneity in public life (Self 24). By declaring wars on crime, drugs and cancer, Nixon used struggles against a shared, monolithic foe to push white America into his political majority, reminiscent of post–World War II patriotic unity (Simon 262).

Largely, such domestic policy–based wars relied on fear of anticipated harm as opposed to actual harm (Glassner 3). As an example, in 1971, when Nixon went so far as to announce a War on Cancer initiative, the average American was 2.5 times more likely to die of heart disease than cancer ("75 Years of Mortality in the United States" 6). Why a war on cancer, then? Simply put, Americans were more afraid of cancer than they were of heart disease (Simon 263). In a time of growing poverty, with an active draft sending young American men to a messy conflict—an actual war, in fact—in Vietnam, Nixon chose his fights wisely, opting to battle what Americans were afraid of, not what issues truly plagued them most. And certainly, Nixon excelled at fear-based manipulation.

The two longest-running political examples of the culture of fear are the wars on drugs and crime, again originated by President Nixon. Subsequent presidents gladly accepted the reins of Nixon's war horses and the government set forth policies to curb crime and drug use, which were largely viewed as black issues ("Race & the War on Drugs"). Again we see that policy agendas were couched in the rhetoric of war to make the struggle seem monolithic. Issues of drug abuse, which are nuanced, difficult, and dependent upon myriad factors to change, were oversimplified in order to garner support for complicated legislation. Plainly, Nixon could not garner white support for drug and crime policy if he portrayed a nuanced view of crime and drugs, so instead he instigated fear of blacks.

In the end, these "wars" were largely ineffective in solving their goals, as their inherent oversimplification failed to address messy root causes. The drug abuse rates actually increased in the first five years after the beginning of the War on Drugs ("The War on Drugs"). Furthermore, the wars on crime and drugs escalated in media coverage and political importance only as crime rates sank in the 1990s. In his book Barry Glassner explains, using road rage as an example:

> In just about every contemporary American scare, rather than confront disturbing shortcomings in society, the public discussion centers on disturbed individuals. [...] [R]eporter Patrick O'Driscoll notes that 70 percent of urban freeways are clogged [...] and that traffic exceeds road capacity in most U.S. cities. Did he then go on to consider possibilities for relieving congestions? On the contrary, his new sentence began, "Faced with tempers boiling over like radiators [...]."

Yet despite all evidence to the contrary of their ineffectiveness, Nixon and many who followed in his footsteps pursued these pet wars on fictional "bad guys," with the most clear present example being the War on Terror. Of course, black-and-white wars against timeless, unbeatable evils like drugs, crime, and terror seem more the stuff of comic books—don't they?

The Monolith Breaks

Though, as mentioned, the X-Men franchise has always been powered by real-world struggles, much like President Nixon and his followers, its creators tend to focus on oversimplified, dichotomous struggle for the soul of mutantkind—Manichean divisions of good and evil mutants fighting each other to achieve a single, conceptually simple goal: mutant rights. Up to 2001, mutant philosophy possessed, for the most part, simple cut-and-dry viewpoints with distinct boundaries. Equality with or dominance of humans were but the good and evil paths, respectively, to the shared goal.

This simplistic divide decidedly does not exist Morrison's *New X-Men*. Though he set many goals across his 40 issues on the title, Morrison's chief occupation is characterizing mutantkind as social group rife with interdiversity.

Countless "factions" of mutants exist, each with their own culture and mores. The classic good/evil binary takes a serious backseat to other, less super-hero-y expressions. Morrison himself explains this in his 2011 book *Supergods*:

> I imagined mutant culture not as a single monolithic ideal or the warring ideologies of "evil mutants" and "good ones," but as a spectrum of conflicting viewpoints, self-images, and ideas about the future. Artist Frank Quitely and I tried to imagine the emergence into our midst of a weird new culture, with mutant clothes designers creating six-armed shirts or invisible couture, mutant musicians releasing records that could by [*sic*] heard only on infra- or ultrasonic frequencies, art that used colors only mutant eyes could see. Instead of just a team, or even a tribe, we imagined a fully formed Homo superior society finally emerging into the light of emancipation [356].

With the expanded focus on mutantkind's diversity, Professor Charles Xavier's School for Gifted Youngsters truly comes alive in these pages—less a boot camp for mutant soldiers (as in some previous incarnations), more an incubator for the world's hippest subcultures. To match this, the outside world responds accordingly: human journalists are embedded at Xavier's to tell the school's story; geeky suburban white kids begin to think that having mutant powers makes a person cool and unique.

Of course, this fascination with the Other does not come without threats. There are human rights activists. There are (what else?) politicians capitalizing on mutant-phobia. There are military-industrial complex scions who want to manipulate mutant abilities for their own gain. There are corrupt cult-like leaders who see mutant powers as a way to attract more wayward followers. And the list goes on. There's no mistaking the diversity on both sides of the line in these pages.

It's is the addition of the cultural richness on both sides of the mutant rights debate where Morrison's presentation of the world feels the most potent. By enriching the social groups in the X-Men's universe and exploring facets of mutant existence and conflict that have gone previously untread, we see that Morrison sets the stage to pick apart the false oversimplicity of the culture of fear. The world of the 21st century is wildly complex and diverse; technological and cultural advances have made the idea of a "melting pot" of peoples more possible than ever. Yet when the acceptance of this melting pot conflicts with a leader's agenda, the richness and diversity is denied.

Morrison Anticipates and Responds to 9/11

Twelve years after the fact, it seems almost passé to talk about 9/11 as a cultural milestone—everybody experienced it, everybody reflected on it in some way, and everyone has shared those reflections. But when Morrison was crafting *New X-Men*, the terrorist attacks of September 11, 2001 were fresh in the zeitgeist. In many ways, Morrison's work on *X-Men* is a response to 9/11 and its cultural fallout.

Eerily, it seems like Morrison almost saw this all coming. Most exemplifying this seeming prescience, in the second issue of his run, published in June 2001,[1] villain Cassandra Nova perpetrates a genocidal attack on the mutant island of Genosha, killing millions and dealing a huge blow to the worldwide mutant population. In the process, an entire booming cityscape is reduced to rubble, buildings and all.

Four months before the actual event, then, Morrison's *New X-Men* #115 eerily sets the stage for a Marvel Comics world that closely aligns with cultural conditions of post–9/11 America. In the later back-to-back issues of #132 and #133, though, Morrison explicitly draws this parallel, addressing both symbolically and literally a number of major elements involved in the attack, including violent plane hijackings, the ruins of massive urban architecture, and grief over loved ones lost. Of this explicit parallel, Morrison later wrote: "Over its forty-issue run, *New X-Men* turned into a diary of my own growing distrust of a post–9/11 conformity culture that appeared to be in the process of greedily consuming the unusual and different" (*Supergods* 356). "Conformity" here is essentially a stand-in for the process of homogenization and marginalization that the culture of fear wrought in the real world.

New X-Men #132 and #133 can in fact together be seen as a kind of two-part treatise on 9/11. In the former, set in the bombed-out ruins of Genosha, Morrison looks backwards to help the survivors of a world destroyed by violence. Meanwhile, *New X-Men* #133 is all about existing in a world where terror and its resulting War are reality. This latter issue opens on the Afghanistan/ Pakistan border, with the mutant hero Wolverine attacking a group of slave-traders who specialize in captives with special powers (another of Morrison's new and diverse threats) and who are dressed an awful lot like typical depictions of Middle Eastern terrorists. The plot also involves Professor Xavier and Jean Grey disrupting an attempt to hijack a commercial airplane to Mumbai and turn it into a suicide bomb. Immediately afterwards, Xavier survives an execution attempt via sniper.[2]

Most notably, *New X-Men* #133 also includes the introduction of the first major Middle Eastern/Sunni Muslim X-Man, a young Afghani woman by the name of Sooraya. Although Morrison mostly leaves Sooraya's development to later writers, it's surely not accidental that he opts to turn to the Middle East for expanding the X-Men's global membership at a time when being Muslim was not always greeted kindly in the West. In fact, we can see the inclusion of

Sooraya as part of Morrison's above-cited rebellion against post–9/11 homogenization.

Even the covers of #132 and #133 indicate the dual nature of these issues and their reflections on terror. In both, which present the image only of a head, viewer focus is drawn to the eyes—the red/purple of a statue (a monument, really) of Magneto's helmet in #132, the black of Sooraya's burka in #133. But despite the parallel construction of these covers, there's an important contrast: in #132, Magneto's eyes are closed forever. In #133, Sooraya's eyes are very much wide open. Moreover, as cover artist Frank Quitely's pencils indicate, Sooraya's struck with fear—in this case, fear of the silhouette of Wolverine, her purported rescuer. Sooraya the survivor greets the future with wide and somewhat hopeful eyes (note the tiny X-Men logo reflected in her gaze as well), but that future comes with some trepidation. Again, even though both Sooraya and Wolverine are "good guys," Morrison denies any homogenization—if a man like Wolverine is your rescuer, even the "good guys" can be frightening.

Jingoism and "Us" vs. "Them"

We've mentioned how the world around mutants has adapted to account for their rich interdiversity, but we've not yet talked about one of the X-Men's greatest adversaries relates to that theme. Let's return for a moment to #132 and its central character, Magneto. Magneto, attempting to rouse vengeful feeling among mutantkind in the wake of the attack on Genosha, clearly indicates in his supposed deathbed speech that in the wake of the terrible destruction of Genosha mutant issues remain a simple question of "us" versus "them" (or "they" versus "us"):

> This is the voice. This is the voice of Magneto. This is the voice of the Genoshan Nation. It's a strange thing, to die in the darkness. It's a strange thing to die. I was Magneto, the master of magnetic forces. Now I will be a voice in the darkness, echoing forever. Once, I was a mortal man. Now I am becoming memory, immortal. They must have thought they could silence us forever. Instead we have become magnetic. Unstoppable [November 2002].

This language bears surprising similarity to a speech from President George W. Bush in which he unveiled his plans for the War on Terror, Richard Nixon's symbolic godchild. Only nine days after the Twin Towers fell, President Bush addressed the joint session of Congress, laying out his plan to engage in a heroic battle against terrorism in the form of Al Qaeda and the Taliban.

> All of this was brought upon us in a single day, and night fell on a different world, a world where freedom itself is under attack. [...] It will not end until

every terrorist group of global reach has been found, stopped and defeated. [...]
Great harm has been done to us. We have suffered great loss. And in our grief
and anger we have found our mission and our moment.

In both speeches the words are simple, persuasive, passionate, and frightening:
"Freedom itself—our very way of life—is under attack." Both Magneto and
President Bush's words utilize recent tragedy and fresh emotion to motivate
the listener to action. And while some in both the real and fictional worlds
are convinced, the complex responses that result to these passionate pleas in
New X-Men demonstrate Morrison's keen awareness of how American political
culture has changed. Those who've read through the entirety of Morrison's
X-Men know that in fact Magneto's stirring speech is far from his last words—
it is instead symbolic of Magneto's ailing clout.

Magneto Redefined

> "[Magneto] had depth and dignity, so I turned him into a demented
> drug addict, unable to connect with a younger generation of mutants
> who wanted only his face on their Magneto Was Right T-shirts, like
> a latter-day Che Guevara."
> —Grant Morrison (*Supergods* 357)

Though prior to the penultimate "Planet X" story arc Magneto's most
directly glimpsed in #132, his presence has been spotted all throughout Morrison's *New X-Men* run—mostly on t-shirts and posters. In death, Magneto
has become a rallying figure for mutants who still don't feel as though they
have a place alongside humankind. As Morrison points out, the former evil
mutant leader has become a Guevara-type inspiration for disaffected youth.
This change more than perhaps any other clearly symbolizes how the mutant
culture has shifted. In a post–9/11 world, a man who once donned a colorful
battle helmet to lead paramilitary assaults has found his home in countercultural marketing. One can imagine his shirts being sold at Hot Topic—and
likely not just to mutants.[3]

Of course, the big twist in Morrison's *X-Men* is that Magneto did not die
in Genosha—not literally, anyway. Instead, he spends most of *New X-Men* under
Charles Xavier's nose masquerading as the mutant Zen healer Xorn, essentially
Magneto's parody of a righteous Xavier follower. He finally reveals his presence
in *New X-Men* #146 in a stunning last-page spread by artist Phil Jimenez, as
the unmasked Xorn stands above a prostrate Xavier grinning cockily and toss-
ing his false helmet in the air like a baseball. "X-Men emergency *indeed*, Charles
... the dream is *over*" (November 2003). Ominously, one of those aforemen-

tioned Guevara-isms—a "Magneto Was Right" poster—looks judgingly upon Erik Lensherr, who's about to launch his greatest attack on humankind.

Yet throughout the "Planet X" story, something becomes increasingly clear about Magneto's crusade against both humankind and his mutant opposition—it's incredibly outdated. His impassioned speeches and bold actions that worked wonders in days past don't hold up in this new world. His throngs of mutant followers get bored with his proclamations easily; his scare tactics barely even register as a blip on the radar with most of his followers. Magneto can barely control the half dozen children of the "Special Class" directly under his watch. What causes this failure?

Essentially, Magneto (whose eyes were closed on the cover to #132, remember) is unable to realize that the world has changed—his particular terror tactics haven't adjusted to a post–9/11 world. He's one of the only characters (one of the only mutants especially) in Morrison's run who still refers to mutants as a monolithic group, and as we saw earlier, this is a philosophy that treads no water any more. Emblematic of this approach, note the Manichean duality in such proclamations as a speech from issue #147 that finds him describing his "new world" as a place "Where the outcasts, the despised, the rejected ... are champions" (November 2003), ignoring the fact that not all mutants are necessarily outcasts any more; to some, mutants are actually kind of cool.

Though ostensibly part of the marginalized and targeted group, Morrison's Magneto easily stands in for President Bush in his use of the War on Terror to push neoconservative ideas. President Bush, remember, used the same rhetoric: "us" versus "them," a "world remade." Yet the conflicts in Iraq and Afghanistan did not receive especially wide public support ("Public Attitudes Towards the War in Iraq"). Even with fueling the culture of fear with real terror in addition to the patriotism and unity of post–9/11 America, Bush was unable to garner the same near-unflinching support Nixon received for his wars on cancer, drugs, and crime (as ineffective as those wars were). Many Americans (even white Americans) understood, partly because Bush himself emphasized this in his first post 9/11 address,[4] that the peoples of Iraq and Afghanistan, and the larger Muslim community in the Middle East, couldn't be painted with a wide brush. Without this oversimplification, the culture of fear was easier to poke holes in.

As Bush attempted to channel the previously successful tactics of Richard Nixon to push his agenda but found greatly diminished returns in an increasingly complex post–9/11 America, so too does Morrison's Magneto look to previous efforts to execute an agenda that end up being wildly ineffective. The notable difference with Magneto is that the previous tactics he's channeling are his own (many of which were originally written, it should be noted, more contemporaneously to Nixon); Magneto admits that his plan in "Planet X" is literally a recycled scheme from his younger days that he's finally decided to give another go. Note, too, that Magneto is almost the only character in Morrison's run who still wears his gaudy costume from simpler times; even his most loyal follower, Toad, has switched from an orange and brown jumpsuit to jeans, a t-shirt, and a leather jacket.

Magneto's ultimate folly is that he fails to understand the very idea we've been discussing—that mutant culture has reached a place where it cannot be encapsulated by a single ideal anymore. Helpfully, in the climax of "Planet X" Professor Xavier acts as a stand-in for Morrison himself[5]; in his X-Men's final battle with Magneto, Xavier crushes his one-time enemy's dreams by stating that Magneto has "nothing this new generation of mutants wants ... except for your face on a T-shirt." He further explains: "They have ideas of their own now. Perhaps it's time we put away the old dreams, the old manifestos ... and just listened for a while" (February 2004).

Fallout and the Future

Despite Magneto's failure as a mutant leader in a post–9/11 world, his final assault on the Marvel Universe version of New York City bears fruit worth considering. Specifically, it's interesting that Magneto's insistence on a simple cultural duality between human and mutant leads others to this Manichean perspective as well. Consider that, though certainly humans have opposed mutants in myriad ways throughout Morrison's run, these have mostly been more subtle, complicated threats than what comes out as a reaction to Magneto. In New X-Men #150, the final issue of Magneto's attack, an advisor to the U.S. President (not Bush himself, but it might as well be) cautions him that "Ours is a species fighting for its life" and subsequently suggests that the President drop neutron bombs on New York City, now rechristened New Genosha by the enemy. Tellingly, the advisor also informs the President that each bomb "Kills all known mutations stone dead, leaves our architectural heritage intact" (February 2004). These neutron bombs are arguably the largest threat humankind brings to bear against mutants in Morrison's entire run; they are certainly the most blunt.

With "Planet X," Morrison creates a complicated intermingling of fiction and reality to leave his ultimate comment on the War on Terror. Here Morrison inverts his initial (and originally unintended) Genosha/New York City comparison. Genosha begins as a mutant land destroyed in a terrorist attack that recalls New York City on 9/11. To compensate, Magneto ravages New York City, using his own style of terror for manipulating and distorting its architecture to become "New Genosha." And his human enemies want to destroy it, but their weapons will leave the architecture intact, a poignant reminder of what the last attack on U.S. soil precisely did not do.

Jumping back to reality a minute, in response to the 9/11 attacks, American forces, driven by the belief of a small group of leaders peddling fear, invaded Iraq and Afghanistan, killing civilians and destroying local communities ("Iraq War Casualties"). In a bittersweet comparison, in the initial battle between U.S. forces and Saddam Hussein in Iraq, American bombs destroyed millennia-old architecture of immense historical value ("Ancient Iraqi Sites Show Theft, Destruction").

In both our fictional scenario and our real one, it is a small group of attackers from a marginalized/homogenized community that commits grave acts of violence, and in both cases the entire group to which those attackers belong suffer. Beyond that, the attacked exacerbate their own suffering. And while everything wraps up relatively nicely for the X-Men in the end, the real world may not be as forgiving.

"Another result of 9/11 meant that the wanton destruction of fictional representations of real cities ... was no longer acceptable. Stories had to stay with the survivors, examine the repercussions, and treat formerly gratuitous scenes of carnage with some sensitivity," says Morrison (*Supergods* 354). But despite some more attention being paid to destructive aftermath, the rules of the medium remain: in Marvel Comics, the survivors go on to have adventures for years and years, their two-dimensional beings bearing only whatever scars of the past their current creator has deemed relevant.

But in the real world, survivors don't have the benefit of selective continuity. We have to learn from our mistakes, because we're probably not going to get rebooted and rewritten in three years. And hopefully what we learned from the fallout of 9/11—and what Morrison's run on *X-Men* portrays so well—is that attempting to marginalize a minority group as a monolithic, evil Other is a mistake. Asking an entire culture of individuals to pay for the mistakes of one or two has repercussions on everybody. And though Morrison uniquely explores the specifics of a post–9/11 world with Marvel's mutants, in a way, his ultimate message is exactly the same one Stan Lee and Jack Kirby emphasized way back in 1963: pay due respect those who are different from you and the world will be a much better place.

Notes

1. Note that the official publishing dates in the Works Cited page are two months later due to traditional comic book industry practices.

2. Granted, the would-be assassin turns out to be a space empress/jilted ex-lover of Xavier's, but still, the point stands that impressions of terror abound in this issue.

3. Speaking of commercialism, President Bush himself implored the American people

to show they weren't afraid by opening their pocketbooks. "Get down to Disney World," he told us in a famous post–9/11 quote.

4. To extend our metaphor, perhaps this is one of President Bush's "Xorn moments."

5. And certainly they share some physical similarities as well.

WORKS CITED

"Ancient Iraqi Sites Show Theft, Destruction." *National Geographic*. National Geographic Society, 11 Jan. 2003. Web. 30 Apr. 2013.

Glassner, Barry. *The Culture of Fear: Why Americans Are Afraid of the Wrong Things*. New York, NY: Basic, 1999. Print.

"Iraq War Casualties: The Toll of War." *NPR*. National Public Radio, 1 Jan. 2013. Web. 25 Apr. 2013.

Morrison, Grant. *Supergods: What Masked Vigilantes, Miraculous Mutants, and a Sun God from Smallville Can Teach Us About Being Human*. New York: Spiegel & Grau, 2011. Print.

Morrison, Grant (w) and Ethan Van Sciver (a). "Dust." *New X-Men* #133 (December 2002). New York: Marvel Comics. Print.

Morrison, Grant (w) and Frank Quitely (a). "E is for Extinction (Part 2)". *New X-Men* #115 (August 2001). New York: Marvel Comics. Print.

Morrison, Grant (w) and Frank Quitely, et al. (a). *New X-Men Omnibus* (August 2012). New York: Marvel Comics. Print.

Morrison, Grant (w) and Phil Jiminez (a). "Ambient Magnetic Fields." *New X-Men* #132 (November 2002). New York: Marvel Comics. Print.

_____ and _____. "Planet X (Part 1)." *New X-Men* #146 (November 2003). New York: Marvel Comics. Print.

_____ and _____. "Planet X (Part 2)." *New X-Men* #147 (November 2003). New York: Marvel Comics. Print.

_____ and _____. "Planet X (Part 5)." *New X-Men* #150 (February 2004). New York: Marvel Comics. Print.

"Public Attitudes Toward the War in Iraq: 2003–2008." *Pew Research Center*. Pew Research Center, 19 Mar. 2008. Web. 25 Apr. 2013.

"Race & the War on Drugs." *American Civil Liberties Union*. American Civil Liberties Union, 17 Oct. 2003. Web. 25 Apr. 2013.

Self, Robert O. "Industrial Garden." Introduction. *American Babylon: Race and the Struggle for Postwar Oakland*. Princeton, NJ: Princeton University Press, 2003. N. pag. Print.

"75 Years of Mortality in the United States, 1935–2010." *Centers for Disease Control and Prevention*. Centers for Disease Control and Prevention, 13 Mar. 2012. Web. 20 Apr. 2013.

Simon, Jonathan. *Governing through Crime: How the War on Crime Transformed American Democracy and Created a Culture of Fear*. Oxford: Oxford University Press, 2007. Print.

"Transcript of President Bush's Address." *CNN.com*. CNN, 21 Sept. 2001. Web. 25 Apr. 2013.

Vorenberg, James. "The War on Crime: The First Five Years." *The War on Crime by James Vorenberg*. The Atlantic Magazine, n.d. Web. 25 Apr. 2013.

From Columbine to Xavier's: Restaging the Media Narrative as Superhero Fiction

Nicolas Labarre

During the Columbine shooting, on May 20, 1999, young students using information found on the Internet to create and obtain weapons mounted a violent assault on their school with a tragic outcome. The same schematic description would apply to "Riot at Xavier's"—a narrative arc from Grant Morrison's *New X-Men* published from January to May 2003 (#134 to 138).[1] Obviously, despite broad similarities there are also significant difference. While the two Columbine shooters, Eric Harris and Dylan Klebold, used guns and bombs to kill as many of their fellow students as possible (Cullen 326–36), Quentin Quire, who leads the assault in *New X-Men*, causes death through miscalculation and is never presented as wishing a massacre. Other differences would the conspicuous absence of guns in *New X-Men*, while firearms were one of the primary subjects of commentary and debate following the events at Columbine; Michael Moore famously used Columbine as an founding example for his indictment of gun culture in the USA, in *Bowling for Columbine* (2002). To a large extent, the disparities stem from the nature of "Riot at Xavier's," a work framed by a specific genre, by a larger narrative, and by the constraints of serial publishing. "Riot at Xavier's" can be described as one of the "strangely hybrid works" resulting from what Linda Hutcheon calls "indigenization," what happens when a story is adapted and transplanted from a context to another (Hutcheon 150–1).

In 2003, as Grant Morrison was about to conclude his work on the series, he described "Riot at Xavier's" as "every school story [he] could think of mashed into one 'comicsclash' in the '2 many DJs' style" (Morrison and Singh, The End of An X-Era). This cultural blend would necessarily include school shootings, which had by that time become one of the dominant narratives surrounding schools and education in the United States. Morrison was transplanting a real world narrative into the superhero genre. At the simplest level, this change of context involved straightforward transpositions. For instance, there is a difference in the nature of weapons used. Instead of looking up bomb recipes on the Internet, as Harris and Klebold had done, Quire uses the Internet to find a copy of Magneto's helmet in order to neutralize Xavier's powers (#137). This paper purports to examine the circumstances and the extent of this indigenization of the Columbine shooting in the context of *New X-Men* specifically and the larger X-Men narrative. It will also seek to show how this displacement is used to reframe the Columbine shooting as a containable event, rather than a symptom of an "epidemic" of violence, a term which was used both by the media and by politicians in the wake of the catastrophe (Killing at Columbine High; Holt 5269)

While there had been a spree of killings in school from 1997 to 1999, the Columbine shooting was "the primary reference point for such acts of school violence" (Forman 67), the "iconic shooting" (Marsico 66–79) that came to symbolize a changed condition in American schools. The notion that the United States had entered a "post–Columbine era" was expressed as late as 2004.

> Since the incident, our society can speak of a post–Columbine era in a meaningful way. The temporality of the term simultaneously connotes a period of individual pain, familial suffering, anger, solace, healing and national soul searching as well as a new historical period into which Americans have collectively entered [Forman 66].

In the period during which "Riot at Xavier's" was written and drawn, the debate around Columbine had been reignited in the media by the release of Michael Moore's film, which premiered in June 2002 in Cannes and was subsequently released worldwide between August and September of the same year. We do not have access to the exact timeline of the conception of the story-arc, but a typical comic book produced by Marvel Comics takes roughly five months from the first script to the moment it appears on the stand (Rhoades 144). The prologue to the story arc appeared cover-dated January 2003. Grant Morrison never mentioned Columbine specifically as an influence on "Riot at Xavier's," nor is any shooting mentioned in the various promotional material surrounding these issues (Marvel solicitations, blurbs, etc.). However, the creators behind any depiction of an attack on a school in the post–Columbine and post-*Bowling for Columbine* period were likely aware with the then-defining narrative on school shootings.

Furthermore, fourteen months before *New X-Men* #134, readers of *New-X Men* were presented with a three page scene which contains a quote that seems to reference information that surrounded the Columbine shooting. In

New X-Men #118 (Nov. 2001), a high school student interrupts a school ceremony, shoots down an athlete and explains his action by his pride to be
"weird," before being shot down by the police. The line specifically echoes a
much repeated quote from the coverage of the Columbine shooting "Who
says we are different? Insanity's healthy!" Though the quote—from the school
yearbook—was later shown not to be related to the killers, it was widely
repeated initially, from CBS to the Associated Press. The entire scene is colored
in blue hues and introduced as separate from the main narrative. Its function
is to introduce a new deviant ideology which justifies an assault Xavier's institute in the two subsequent issues. However, this priming function expands
beyond that specific story-arc: the shooter's t-shirt is later worn by Quentin
Quire, in *New X-Men* #135 (Feb. 2003), establishing a subtle but unmistakable
connection between the two and confirming that Quire is to be read as a villain. This issue also informs the readers' perception of the genre itself. While
it keeps the X-Men separate from the shooting—they never appear in these
three pages—the representation of the school shooting integrates the event
into the fictional world. Literary theorist Jonathan Culler points out that "each
genre constitutes a special *vraisemblance* of its own," where *vraisemblance* is
"whatever tradition makes suitable or expected in a particular genre" (Culler
162,172). The inclusion of this scene thus redefines the contours of the *X-Men*
sub-genre, by making school shootings a narrative possibility. Morrison's intent
to target a "media-literate audience" (Morrison, Morrison Manifesto 2) suggests that this framing and priming should be read as a deliberate attempt to
establish a dialogue between a codified form of entertainment and other media
narratives, bringing a news event to bear on the fictional work inhabited by
the X-Men. This dialogue between news and super-heroes is established in
"Riot at Xavier's" through an indirect yet recognizable adaptation of the
Columbine narrative.

Referring to Columbine shooting as a story, a narrative or even as adapt-
able text may seem callous. However, part of the specificity of the event lies
in the media frenzy which surrounded it. In his meticulous depiction of the
shooting and its context, journalist Dave Cullen suggests that the coverage of
the shooting was a "gross caricature" of the event as described by first-hand
witnesses (Cullen 159). Reconstructing the origin of these distortions, he
shows that initial hypotheses put forward in the TV coverage as well as in
the *Denver Post* (152) quickly "tainted" testimonies (159), creating a self-
reinforcing spiral and finally aggregating into a series of myths which were
then repeated and perpetuated long after they were disproved:

> We remember Columbine as a pair of outcast Goths from the Trench Coat Mafia
> snapping and tearing through their high school hunting down jocks to settle
> a long-running feud. Almost none of that happened. No Goths, no outcasts,

nobody snapping. No targets, no feud, and no Trench Coat Mafia. Most of these elements existed at Columbine—which is what gave them such currency. They just had nothing to do with the murders. The lesser myths are equally unsupported: no connection to Marilyn Manson, Hitler's birthday, minorities or Christians [Cullen 149].

These early myths were all the harder to dispel since the police withheld or even dissimulated for a long time the documents which would have allowed a more complete version to emerge. From the point of view of adaptation, however, the actual events as they can now be reconstituted by Cullen and others matter less than their public perception at the time of the coverage. The post–Columbine era was mostly informed not by these retrospective analyses but by the myths enumerated in the above quote, and so is "Riot at Xavier's." This story references the cultural mythology of the shooting, not the presently established but less disseminated facts.

One of the factors facilitating the indigenization of the Columbine mythology is the fact that during Morrison's tenure, the X-Men were anchored around "Xavier's Institute for the Gifted Children," presented as an actual school rather than a private resort for a group of young adults. Xavier's institution, a quiet and wealthy place constantly assaulted by catastrophes echoes one of the apparent paradoxes of the school shootings: their tendency to occur "not at inner-city high schools filled with disadvantaged children" but rather in well-off suburban schools (Lewin). When he started writing the series, Morrison made clear his intention not to rely on the X-Men's convoluted history, and the school assault therefore remains open to more sinister readings.

As to the dominant theme of the Columbine coverage, the status of outcasts in high school, examining the place and role of misfits has arguably been the dominant motif in the various X-Men series since their creation. Various other creators working within the franchise before and after Morrison did indeed combine these elements to create stories of alienation and rejection in school, in series such as *Generation X* (1994–2001) or *New X-Men: Academy X* (2004–08). However, as part of his plan for the series, Morrison intended to make glamorous rebellion not only a thematic element of the series but one of its selling point: : "The X-Men are every rebel teenager wanting to change the world[...]. College kids will buy [*New X-Men*] for the rebel irony" (Morrison Manifesto 2). It is with "Riot at Xavier's" that Morrison undertakes a thorough examination of this theme of school rebellion. Though the school and its students are featured on several occasions prior to that arc, the focus in every case is on a confrontation with the outside world rather than on internal tensions within the institution.

New X-Men #134 opens with a two-page murder sequence colored in blue and grey hues—echoing the scene depicting the school shooting in #118—

before shifting abruptly to a depiction of a classroom, in pastel colors and from an askew angle. Five more pages elapse before a senior member of the X-Men appears. Later in the same issue, another three-page sequence again focuses solely on the interaction between students, with no adult present. This constitutes a significant departure from the established narrative strategy in the series. In no previous issues are the titular heroes absent for more than two or three consecutive pages. One of the functions of these two scenes between students is to introduce Kid Ω, Quentin Quire, before he leads the assault on the school. He is bespectacled and looking down, wearing a white shirt under a sleeveless sweater, while his fellow students are all dressed in fashionable street wear. The image is not necessarily negative in the context of a Marvel comic book, as Quentin's attire and attitude recall the early Peter Parker. A jagged line pattern on his sweater even connects him to Charlie Brown, another positive loser icon. The focus of the scene is on Slick, a popular black young man, who sports a risqué wooly pink jacket with no shirt, displaying his impressive musculature. He humiliates Quire, calls him a loser before leaving the room with a beautiful black woman called Tattoo at his arm, in a panel where the reader's point of view is that of Quire, looking up to this tormentor. In the next two pages, Quire and a fellow reject, Herman, a transparent pink body with visible skeleton and viscera, enviously discuss Slick's success with girls. Quire then asserts that the popular boy "knows nothing about real style," and offers to show his friend the "coolest artifact of all time," an old press cutting warning about mutants, featuring a stylized illustration of a mutant oppressor in striped shirt bossing around human slaves—actually an adaptation from a Jack Kirby drawing in *The X-Men* #14 (Nov. 1965). The reader then learns that Quire does not have a mobile phone, an indication of his social and financial status, as he is shown answering a public phone.

In these five pages Morrison introduces a complete cast of new characters, though Slick and Tattoo had been glimpsed before, and does so by resorting to visual shorthands, stereotypes, and heightened contrasts. The clothes worn by the other students, for instance, are more uniformly trendy and tight-fitting in this issue than in previous crowd scenes. Slick condenses most of the characteristics of the high school elite, with his elaborate hair, distinctive fashion sense, implied athleticism and overwhelming charisma. By contrast, Quire's deficiencies in all these domains come to the fore. The protective strategy adopted by Quire and Herman, providing alternative values for an in-group, recalls some of the early descriptions of the Columbine shooters. The day after the shooting, one of the Columbine students told the Colorado Gazette: "Kids get picked on, [...] they were harassed, not included. They were always on the outside looking in. There's always a group that gets picked on, but they seemed to like it that way" (Anton). In the opening panel depicting the classroom, it is worth noting that both Herman and Quire are indeed on the margin, while Slick is at the center and on the point of convergence of perspective lines. Since the meaning of the scene is conveyed at once by the text, the character design, by composition, and by intertextual references, the passage does read as explicitly didactic. Its sole purpose, however, is to introduce these characters in a set of social roles which closely mirror the tensions described in the mediated image of Columbine High before the shooting, as portrayed for instance in this *New York Times* article, published ten days after the shooting:

> The winners are a smaller group than we'd like to think, and high school life is very different for those who experience it as the losers. They become part of the invisible middle and suffer in silence, alienated and without any real connection to any adult [Lewin].

In itself, the situation is not unusual in North American comics, if only because the scenario of the humiliated weakling is the basis for the influential Charles Atlas ads aimed at outcast comic book readers that are so closely associated with mid–20th century comic books. When in the same issue, Quire confronts Slick and reveals his handsomeness to be a mere illusion generated by his mutant power, he is enacting a classical revenge fantasy, mocked as early as 1953 by Kurtzman and Wood in "Superduperman" (*Mad #4*, Apr.-May 1953). Slick, who now has the appearance of a small monkey, is rejected to the side of the weak and the uncool. Tattoo's skin, which spells out her emotion, reacts by printing out "loser," the very insult used by Slick towards Quire at the beginning of the issue. Formally, the page is all the more effective since Slick is never in the frame. Instead, three of the four panels have the reader face Quire. Slick is thus in turn relegated to a marginal space, and his point of view becomes the reader's for a page at least. The form invites us to empathize with the victims, whose point of view we share, while fittingly making the bully the center of attention.

Significant details help connect this archetypal situation to the Columbine dramaturgy, as Quire is shown "snapping up" among adults unable to heed the warning signs. At the end of the first scene, he is shown on the phone, asking "Mom is what?" The reader learns towards the end of the issue that the call was informing him he was an adopted child. Quire's impulse to turn the table on his tormentor is thus presented as the combination of a social dysfunction with a triggering event, an integral part of the early search for scapegoats in the Columbine narrative (Cullen 159). In the same issue and the next, all the adult supervisors of the schools are shown in turn examining Quire's case only to conclude that his attitude is that of a typical teenager (#134 and #135). Again, the idea that violence in schools results from a misreading or a lack of attention to warning signs was present in the Columbine narrative as early as in the speech Bill Clinton gave on the day of the shooting, and was later widely used in the coverage:

> We do know that we must do more to reach out to our children and teach them to express their anger and to resolve their conflicts with words, not weapons. And we do know we have to do more to recognize the early warning signs that are sent before children act violently [Clinton].

The context thus established is remarkably similar to the backstory fashioned by the media in the first day after the attack: a bright but unpopular student being picked on, snapping up and deciding to reverse the roles, under the watch of unprepared adults. This parallels the testimony of one of the members of the "Trench Coat Mafia," published by the Associated Press four days after the shooting:

> Another member of the group told *The Denver Post* that he understood why the teens snapped: One of the reasons the Trenchcoat Mafia existed, he said, was to give its members a sense of belonging in the face of teasing and bullying by other students, especially athletes.
> "I can't describe how hard it was to get up in the morning and face that," the 18-year-old, demanding anonymity, told The Denver Post. "Hell ... pure hell."
> He said that from the time he was a freshman, jocks at the school called him "faggot," bashed him into lockers and threw rocks at him as he rode his bike home [Foster].

New X-Men complicates this reading however, by having the actual violence exerted not upon Quire but upon another mutant, Jumbo Carnation, who is bullied then killed by normal humans in the prologue to "Riot at Xavier's." Quire's rebellion is thus to be understood as an individual act but also as an instance of collective action. By increasing the number of victims to two protagonists, including a character with no direct link to the school, Morrison establishes a dialectic tension between the specificities of the Columbine narrative and the framework of the X-Men. The bespectacled student as a vengeful outcast does not displace the general theme of the mutants as outcasts, it parallels it. The move suggests a reading of the event as an occurrence of the X-Men dominant theme, as opposed to a form of social comment applicable to the situation in actual American schools. Indigenization becomes a form of containment (Hall 478–79) or assimilation into a specific form of popular culture. While Morrison extends the boundaries of the genre by expanding its *vraisemblance*, he also "braids" his story into genre-specific themes (Groensteen 86), thus ascribing it to a tightly bound perimeter.

The notion of subculture, which featured prominently in the Columbine coverage, is similarly reframed and circumscribed in "Riot at Xavier's." In addition to their supposed and later disproved allegiance to the "Trench Coat

Mafia" (Cullen 148), the Columbine killers were also described as "goths," with little or no supporting evidence. That myth was also quickly dispelled, but not before being elevated to the status of national threat, as in this *Washington Post* article:

> Black trench coats are a consistent theme in the Gothic subculture that has attracted many teenagers to the poetry, music and costumes of a scene that ranges from benign fantasy to violent reality.
> Inspired by fantasy games such as Dungeons and Dragons, Gothic has become a fascination of many American high schoolers, some of whom simply dress and paint their fingernails black while others immerse themselves in a pseudo-medieval world of dark images [Fisher].

It was subsequently pointed out that Goths tend to be anything but violent (Cullen 156–7), but the incident suggest the need to use subcultural dynamics, especially such a visible subculture as the gothic movement, as an explanation for the disaster.

This explanation for violence features prominently in "Riot at Xavier's." In #135, Quire is reprimanded for his clothes. He is shown wearing a striped red-and-dark green sweater over a buttoned-up white shirt, with green trousers, an outfit which owes a lot to French designer Jean Paul Gaultier's distinctive tight striped sweaters. He later convinces a group of fellow students, his "Omega Gang," to wear the same outfit for a punitive expedition in town with the aim of avenging Jumbo Carnation's death. The outing ends with several deaths among Carnation's attackers and a promise for more violence. The following day, Xavier tells the school about the assault and the fact that the attackers were wearing "odd" clothing. Striped shirts." As a reaction to the "unrest," he then announces the banning of "certain fashion items," implicitly referring to those worn by the gang.

The striped clothes have by this point in the narrative become a synecdoche for Quire and his associates' violent behavior. The episode echoes not only the media's fascination with the so called "trench coat mafia" in Columbine, a group to which neither of the shooters actually belonged, but also the subsequent dress code changes which many schools sought to implement in reaction to this (Booth). Quire and his gang later wear the forbidden clothes again when attacking the school itself. The type of clothes differ, but the logic of establishing a subculture as a way to demonstrate solidarity and to refuse an oppressive dominant order connects *New X-Men*'s striped shirts and the Columbine trench coat. Furthermore, through their association with old-fashioned representations of the mutant menace, Quire's clothes are actually perceived by other characters as threatening rather than merely distinctive. In *New X-Men*, the heroes are the ones wearing black "brutalist and military" costumes (Morrison, Morrison Manifesto 2). Having Quire and his accomplices adopt a contrasting wardrobe after having established that its function is the same as that of black trench-coats in our world thus appears as an adaptation to the generic constraints rather than a willful deviation from the Columbine scenario.

A dialogue between the members of the Omega Gang as they first try their suits on encapsulates the appeal of the subculture for the outcasts:

> QUENTIN: We're a gang. We all wear the same clothes. We want people to copy us. Ask Tattoo. She's cool.
> TATTOO: Cool? Super Zeitgeist! I am that Blackbird. Glam! Industrial! Clockwork Orange! Next level Quentin—you score!
> QUENTIN: See? It's based on what humans thought we might wear when they were most scared of us. [...] [W]e have to make them scared again [#135].

Morrison thus has his outcasts articulate the specific role of the subculture, made visible through clothing and style: the creation of a shared identity and an ostentatious difference. This is perhaps best expressed by Dick Hebdige in his seminal study of subcultures:

> The communication of a significant *difference*, then (and the parallel communication of a group *identity*), is the "point" behind the style of all spectacular subcultures. It is the superordinate term under which all the other significations are marshaled, the message through which all the other messages speak [Hebdige 102].

As in the case of the school dynamics, Morrison resorts to a simplified and explicit construction of the role of subculture. This appears as a necessity, to fit the story in the constraining frame of the serial narrative. Since he only gets to show two brief instances of collaboration between the members of Quire's group, the long-term use of subcultural devices may otherwise have been missed. The above explanation is located just before the group's first outing, and suitably frames our reading of the incident. In the scene, we also get a glimpse of the wall of Quire's bedroom, on which a series of clipped articles and posters suggest that his actions should be read in the context of a larger subcultural movement: groups such as "The Coming Race" and "Juggernaut" are advertised alongside press clippings more directly related to the story.

Morrison also includes a nod to another Columbine myth in the construction of Quire's specific subcultural blend, the killers' alleged fascination for Hitler and their choice of the 20th April as a nod to the German dictator's birthday, by having Quire wear a "Magneto was right" t-shirt in #136. The garment is an effective example of indigenization. It uses the equivalence between two symbolic arch-villains, but also plays a structural or braiding role in the larger *New X-Men* narrative: as mentioned earlier, a similar t-shirt was worn by the school shooter in #118, and the allusion to Magneto is but one of the many elements foreshadowing his reappearance in #146 (Nov. 2003). Though Magneto is a victim of Nazism, he is also regularly depicted as having a totalitarian ambition, and his creed of mutant supremacy fits with some of the initial testimonies regarding the killers: "They're into anarchy. They're white supremacists and they're into Nostradamus stuff and Doomsday" (Students say group made up of "outcasts"). David Cullen points to a *USA Today* article published two days after the shooting as the source for the syncretic narrative which brought all the disparate myths surrounding the shooting together, from the shooters' fascination with fascism to the Trench Coat Mafia to the Gothic subculture (157). In "Riot at Xavier's," that function is given to a tattooist, who enumerates all the possible readings of Quire's rebellious attitude: "Let me guess... / you're some sissy emo band. / You're suburban Neo-Nazis. / Frat boys on dope!" (#135).

The irony of embedding a subculture within a larger mutant group itself consistently described as a subculture is not lost on the author, and in the final pages of #135, Quire bridges the apparent contradiction by proclaiming he and his group to be "the New X-Men." The metafictional nod to Morrison's own efforts to modernize the franchise is another instance of containment, as the series turns towards itself in the very moment when it most closely approximates the Columbine narrative. Columbine came to be considered as a synecdoche for high schools throughout the country, but Quire's rebellion is explicitly posited as being about the X-Men and only them.

By focusing on the Columbine myths rather than on the events, *New X-Men* provides a form of comment on the construction of a traumatic event, fit for the intended "media-literate" audience. However, the narrative also provides a specific rearticulation of the role of the media in the shaping of the event. While in the Columbine coverage the media looked for explanations from without their own realms, *New X-Men* puts forward the hypothesis of self-generating images of violence. The video game *Doom* was widely blamed for Harris and Klebold's behavior, and so were movies (*The Basketball Diaries*) and bands (including Marilyn Manson, fitting with the Goth hypothesis). Quire, by contrast, is inspired by a press cutting, itself based on a comics drawing. Much of the media's efforts in their coverage were dedicated to finding a scapegoat, a suitably marginal cultural object or subculture, alienated enough from the mainstream to provide a ready-made explanation. Morrison instead provides a specific source for Quire's behavior, but makes the cultural object highly paradoxical. This is a press article presented as fictional in the diegetic world, itself based on a comic book illustration, possibly inspired by a speculative article in *Mechanix Illustrated* (Cronin). The change calls attention to the futility of the blaming process: in *New X-Men*, the article provides Quire with a style, a model and a cultural precedent, but this find merely displaces the roots of violence to an ultimately unknowable object. The blaming process is voided, turned into a self-referential quest for precedents. In turn, this can be read as an indictment of the media's own attitude and of their role in creating violent behaviors and copycats. Klebold and Harris were indeed inspired by previous shootings and the intensity of the Columbine coverage did indeed further violence: a 1999 Gallup poll showed that 20 percent of American teenagers were confronted with copycats in their schools (Cornell 208; Cullen 322–3). Moreover, as indicated before, much of the national response was a reaction to the coverage of the event rather to the events themselves, the instauration of dress codes being a case in point.

By retaining the school dynamics and the emergence of a violent subculture while altering or reframing most of the media context, Grant Morrison further focuses his version of the event on personal rather than societal explanations. This is amply demonstrated towards the end of the assault, when a defeated Quire cries "I started up my own movement and everything ... so you'd look up to me" (#137) as he is being defeated by the Stepford Cuckoos, five beautiful teenage girls. This emotional and earnest outburst contrasts sharply with Dylan and Klebold's psychopathic indifference to the fate of others (Cullen 352). The empathy with Quire, announced when the character is first introduced and the reader is asked to share his point of view, may also explain the dramatic changes in the assault itself. While most of the buildup towards the invasion of the school purposefully echoes the media coverage of Columbine, including the notion that the attack may be a suicide mission ("That's Wolverine you messed up with, you suicidal genius," quips a member of the Omega gang in #137), the attack itself plays out more as a comedy, with a dramatic twist, than as a tragedy. This should also be read as part of the indigenization process: while in Columbine the SWAT teams intervened late and explored cautiously the buildings for hours, the X-Men intervene directly against Quire and his group. The difference in competence between the heroes and regular intervention forces is a feature in the series (in #127 for instance, the police shoots a young mutant who could have been saved by Xorn, then a healer among the X-Men) and the very narrative structure of the super-hero genre promises an eventual victory for the heroes, though with possible sacrifices in between. Thus, while Quire and his associates are living weapons, with powers heightened by a specific drug—possibly an indigenized equivalent of guns—they fail to cause much damage. The only casualty, the death of a fellow telepathic student is accidental though also imputable to the use of the drug. What Morrison offers in "Riot at Xavier's" is thus an indigenized reenactment of the Columbine narrative which ends up in a final act of containment. The assault is folded back into strictly personal motives, and has little lasting consequences in the narrative world itself.

"Riot at Xavier's" thus attests to the continued relevance of the Columbine shooting as late at 2003, to the persistence of the myths spawned by the initial coverage, and to the irrelevance of the quest for explanations and scapegoats which went on after the shooting. Interpreting the changes in the story and its outcome is complicated by what we have been calling the indigenization process. In spite of the many similarities between the Columbine narrative and this *New X-Men* narrative arc, this indigenization ensures the story is read primarily as an episode in the broader X-Men narrative and only secondarily as a reinterpretation of an actual event. This specific balance between reference and code may also have been inspired by the lessons drawn from other representations of school shootings in popular culture. School shootings were indeed deemed a sensitive subject to broach in popular fiction. An episode of *Buffy the Vampire Slayer* delayed its airing in 1999 because its story involved a possible school shooter (McConnel 119–120) and the Columbine shooting occurred the week before its scheduled airdate. "Shoot," a short story written by Warren Ellis on the subject, that was to be published in the DC/Vertigo comic book *Hellblazer,* was also cancelled the same year, though it eventually saw print in 2010 (Ellis). Prior to "Riot at Xavier's," Columbine had been alluded to in the X-Men franchise, but "Correction," published in *Generation X* #63–66 (May–August 2000), had avoided the assault itself, to focus on an exaggerated version of the societal reaction to the shooting. In the story, plotted by Warren Ellis, a government facility kidnaps kids inspired by the Columbine shooters to turn them into robotic monsters. It aligned with the classic X-Men theme of young outcasts faced with socially-sanctioned intolerance. It also read as a form of libertarian comment, while "Riot at Xavier's," as we indicated earlier, focuses on personal rather than social or political causes.

"Riot at Xavier's" thus appears as a contained reenactment of Columbine: containment of the causes to a personal narrative, containment of the story within the codes of the genre, containment of the outcome to one accidental death. It is tempting to see in this containment the effect of the inherent tendency of mass culture as described by Frankfurt School theorist, the "spurious personalization of objective issues," which forcibly reduces the political to the personal (Adorno 485). However, this tightly contained version of Columbine also echoes the notion, then emerging, that the shooting actually did not lead to a dramatic outburst of school violence, making most of the measures taken in its aftermath appear as overreaction, a thesis also put forward in *Bowling for Columbine.* The framing of the incident in the narrative arc replaces the national event with a personal tragedy, a first step towards a reexamination of the media construction surrounding Harris and Klebold which is not entirely dissimilar to the acclaimed and useful reexamination since undertaken outside the realm of popular fiction.

NOTE

1. When Grant Morrison started writing *X-Men* in 2001, the series' title was changed to *New X-Men*. In the rest of this paper, *New X-Men* refers to this series, written by Morrison from May 2001 (#114) to March 2004 (#154), as opposed to ulterior uses of the same title. "Riot at Xavier's" is a collective title for a four part storyline running from #135 to #138; however, #134, "Kid Ω," serves as a prologue to that storyline and is included in the various collected editions.

WORKS CITED

Adorno, Theodor w. "Television and the Patterns of Mass Culture." In *Mass Culture. The Popular Arts in America*. Ed. Bernard Rosenberg and David Manning White. Glencoe: The Free Press, 1957. 474–87.

Altman, Rick. *Film/Genre*. London: British Film Institue, 1999.

Anton, Genevieve. "'Trench Coat Mafia' Fellow Students Describe Members of the Fringe Group as Outcasts and Recluses." *The Gazette* 21 April 1999. A3.

Booth, Michael. "Methods Differ, Aim Same: Making U.S. Kids Safe." *The Denver Post* 15 August 1999. K-03.

Bowling for Columbine. Dir. Michael Moore. 2002. DVD.

Clinton, Bill. "Remarks on the Attack at Columbine High School in Littleton, Colorado." 20 April 1999. *Government Printing Office*. 21 December 2012. <http://www.gpo.gov/fdsys/pkg/WCPD-1999-04-26/html/WCPD-1999-04-26-Pg685–2.htm>.

Cornell, Dewey G. *School Violence: Fears Versus Facts*. Mahwah, N.J: Lawrence Erlbaum Associates, 2006.

Cronin, Brian. "Comic Book Legends Revealed #309." 15 April 2011. *Comic Book Resources*. 17 November 2012. <http://goodcomics.comicbookresources.com/2011/04/15/comic-book-legends-revealed-309/>.

Cullen, Dave. *Columbine*. London: Old Street Publishing, 2009.

Culler, Jonathan. *Structuralist Poetics: Structuralism, Linguistics and the Study of Literature*. 2nd. Lodon, New York: Routledge, 2002.

Ellis, Warren. "SHOOT to Finally Be Published." 16 July 2010. *Warren Ellis Dot Com*. 21 December 2012. <http://www.warrenellis.com/?p=10078>.

Ellis, Warren (w), Brian Wood (w) and Steve Pugh (a). "Correction." *Generation X* #63–66 (May-Aug. 2000). New York: Marvel Comics.

Ellis, Warren (w) and Phil Jiminez (a). "Shoot." *Vertigo Resurrected* #1 (Oct. 2010). New York: DC Comics.

Fisher, Mark. "'Trench Coat' Mafia Spun Dark Fantasy." *The Washington Post* 21 April 1999. A01.

Forman, Murray. "Freaks, Aliens and the Social Other: Representations of Student Stratification in U.S. Television's First Post-Columbine Season." *The Velvet Light Trap* 53 (2004): 66–82.

Foster, David. "Gunmen's Friends Deny Knowing Plan." 24 April 1999. *Associated Press*. 12 November 2012.

Groensteen, Thierry. *The System of Comics*. Trans. Bart Beaty and Rick Nguyen. Jackson: University Press of Mississippi, 2007.

Hall, Stuart. "Notes on Deconstructing 'the Popular.'" Storey, John. *Cultural Theory and Popular Culture. A Reader. 3rd Edition.* Harlow: Pearson Education, 2006. 478–487.

Hebdige, Dick. *Subcultures: the Meaning of Style.* London: Methuen, 1979.

Holt, Rush Rep. *Congressional Record.* Washington: Government Printing Office, 11 April 2000.

Hutcheon, Linda. *A Theory of Adaptation.* London, New York: Routledge, 2006.

Kurtzman, Harvey (w) and Wallace Wood (a). "Superduperman." *Mad* #4 (Apr.-May 1953). New York: Educational Comics.

Lewin, Tamar. "Terror in Littleton: The Teen-Age Culture; Arizona High School Provides Glimpse Inside Cliques' Divisive Webs." 02 May 1999. *The New York Times.* 4 November 2012.

Marsico, Katie. *The Columbine High School Massacre: Murder in the Classroom.* Tarrytown, NY: Marshall Cavendish Corporation, 2010.

McConnel, Katherine. "Chaos at the Mouth of Hell. Why the Columbine High School Massacre had Repercussions for Buffy the Vampire Slayer." *Gothic Studies* (2000): 119–135.

Millar, Mark (w) and Andy Kubert (a). "The Tomorrow People." *Ultimate X-Men* #1 (May 2000). New York: Marvel Comics.

"Minute by Minute: Killing at Columbine High." *NBC News: Dateline.* 20 April 1999. Television transcript.

Morrison, Grant. "Morrison Manifesto." *New X-Men vol.1.* New York: Marvel Comics, 2003. 2.

Morrison, Grant, and Arune Singh. "The End of an X-Era: Grant Morrison Talks Finishing 'New X-Men,' Sex & DC." 26 September 2003. *Comic Book Resources.* 4 November 2012. <http://www.comicbookresources.com/?page=article&old=1&id=2815>.

Morrison, Grant (w), and Ethan van Sciver (a). "Germ Free Generation (Part 1)." *New X-Men* #118 (Nov. 2001). New York: Marvel Comics.

Morrison, Grant (w), and John Paul Leon (a). "Of Living and Dying." *New X-Men* #127 (Aug. 2002). New York: Marvel Comics.

Morrison, Grant (w), and various artists. "Kid Ω" and "Riot at Xavier's." *New X-Men* #134–138 (Jan.–May 2003).New York: Marvel Comics.

Rhoades, Shirrel. *Comic Books: How the Industry Works.* New York: Peter Lang, 2008.

"Students Say Group Made Up of 'Outcasts' 'Trenchcoat Mafia' Were Racists, into Gothic Lifestyle." *The Charleston Gazette* (21 April 1999): P6A.

No Mutant Left Behind: Lessons from *New X-Men: Academy X*

RICH SHIVENER

Comic book publishers have a long history of publishing stories that focus on teenage superheroes and villains as a means of introducing new characters and connecting with younger audiences. Some examples including *Spider-Man, New Mutants, Young Avengers* and *Teen Titans*. In 2004 Marvel debuted *New X-Men: Academy X*, centering on new students of the Xavier Institute for Higher Learning, once known as Xavier's School for Gifted Youngsters, where veteran X-Men serve as faculty. Though a work of fiction, it's clear that *New X-Men: Academy X* reflected contemporary hot-button issues in American education, including violence, bullying, gifted and private studies, and faculty-student romance. Those and more are covered in *New X-Men: Academy X*'s first story arc, "Choosing Sides," published in *New X-Men: Academy X* #1–6 (Jul.–Dec. 2004).

New X-Men: Academy X is not to be confused with *New X-Men*, written by Grant Morrison, from 2001 to 2004. Since *New X-Men*'s conclusion, Morrison has reflected on his tenure with the series. In speaking with the popular comics news publication *Comic Book Resources*, he revealed a fact that helped set the foundation for *New X-Men: Academy X*.

> I asked for the name of the book to be changed from "X-Men" to "New X-Men" during my run for a few reasons, apart from the fact that it made for such a cool flip-over logo. One thing I wanted to do was combine the concepts of the "X-Men" book with the old "New Mutants" idea of the Xavier school as a place where teenagers learn to become super-heroes. "X-Men" + "New Mutants" = "New X-Men" [Singh].

As Morrison's *New X-Men* came to a conclusion, husband-wife team Nunzio DeFilippis and Christina Weir were writing *New Mutants* (Marvel), a series centering on new students of Xavier's school. When *New X-Men* ended, *New*

Mutants was retitled as *New X-Men: Academy X*; DeFilippis and Weir wrote the first story arc, "Choosing Sides," with Randy Green providing the art. *New X-Men: Academy X* maintains the continuity of *New Mutants*, but at the time of writing, DeFilippis and Weir saw *Academy X* as a way to refresh stories about young mutants:

> As proud as we were of *New Mutants*, we wanted this to be a book that stood on its own and didn't require anyone to read the back issues. And the *New X-Men* title serves two purposes. One, it gives the book a higher profile and makes it something more people are likely to check out. And two, it accurately reflects the central theme of the book—these are the *New X-Men*, the next generation of mutant heroes. The difference is, with this book, you get to catch them at the ground floor [DeFilippis and Weir 26].

Weir and Nunzio DeFilippis had anticipated the pressure of following Morrison's manifesto, as well as Marvel's request to keep *New X-Men: Academy X* "young-reader friendly" and "keeping their X-books on message," or consistent with continuity, style, et cetera (Cronin). As a result, the messages Weir and Nunzio DeFilippis brought to *New X-Men: Academy X* are worth examining while considering critical moments in U.S. education.

Private and Gifted

Debuting in July 2004, "Part One" of "Choosing Sides" depicts Xavier's Institute for Higher Learning in Westchester County, New York, where new mutants learn and control their powers—and perhaps become the next generations of X-Men. Cyclops and Emma Frost, a villain-turned-hero (or vice versa, depending on who one asks) serve as the headmasters of Xavier's Institute for Higher Learning, and veteran X-Men serve as faculty who advise and teach. The new students, who board at the school, are assigned to squads, each of which has an advisor. "Part One" introduces new mutants who will likely be central to the story arc. For instance, Josh Foley, age 16, has "omega-class healing ability"; Laurie Collins, age 15, has "pheromone-based manipulation of emotions," and David Alleyne, age 17, has "limited telepathy" that allows him to absorb skills and knowledge (DeFilippis and Weir 10–15).

When paralleled with U.S. education, "Part One" demonstrates effectively that the Xavier's Institute for Higher Learning has the ideals and structure of private schools with boarding, more specifically those in New York. Take the Hackley School, located in Tarrytown, New York, part of Westchester County, where the fictional Xavier Institute for Higher Learning is located. Hackley's mission statement reads:

Hackley believes that students will grow in character and responsibility by participating in structured activity that serves the needs of people outside the spheres of home and school. By committing their energy, time, and imagination to serving those needs, students can experience the satisfaction of helping others and can gain some appreciation of the complexity and concerns of the larger community [Hackley].

Hackley's beliefs and values aren't too far from those of Xavier's Institute for Higher Learning, as evidenced by headmaster Cyclops. In "Part One," Mr. Cyclops, as the students call him, notes that "This is a school first and foremost. You are here to learn how to control your powers, and to attend classes like another teenage" (DeFilippis and Weir 5). In "Part Two," he notes that "Professor Xavier is away, pursuing other aspects of his dream. A dream of humans and mutants coexisting peacefully. But that dream is still alive here" (DeFilippis and Weir 21).

Furthermore, thanks to what Cyclops states and the population he serves, Xavier's Institute for Higher Learning is a reflection of U.S. institutions that support "gifted" students. Xavier's gifted is synonymous with fictional mutants, but in the real world the National Association for Gifted Children (NAGC), regards: "Gifted individuals are those who demonstrate outstanding levels of aptitude (defined as an exceptional ability to reason and learn) or competence (documented performance or achievement in top 10 percent or rarer) in one or more domains" (NAGC).

Institutes supporting gifted program are widely available in the U.S. (NAGC), but levels of funding and state recognition for such institutes vary by state. Specifically in New York, the NAGC notes, the state hasn't allocated abundant funding in recent years, though it does recognize gifted as "intellectually gifted; Academically gifted; Performing/visual arts" (NAGC).

In recent years, as the NAGC continues to watch federal and state actions, it also notes an alarming decline in funding for gifted programs across the U.S., thanks to the President Bush's No Child Left Behind Act. The federal act, effective 2001, focuses on increasing competencies of low-achieving students and holding schools more accountable for high achievement (*The New York Times*).

Furthermore, in regards to Xavier's approaches to education, "Part Two" of "Choosing Sides" centers on the new squads of Xavier's Institute for Higher Learning (DeFilippis and Weir). The last half of the story outlines what will be the central conflict of "Choosing Sides": The New Mutants are at odds with Hellions. The New Mutants consist of the aforementioned mutants— Foley, Collins, and Alleyne—plus a few more, including Noriko Ashida, later codenamed Surge. Hellions are led by Julian Keller, codenamed Hellion, viewed as a troublemaker-cum-leader among the students; his clique, if you will, includes, among others, Santo Vaccarro, codenamed Rockslide, and Sooraya Qadir, codenamed Dust, for her ability to morph into her namesake. What's interesting is that both New Mutants and Hellions have qualities of heroism and villainy, not to mention diverse thinking and being.

More importantly, *New X-Men: Academy X*'s depictions of squad-based learning and formations, with respect to New Mutants and Hellions, further reflects practices among private schools, as well as military schools. Hackley School, for instance, assigns to students to "houses" and invites students to participate in social and academic-based activities and competitions (Hackley). Also in upstate New York, the New York Military Academy, founded in 1889, focuses on squad-based learning and application, as evidenced by the following:

> NYMA cadets pursue a cutting-edge and relevant 21st century curriculum alongside a structured, leadership and life-skills focused military program guided by the school's decade's long affiliation with the United States Army JROTC. Not only is this whole-child method a proven educational approach for intentional and forward-looking students, but this unique model also offers more peer leadership opportunity, self reliance, personal accountability, and thoughtful structure than is available to aspiring young leaders in most other public, independent and charter schools [NYMA].

In summary, *New X-Men: Academy X*, thanks to DeFilippis and Weir, has the tone and character of educational institutions that offer private, gifted and military programming, appearing as a mutation, if you will, of all three.

Wartime Tension Veiled?

"Part Two" of "Choosing Sides," in addition to its reflections of educational practices among private and gifted schools, contains a short scene, about a page long, that speaks to wartime tensions among the United States and the Middle East and the difficulty adolescents may have had in negotiating these newly heightened tensions.

The scene consists of Surge and Dust, who are roommates at Xavier's Institute for Higher Learning. Dust is wearing a burqa, loosely reflecting the Islamic traditions of Afghanistan (Dar 107). Noriko comments on it, asking if Dust does "Cover yourself from head to toe in shame and be subservient to men?" Dust replies, "No, the burqa is about modesty. There are boys and men on campus. And it is not right for me to show off by exposing myself or my flesh to them." To which Noriko later retorts, "I don't need to be lectured by someone who's setting women back fifty years just walking around like that" (DeFilippis and Weir 7).

In July 2004, when "Part Two" was published, United States military branches and NATO were still battling the lasting formations of the Taliban, while Afghanistan as whole, now war-torn, was preparing for its first parliamentary elections in 30 years (BBC). At the same time, in light on the 9/11 attacks, violence against Muslims in the United States was on the upswing; a report by the The Council on American-Islamic Relations (CAIR) found the following:

> ...CAIR received 141 reports of actual and potential violent anti–Muslim hate crimes, a 52 percent increase from the 93 reports received in 2003. Overall, 10 states alone accounted for almost 79 percent of all reported incidents to CAIR in 2004. These ten states include: California (20.17%), New York (10.11%), Arizona (9.26%), Virginia (7.16%), Texas (6.83%), Florida (6.77%), Ohio (5.32%), Maryland (5.26%), New Jersey (4.53%) and Illinois (2.96%) [CAIR].

Though "Part Two" reflects American views on Islam, the story, as well as "Choosing Sides" overall, never mentions Dust's faith or the United States' involvement overseas, but the connections to reality are clear. Some authors, including Dar, point out that Dust's representation of Islamic practices is loosely accurate (108).

Faculty-Student Romance

Among academic circles and the public at large, a long-standing hot button issue is the ethics of faculty-student relationships. Particularly troublesome are such relationships between American high school students, who are almost universally minors, and their adult teachers. There are numerous cases of such relationships involving sexual misconduct and harassment, affairs that have affected school policies as well as state legislations (Chen and McGeehan). Some cases have led to firings, lawsuits, and jail time.

"Part Three" of *New X-Men: Academy X*'s "Choosing Sides" story arc underscores this issue with a brief scene. New Mutants squad member Foley, now codenamed Elixir, is seen kissing and flirting with faculty member Rahne Sinclair, codenamed Wolfsbane, once a New Mutant herself. Elixir is 16 years old, and Wolfsbane is 19, though she believes she is "so much older." While they both seem to like each other, Wolfsbane airs her concerns about their secret relationship (DeFilippis and Weir 11).

"What does it tell you that we're keeping this from everyone?" she asks. "I'm a teacher now. And Mr. Summers reminded me that I have to act like one."

"So that's it, then? We're not even gonna try to make it work?" Elixir replies. "I really thought you liked me."

"Part Three" was published in September 2004, an interesting year for faculty-student relationships. In May 2004, teacher Debra Lafave, then age 23, was arrested for sexual relations with a 14-year-old student in central Florida. Her case is one of the most notorious in recent years (Lafave). Another noteworthy case includes Mary Kay Letourneau's release from prison in 2004. The former teacher had been sentenced for having an affair with a 13-year-old, Vili Fualaau, by whom she had two kids and later married (King).

As these cases and existing discourse show, the issue of faculty-student relationships is complex, just like the relationship between Elixir and Wolfsbane. "Part Three" isn't the end of their relationship, as noted in "Part Six" (DeFilippis and Weir 25).

Bullying and School Violence

In recent years, federal and state entities have stepped up support for addressing the issue of bullying, especially as it relates to schools. In 2004, the U.S. Department of Health and Human Services (HHS), launched its "Stop Bullying Now!" campaign. It now manages StopBullying.gov, a comprehensive resource regarding the issue. It defines bullying as:

...unwanted, aggressive behavior among school aged children that involves a real or perceived power imbalance. The behavior is repeated, or has the potential to be repeated, over time. Both kids who are bullied and who bully others may have serious, lasting problems [HHS].

HHS goes on to define types of bullying and such associated acts as "name calling," "taunting" and "hitting/kicking/pinching." These and more are present throughout *New X-Men: Academy X*.

With concerns similar to HHS, the Bureau of Justice Statistics and National Center for Education Statistics files an annual report regarding "Indicators of School Crime and Safety," which addresses bullying. Their joint report of 2005 found that:

In 2003, students ages 12–18 were victims of about 740,000 violent crimes and 1.2 million crimes of theft at school. Seven percent of students ages 12–18 reported that they had been bullied, 29 percent of students in grades 9–12 reported that drugs were made available to them on school property, and 9 percent of students were threatened or injured with a weapon on school property [Bureau of Justice Statistics and National Center for Education Statistics].

Using these definitions of bullying, *New X-Men: Academy X's* "Choosing Sides" story arc addresses bullying in more than one instance. The central bully is Hellion, who on numerous occasions threatens the New Mutants, seen as a threat to his self-assumed leadership at the Xavier Institute for Higher Learning (DeFilippis and Weir). "Part Four" of "Choosing Sides" finds Hellion once again trying to get a rise out of his so-called opponents, namely Winddancer. In one scene, they argue about cheating in what should be a friendly competition between New Mutants and Hellions. Hellion had used a telekinetic wall to prevent his opponents from finding a hidden item (DeFilippis and Weir 4).

"I simply put up a wall and you flew into it. What's offensive about that?" Hellion asks.

"Well, the fact that the wall came from you makes it offensive," Windancer says.

"You wound me, Sofia," Hellion responds. "Let's face it. I've got to be getting under your skin if I can get you this riled up!"

While that scene and others indicate that Hellion is rather antagonistic, he takes a turn for the better in "Part Five," which touches on notions of bullying prevention. In it, a new student named Kevin Ford, codenamed Wither, can disintegrate organic matter, making him a high-level threat to many. When he is being investigated for the death of his father, students begin gossiping about him, and in response he becomes reclusive. Hellion, in turn, takes a stand for him. "This is a place we go to be safe. They want to take one of us away and all you can do is gossip. You're terrible mutants. You're not fit to be called homo superior" (DeFilippis and Weir 20).

Hellion's turn of character speaks Health & Human Services' notion that students can "be more than a bystander" (HHS). Still, as subsequent pages show, Hellion again embraces his bullying side, raising questions about his own title as homo superior (DeFilippis and Weir 23).

As it addresses bullying, "Choosing Sides" also downplays school violence, seen as the next step of bullying (APA). In fact, in "Part Three" of the story arc, New Mutants and Hellions are tasked with locating a hidden item, the caveat being "One last rule. No offensive use of powers on members of the opposing squad," according to Cyclops (DeFilippis and Weir 23). Cyclops later notes that "the rule was put in place to prevent violence between students." In "Part Six," he and the faculty stop the Hellions and New Mutants from engaging in a serious battle, one that could have exposed many mutants to the FBI (DeFilippis and Weir 19). These instances, as well as others, speak to Marvel's overarching request to keep *New X-Men: Academy X* young-reader friendly. In 2004, DeFilippis and Weir were aware of the Marvel's aforementioned request, something that affected them in late 2003, when they were tasked with removing suicide and gay scenes in the eighth issue of New Mutants (Cronin).

Lessons Learned

As a whole, the first story arc of *New X-Men: Academy X* offers timely reflections of such issues as bullying and violence, faculty-student romance, gifted studies—issues that are still being debated in schools. DeFilippis and Weir continued their relevant work through October 2005, when issue 19 of *New X-Men: Academy X*, marked the end of their run. Their successors were Craig Kyle and Chris Yost, whose writings no doubt offer lessons not unlike their predecessors (Kyle and Yost). In fact, they sought to make New X-Men's tests harder than ever before:

> They've struggled as teenagers (as all teenagers do), they've struggled as mutants (as all mutants do), and they have stood in the shadows of the best heroes in the Marvel Universe.... But that is not enough. These kids should suffer all of those problems *while* being forced to endure conflicts and battles that even the X-Men would struggle to survive. The choice that a person makes in his or her darkest hour defines them. It's time we found out what these kids are made of [Kyle and Yost].

WORKS CITED

American Psychological Association. "School Bullying Is Nothing New, But Psychologists Identify New Ways to Prevent It." *American Psychological Association*. American Psychological Association, 29 Oct 2004. Web. 1 May 2013. <http://www.apa.org/research/action/bullying.aspx>.

Birkland, Thomas A., and Regina G. Lawrence. "Media Framing and Policy Change After Columbine." *American Behavioral Scientist* 52.10 (2009): 1405–25. ProQuest. Web. 29 May 2013.

British Broadcasting Corporation. "Afghanistan Profile—Timeline." *BBC News*. British Broadcasting Corporation, 13 Mar 2013. Web. 1 April 2013. <http://www.bbc.co.uk/news/world-south-asia-12024253>.

Callahan, Timothy. "When Words Collide." *Comic Book Resources*. Comic Book Resources, 16 Nov 2009. Web. 15 April 2013. <http://www.comicbookresources.com/?page=article&id=23729>.

Chen, David, and Patrick McGeehan. "Social Media Rules Limit New York Student-Teacher Contact." *New York Times*. 1 May 2012: 1. Web. 30 May. 2013. <http://www.nytimes.com/2012/05/02/nyregion/social-media-rules-for-nyc-school-staff-limits-contact-with-students.html?pagewanted=all&_r=0>.

The Council on American-Islamic Relations. "2005 Civil Rights Report: Unequal Protection." *The Council on American-Islamic Relations*. The Council on American-Islamic Relations, 29 Mar 2013. Web. 30 May 2013. <http://www.cair.com/civil-rights/civil-rights-reports/2005.html>.

Cronin, Brian. "Comic Book Urban Legends Revealed #176." *Comics Should Be Good*. Comic Book Resources, 9 Oct 2008. Web. 30 May. 2013. <http://goodcomics.comicbookresources.com/2008/10/09/comic-book-urban-legends-revealed-176/>.

Dar, Jehanzeb. "Holy Islamophobia, Batman! Demonization of Muslims and Arabs in Mainstream American Comic Books." *Teaching Against Islamophobia*. Shirley R. Steinberg, ed. 1st ed. New York: Peter Lang, 2010. 107. Print. <http://www.peterlang.com/index.cfm?event=cmp.ccc.seitenstruktur.detailseiten&seitentyp=produkt&pk=53817&concordeid=310336>.

DeFillippis, Nunzio, and Christina Weir. Interview by Brian Cronin. "CBR Chat Transcript: Nunzio DeFillippis and Christina Weir." *Comic Book Resources*. 1 Aug 2005. Comic Book Resources. 1 Aug 2005.. Web. 10 May 2013. http://www.comicbookresources.com/?page=article&id=5440.

DeFillippis, Nunzio (w), Christina Weir (w), Randy Green (a), et al. "Part One." *New X-Men: Academy X* #1. Jul. 2004. Print.

_____, _____, _____, et al. "Part Two." *New X-Men: Academy X* #2. Aug. 2004. Print.

DeFillippis, Nunzio (w), Christina Weir (w), Staz Johnson (a), et al. "Part Three." *New X-Men: Academy X* #3. Sept. 2004. Print.

_____, _____, _____, et al. "Part Four." *New X-Men: Academy X* #4. Oct. 2004. Print.

DeFillippis, Nunzio (w), Christina Weir (w), Michael Ryan (a), et al. "Part Five." *New X-Men: Academy X* #5. Nov. 2004. Print.

_____, _____, _____, et al. "Part Six." *New X-Men: Academy X* #6. Dec. 2004. Print.

DeVoe, Jill F.; Peter, Katharin; et al. "Indicators of School Crime and Safety: 2005." *National Center For Education Statistics* (2005): *ERIC*. Web. 1 May 2013.

Elliott, Andrea. "Reported hate crimes against Muslims rise in U.S." *New York Times*. 13 May 2005: n.p. Web. 30 May. 2013. <http://www.nytimes.com/2005/05/12/world/americas/12iht-islam.html?_r=0>.

Hackley School. "Hackley School Mission and History." *Hackley School*. Hackley School. Web. 1 May 2013. <http://www.hackleyschool.org/podium/default.aspx?t=115776>.

Heinberg (w), Allan, and Jim Cheung (a). *Young Avengers: Sidekicks*. 1st ed. 1. New York: Marvel, 2006. 1–144. Print. <http://marvel.com/characters/bio/1010698/young_avengers>.

Johns (w), Geoff, and McKone (a) Mike. *Teen Titans: A Kid's Game*. 1st ed. 1. New York: DC Comics, 2004. 1–192. Print. <http://www.dccomics.com/graphic-novels/teen-titans-a-kids-game>.

King, Larry; CNN. "Interview with Mary Kay Letourneau and Vili Fualaau." (n.d.): *NewsBank: Access World News*. Web. 30 May 2013.

Kyle, Craig, and Chris Yost. "Checking In with the New X-Men's New Teachers." *Newsrama*. 13 Oct 2005. Benjamin Ong Pang Kean, New York. 13 Oct 2005. Web. 1 May 2013. http://www.newsarama.com/marvelnew/NewXmen/ish20/Kyle_Yost.htm.

Lafave, Debra. Interview by Matt Lauer. "Crossing the Line." *NBC News*. NBC News Digital, New York. 13 Sept 2006. Web. 1 May 2013. http://www.nbcnews.com/id/14499056/

Moore, Michael, dir. *Bowling for Columbine*. United Artists, 2002. Film. 30 May 2013.

National Association for Gifted Children. "What Is Giftedness?" *National Association for Gifted Children*. National Association for Gifted Children, n.d. Web. 1 April 2013. <http://www.nagc.org/WhatisGiftedness.aspx>

New York Military Academy. "New York Military Academy: Mission." *New York Military Academy*. New York Military Academy, 2013. Web. 1 May 2013. <http://www.nyma.org/page.cfm?p=9>.

New York Times. "No Child Left Behind? Ask the Gifted." *New York Times*. 5 Apr 2006:

n. page. Web. 1 May. 2013. <http://www.nytimes.com/2006/04/05/nyregion/05edu-cation.html?pagewanted=1&_r=1>.

Singh, Arune. "The End of an X-Era: Grant Morrison Talks Finishing 'New X-Men,' Sex & DC." *Comic Book Resources*. 26 Sep 2003: n. page. Web. 1 April 2013.

U.S. Department of Health and Human Services. "Risk Factors." *StopBullying*. U.S. Department of Health and Human Services, 14 May 2013. Web. 1 April 2013. <http://www.stopbullying.gov/at-risk/factors/index.html>.

_____. *Be More Than a Bystander*. 2013. Infographic. U.S. Department of Health and Human Services, Washington, DC. Web. 10 April 2013. <http://www.stopbullying.gov/respond/be-more-than-a-bystander/index.html>.

Autism and
the Astonishing X-Men

TODD KIMBALL MACK

Since my two oldest children were diagnosed with autism spectrum disorder (ASD) almost two years ago, it has been impossible for me not to notice how many recent fiction films, books, and TV series portray people with the condition. As a humanist interested in the crossroads of aesthetics and everyday life, I believe that these works have much to offer in the way of understanding both autism and the human condition in general. Recently, however, I have found insight into autism not in fictional representations of people with ASD, but in the X-Men—specifically in *Gifted* (2004), a collection of the first six issues of the *Astonishing X-Men* written by Joss Whedon and drawn by John Cassaday. Along with the great writing and beautiful art in this comic, I have gained understanding as I have looked at this story arc through the lens of autism. I believe that there are enough points of contact between the concerns of these *Astonishing* X-Men and those of people on the autism spectrum to make the comparison worthwhile.

Nothing can fully prepare a parent to receive a diagnosis of autism for one of their children. For me that day came early in 2012. Our oldest son had suffered some mild brain damage when he was born, which resulted in atypical neural development. He was always different, and we attributed that to the trauma he had suffered. However, when our second child, a daughter, began to exhibit the same types of developmental delays, we began to suspect something more serious. After months of careful observation we spoke with our pediatrician and our then four-year-old daughter was diagnosed with autism. Diagnosis for our six-year-old son followed shortly.

Not long after, while my wife and I were still reeling from this news, the Centers for Disease Control released a study with some alarming statistics: 1 in 88 children in the U.S. has autism. This is a 78 percent increase in just six years. The prevalence of autism among boys is an even more staggering 1 in 54 (Baio).

The CDC's study caught national headlines, drawing important attention to autism in America and throughout the world. Unfortunately, the condition again made national headlines that same year when, on December 14, Adam Lanza opened fire at Sandy Hook Elementary School. This cold-blooded act left 20 first-graders and six faculty and administrators dead. Before anyone had had time to process what had happened in this most senseless of tragedies, it was reported that Adam Lanza had Asperger's Syndrome, a form of autism (mediaite.com). Fearing (not irrationally) that society would twist that news in order to profile people on the autism spectrum as violent, the national autism community took up arms to defend people with ASD—reminding the nation that the vast majority of people on the spectrum are peaceful (Ditz).

While both the CDC's report, and the outcry over sketchy reporting in the wake of Sandy Hook drew significant public attention to the topic of autism as a national problem, it did little to address autism as a personal one. Even as the world around us speaks in terms of numbers, we parents of children with autism are left with the day to day battle of living with and trying to help someone on the spectrum to live a happy and fulfilling life. Perhaps more tortuous than the days are the nights, when we lay awake wondering what the future might hold for our children.

The *Diagnostic and Statistical Manual of Mental Disorders* (DSM-5) gives professionals the criteria necessary for a diagnosis of autism (Autism Speaks). According to this manual, people with autism struggle with social communication, and they struggle as they try to navigate social situations. Their interests turn into obsessions, and many struggle with a nervous system that consistently sends inconsistent messages from the sensory systems to the brain. All of this combines to turn everyday life into a living hell for many people on the spectrum (and for the people who live with them). Autism isolates those who have it from the world around them and is often the source of extreme physical discomfort and even pain. With few exceptions, our society has yet to find a way to help integrate any but the highest functioning individuals with autism into communities, or to help them become self-sufficient. Many adults with autism end up on welfare, unable to fit into a world that they do not understand and which does not understand them.

But there is another side to the story. Not in spite of, but because of their condition, many people with autism are among the most astonishing and gifted individuals you will find anywhere. They see the world through a different lens. Their sensory systems, which often cause them so much grief, also allow them to hear tones and rhythms, to see light and colors, to feel sensations that neurotypical people will never hear, see, or feel. Because of how their brains uniquely process information, they often excel at problem solving. In fact, it is easy to view the autism in some of these gifted individuals as their greatest asset—an idea that has not been lost on the creators of a number of recent films, television shows, books, and comics. People like Liz Salandar from *The Girl with the Dragon Tattoo* (2008), the eponymous Sherlock from the successful BBC TV series (2010–), Jake Baum from *Touch* (2012), and Temperance Brennan from *Bones* (2005–) are all either explicitly described as having autism or display characteristics that are remarkably consistent with the spectrum. And each in their own way displays characteristics that border on the fantastic.

The problem with portraying autism either as a horrible handicap or as a near superpower is that neither portrayal accounts for the baffling and beautiful variety across the autism spectrum. Not only does the condition never show up the same way in any two individuals, it often does not manifest the same way from one day to the next. Because autism has so many faces, and because it affects people's lives in such a variety of ways, it is particularly challenging to portray people with autism in art without grossly reducing the highly complicated issue. It is just as easy to watch a film like *Temple Grandin* (2010) or *Rain Man* (1988) and complain that the filmmakers romanticize autism as it is to complain that they demonize it. But what if instead of looking for direct artistic representations of people on the autism spectrum, we were to cast a wider net and look for works of art that indirectly index that condition—perhaps even by accident? I believe that such is the case with Whedon and Cassady's *Gifted.*

The story opens with a nightmare. A creepy voice states: "Mommy ... is screaming. Her screams are ... yummy. Daddy ... is next ..." (4). The dream and the voice belong to a young girl named Tildie Soames—a mutant whose horrifying power manifested while she was just a child. Tildie's mutant power is that her nightmares come to life. She sat inside the monster her own imagination created as she killed first her sleeping mother, then her father, and finally a police officer who had been called to the scene. The nightmare images in the opening pages of the story are merely a memory. Dr. Kavita Rao has cured the child with her newly developed Hope Serum.

Meanwhile, at Xavier's Institute for Gifted Children, Cyclops and Emma Frost have teamed up and re-opened the school. They have put together the crack team of Beast, Wolverine, and Kitty Pryde to help them. But not all is proceeding as planned. In a meeting inside the Danger Room Cyclops reminds his team that despite having saved this and other worlds time and again, society still largely rejects them because "Hank's articulate as anything, but what people see is mostly ... well, a beast. Emma's a former villain, Logan's a thug.

And me... I can lead a team. But I haven't looked anybody in the eye since I was fifteen [17, 19].

This final line stands out to anyone familiar with autism. One of the most easily identifiable characteristics of people on the spectrum is that they struggle to make and hold eye contact. Given the importance of eye contact in the creation of trust and emotional attachment, it is no wonder that Scott Summers feels the weight of his mutation. Likewise, many people with autism feel isolated from the people around them. Nor is it a surprise that those who spend time around people with autism find themselves feeling cut off from the inner world of their loved ones. It would be nonsense to argue that Scott Summers has autism, but his particular mutation certainly makes it easy for people familiar with the autism spectrum to identify with his sense of isolation.

Next in the story comes Kavita Rao's announcement of the cure. She states:

> What is a mutant? They've been called angels, and devils. They've committed atrocities, and been victim to atrocities themselves. They've been labeled monsters, and not without reason. But I will tell you what mutants are. [...] Mutants are people. No better or worse by nature than anybody else. Just people. People with a disease. Mutants are not the next step in evolution. They are not the end of humankind. The mutant gene is nothing more than a disease. A corruption of healthy cellular activity. And now at last... We have found a cure [21–25].

Rao's speech is interesting when viewed through the lens of autism because it bumps up against some of the theoretical battlefields that make it so tricky. Many would stereotype people with autism as completely isolated individuals with no ability to empathize with other human beings—making them prime candidates for socially deviant (if not violent) behavior. This clearly happened after Sandy Hook, when talking heads equated the difficulties of people on the spectrum have when trying to understand the subjectivity of others with an inability for them to view other humans as humans. If they view other humans as mere objects, these people argue, what would stop them from doing violence to those around them? On the other side of the issue, there are people that would make us believe that people with autism possess near super powers. They could even be the next stage in human evolution as is portrayed in series like *Touch*, in which Jake Bohm can see or sense the connections between all human beings, or *Alphas* (2011), in which Gary Bell, a *transducer* can intercept electromagnetic waves with his mind.

Half of what Rao says here will ring true for many involved with Autism Spectrum Disorder (ASD), who long for society to see people with autism not as evil geniuses or superheroes in embryo, but as human beings who process their surroundings and interact with the world in a unique way. The chilling part of Rao's speech, the part that gets under the skin of people like Emma Frost and Wolverine, is that she calls mutation a "disease." This is unforgivable for the X-Men, who generally see their mutation not as a disease, but as their greatest asset.

After Rao shows grisly images of the carnage at Tildie Soames's house, the doctor explains that the "mutant strain can be eliminated. Safely and irreversibly" (29). These words come with as compelling a backdrop as one could imagine: an image in which the sleeping Tildie floats inside her nightmare incarnate. It's arms impale her father and officer Hoyt—pinning them to opposite walls of the bedroom while a leg pins her mother to the bed. In the background, in the conference hall, slightly out of focus, Tildie wraps her arms around Dr. Rao who firmly states: "There is such thing as a second chance" (29).

It is easy to romanticize the mutant powers of the X-Men and the other mutants that inhabit the Marvel universes. Who wouldn't want Kitty Pryde's intangibility, Emma Frost's telepathy, or Wolverine's healing factor? It is even possible to overlook Beast's blue fur because his brains and his agility are amazing. Cyclops may not be able to look people in the eye, but he is sharing a bed with Emma Frost, so intimacy does not appear to be an issue for him. The benefits of a cure in any of their cases would be debatable at best. But for a mutation as damaging and debilitating as Tildie's, there can be no debate.

While Rao is finishing her speech, the X-Men have just finished narrowly defeating Ord, an extraterrestrial who has come to Earth to destroy the X-Men, and have freed his captives—a bunch of rich socialites who were attending a high-class party. Cyclops tells his team: "Zero casualties. Which is good. But any way you slice it, we just got thrashed. So now let's do the hard part" (40). The hard part is dealing with people. This super-powered band of heroes all feel like fish out of water around typical humans. Wolverine states: "Being hated and feared by a world that doesn't understand us beats this circus any day" [40].

People with autism will easily identify with this sentiment because they likewise often feel uncomfortable when placed in the spotlight. This discomfort comes because people with ASD have a difficult time intuitively interpreting social cues. Most neurotypical people have a highly developed theory of mind. This means they can project subjectivity onto the people around them. They understand that other people have beliefs, desires, and intentions, and they can usually instinctively interpret what those beliefs, desires, and intentions are based on physical cues including facial expressions, body position and tone of voice. Most of us never think about it. People with autism, on the other hand, struggle with theory of mind in varying degrees. Some have difficulty recognizing subjectivity in other people at all. Others recognize the inner world of the people around them but struggle to interpret it. There is also a flip side to this. For many people with ASD it is just as difficult to understand and express their own subjectivity as it is to interpret that of others, making it difficult for the neurotypical people around them to understand their inner world. Social situations, then, are doubly uncomfortable since people on the spectrum (like the mutants in this scene) are surrounded by people whom they do not understand and who they are certain do not understand them.

When Henry McCoy hears about the cure, he immediately becomes even more pensive than usual. We can see that the idea of the cure has him rattled. He is not the only one. Emma and Cyclops are worried because they are quickly losing control of their students. In one scene Frost, Cyclops, Wolverine, and Kitty are discussing what to do about the situation. In the background we see the stooped-over silhouette of a brooding Beast—his back turned to the room. Kitty states that some students are terrified, some confused, some ecstatic. The ever-cool Cyclops states that they first ought to find out if the cure is a hoax. Without turning, Beast speaks: "Dr. Kavita Rao. She's one of the greatest geneticists alive. And not prone to pranks. I don't know this corporation 'Benetech,' but if Dr. Rao says she can reverse mutation, there's a very good chance that she can" (41). While Kitty, Wolverine, and Emma debate the benefits of killing Rao, we again see a thoughtful looking Beast, his yellow eyes staring into some void (42). That night he breaks into Benetech and meets with Dr. Rao. At first he looks dangerous with his glowing eyes and his dark hulking shoulders. Rao warns him that there are armed guards surrounding the place. When Beast tells her people will die because of her cure, she quickly and sternly counters but Beast cuts her off: "Stop. I'm not here to discuss the ethics of your 'mutant cure.' And I'm not here to destroy it. I just want to know if it works" (48–49). He no longer looks threatening. In fact, he is unable to look Rao in the eye. The articulate, powerful, brilliant Beast is ashamed because at least part of him *wants* to be cured.

Contrast Beast's reaction to news of the cure with that of the young mutant called Wing. We first meet him as he is conversing with Kitty Pryde on a bench outside the mansion. He explains to Kitty that he broke his legs the first time he flew, then he freaked out because the whole concept seemed "unnatural" to him. Wing continues: "But when I got good at it. When I *got* it. I mean... Flying. God. When you're flying, in a very literal sense the world goes away. It makes everything else ... smaller. And sort of *okay*, too. It's the most important feeling. I can't lose that" (51). Kitty tries to reassure him that that will not happen. "Mutants are a community," she tells him. "We're a *people* and there's no way anybody can make us be what they want. We stick together and don't panic or overreact ... you'll see. We're stronger than this" (52).

"Miss Pryde..." Wing stares at her incredulously. "... Are you a #&$%ing retard?" (52).

The key issue for both Beast and Wing (as it so often is with people on the autism spectrum) is isolation. Beast's blue fur and feline features might be cool to some, but he is ultimately convinced that he will never have a normal relationship. His isolation weighs on him, and Rao's Hope Serum truly tempts him with its promise of normalcy. In this sense he is not so different from the hundreds of mutants lined up outside of Benetech Laboratories (53). These individuals form a stark contrast to Wing's miraculous ability to fly and his dashing good looks. Wing's flight gives him an exhilarating sense of freedom and peace—a welcome buffer from the world. His mutation gives him freedom, not isolation. The idea of losing all of that through some kind of "cure" both angers and terrifies him. Most of the people lined up in front of Benetech, on the other hand, are are grotesquely deformed. These people's mutations cause them painful isolation. They desperately want to be cured.

On the next page we see that the image of people waiting outside Benetech is from a news report that Logan is watching. Kitty storms in complaining about her conversation with Wing. Emma criticizes Kitty's naiveté, but Beast interrupts their conversation. He has been up all night testing a sample of the serum that Dr. Rao let him have. After grabbing a cup of coffee, he heads back to the lab. Wolverine follows him and questions Beast about the viability of the sample. When McCoy tell him the serum looks legitimate Wolverine flatly tells him to "get rid of it now or I'll go through you to do it" (62).

Beast turns to look at him, realizing that Emma has read his mind divulged his thoughts to Wolverine. "She said she couldn't help it," answers Wolverine. "She said you were like a billboard. Like neon. Big neon sign. Flashing. 'I wanna get off.' 'I wanna get out.' Is that how it goes McCoy? You've had enough? You wanna see how the other half lives their half-lives?" (63).

Beast's eyes narrow.

> The truth is that I don't know what I want. And that is none of your damn business [...] I don't know what I am," confesses McCoy in anguish—contemplating his beastly paws. "I used to have fingers. I used to have a mouth you could kiss. I would walk down the street and [...] Maybe I'm devolving. My mind is still sharp, but my instincts, my emotions ... you know what it's like to be out of control. What am I supposed to do, Logan? Wait until I'm lying in front of the students. Playing with a ball of string? I am a *human being*" [65].

"Wrong." Logan glares at McCoy. "You're an X-Man" [65].

Beast is contemplating curing his mutation not because he is dangerous—as was the case with Tildie Soames. He wants the cure because he feels lonely and isolated and because he is afraid of his emotional self. The fact that he is such a genius must compound the fear he feels in the face of the great unknowable void of his subjective self. As I stated earlier, people familiar with autism would easily be able to identify with this sense of isolation. McCoy's beastly appearance has long caused him grief, and it is easy to see how his mutation has become more marked over time, but what makes this conversation with Logan so interesting is the combination of the physical isolation with the emotional alienation he has come to feel with himself. Like a person with autism he literally does not understand his own emotional self.

While Wolverine actually sympathizes with Beast's sense of isolation, he worries that the cure will be forced on the mutants. While Rao insists that mutants would never be cured against their will, that unfortunately has already happened. While the X-Men are raiding Benetech, Ord raids their mansion. Unable to find any of the X-Men, he decides to send them a message by "curing" Wing of his mutation. In one of the truly heartbreaking panels of the book, we see the boy wake up after being knocked out. "Oh God. Oh no," he moans. "My powers... Oh God... I'm cured" (103). Tears fill his eyes as realization hits him. He is now painfully, irreversibly, normal.

As *Gifted* ends, Cyclops and Beast are on a walk inside the mansion— talking about all that has happened over such a short time. Cyclops asks Beast if he will use the cure and McCoy responds:

> I know. I don't know. I heard about the cure. It was like this great weight had been lifted from my shoulders. I never felt that weight till I felt it gone. If Ord had tapped me instead of that poor kid ... maybe this would all be simple. But it's not. I've seen so much self-loathing. These desperate people... Logan was right. And I'm counting on you never to tell him I said that.... An X-Man doesn't quit. Not with the world watching. I'm not saying never [142–43].

As is the case with Beast and the Hope Serum, I have my own personal struggles whenever anyone mentions a cure for autism. One of the first things our pediatrician told us when he diagnosed our children with autism is that there is no cure for it. This is something we would deal with our entire lives. Not twenty-four hours went by, however, before well-meaning people started to tell us that the doctors are all wrong. That there really *is* a cure for autism. If we could just get them into the right school, or get them on the right diet, our children might be cured. If we eliminated gluten, or went completely organic, or if we get our children iPads, or if we did ABA therapy or floortime, or used the right essential oils or eliminated electronics from their lives, our children could be cured.

The problem is that for every child who sees a dramatic reduction in autistic behavior after a certain therapy, treatment, or lifestyle change, countless children will see little or no improvement at all from any or all of these treatments. The result is often either resignation to the fact that nothing can be done or a frantic search for the next promised cure.

For me, however, talk of a cure always raises deep and intensely personal philosophical questions about *what* exactly is being cured. The DSM-5's definition of autism focuses on the negative aspects of ASD, but many people who work with the condition, and many people on the spectrum themselves, choose to view autism not as a disease or even a disorder but simply a unique way of viewing the world—a *different* ability rather than a *dis*-ability. They may struggle with some things that neurotypical people take for granted, but they also possess a level of intelligence, an attention to detail, an ability to focus on one single thing, a unique set of eyes through which they see the world—and all of this comes not *in spite* of their autism but *because* of it.

Some people may see my exploration of this topic as too reductive, but that is exactly what I am advocating against. The benefit of exploring autism through the lens of something like *Gifted* is that, as is often the case with the best science fiction and fantasy writing, the *distance* between the text and the real world liberates interpretation. Because Whedon never explicitly mentions autism, I can identify the moments in which the comparison works and discard those comparisons when they break down. In *Gifted*, no one protests when Tildie is cured of her mutation. Likewise, one could come up with countless examples of people with autism who would *absolutely* benefit from some kind of cure because their autism makes it impossible for them to function in society. Some people on the autism spectrum suffer so much—physically and emotionally—or cause so much suffering in the people around them, that it would be unethical *not* to give them a cure if it were available.

In my own case, however, I find that I identify much more with Beast than with the mutants lined up outside Benetech. I have seen plenty of dark days when I would give anything to make autism disappear from my children's lives; but there are other times when, like Beast, I realize just how *gifted*—even *astonishing*—they truly are.

Works Cited

Autism Speaks. "DSM-5 Diagnostic Criteria." 2013. Web. 18 Nov 2013.

Baio, Jon. "Prevalence of Autism Spectrum Disorders Autism and Developmental Disabilities Monitoring Network, 14 Sites, United States, 2008." 2012. Web. 14 June 2013.

Ditz, Liz. "Gun Violence and the Search for a Scapegoat, Autism Edition." December 2012. Web.

Gatiss, Mark, and Stephen Moffat. *Sherlock*. BBC, 2010. Print.

Hanson, Hart. *Bones*. FOX. Print.

Karnow, Michael, and Zak Penn. *Alphas*. BermanBraun, 2011. Print.

Kring, Tim. *Touch*. FOX, 2012. Print.

Larsson, Stieg. *The Girl with the Dragon Tattoo*. New York: Alfred A. Knopf, 2008. Print.

Levinson, Barry. *Rain Man*. United, 1988. Print.
mediaite.com. "Report: CT Shooting Suspect Had Personality Disorder and Autism; Update: Girlfriend Safely Located." N. p., October 2013. Web.
Whedon, Joss, and John Cassaday. *Gifted*. Comixology. New York: Marvel Comics Group.; Marvel, 2011. Print.

Prophet of Hope and Change: The Mutant Minority in the Age of Obama

MORGAN B. O'ROURKE *and*
DANIEL J. O'ROURKE

The dawn of the twenty-first century was a tumultuous time in American history. A contentious presidential election was decided not at the ballot box but in the Supreme Court. Planes hijacked on September 11, 2001 introduced the country to a new era in terrorism and guerrilla warfare. The United States invoked the Bush doctrine to initiate a military response in Iraq to perceived "threats of weapons of mass destruction." The war against terrorism spread into Afghanistan as the search for Osama Bin Laden and the leaders of Al Qaeda broadened. Finally, the failure of the home mortgage industry threatened major banking institutions and the country with the prospect of economic depression. The United States seemed to be lurching from one crisis to the next. It is little wonder that a majority of Americans were hoping new leadership would offer prospect of change in the presidential election of 2008.

Popular culture can hold a mirror to society to give people a new perspective on their world. Metaphors and creative narratives can sometimes simplify and illustrate the nearly incomprehensible dramas being played out before our eyes. Indeed, if the United States was in the state of crisis, things were far worse in the 21st century world of the X-Men. On M-Day, the Scarlett Witch nearly accomplished what politicians, Sentinels, and religious zealots had been striving to achieve in the Marvel Universe for decades: the eradication of all mutants. Three simple words, "No More Mutants," uttered by a mutant with the power to alter the fabric of reality initiated a mutant genocide that altered the genetic codes of millions of people around the planet. By best estimates, a mere two hundred mutants survived the magical assault. Fortunately, the survivors were mostly X-Men, so the struggle for (and story of) mutant equality continued.

The study of crisis rhetoric informs us that the very term "crisis" is composed of two Chinese characters symbolizing the concepts of "threat" and "opportunity" (Bostdorff). When a situation is defined as a "crisis," it requires immediate and decisive action to meet the perceived "threat." "Opportunity" presents itself when a leader successfully manages the challenging circumstances. New ideas, unconventional approaches, or innovative strategies can be the hallmark of successful responses to crisis. Great leaders and heroes are born or acknowledged in times of crisis. Be it a politician who rallies the nation, a corporate leader who envisions the future, or the firefighter who sacrifices her life to save others, faithful followers recognize the qualities and actions of those who rise above the fray to act in their behalf. Sometimes when leaders fail to appear in real life, writers and artists create them for us.

The purpose of this essay is to explore the metaphoric relationship between the rise of the "Mutant Messiah," Hope Summers, and the political assent of President Barack Obama. To be clear, the authors of this chapter are not arguing that Obama is a Messiah or political savior for the country. In the politically divisive environment of the United States today, it is difficult to imagine any candidate who could overcome the conservative-liberal divide to unite the American people. A decade of war that cost far too many American lives and treasure coupled with an economic collapse created a historic budget deficit that drove both political parties to ideological extremes. Conservatives saw the rise of the Tea Party Movement that demanded austerity in government, reductions in taxes to stimulate a free-market economy, and a return to traditional American values. Liberals, conversely, argued for an expansion of the government with a federally financed health care program, an economic bailout of the American auto industries, an economic stimulus to create jobs, and an expanded role for the federal government on immigration issues and the civil rights of LBGTQ citizens. Rather, this essay explores some of the parallels between Obama's political rise and the character of Hope in X-Men comic books. Republicans and Democrats were as divided as homo sapiens and homo superior. Unfortunately, the fear and acrimony directed toward "the mutant menace" was beginning to sound like the conspiracy theories and name-calling fostered in talk radio, advocacy television, extremist websites, and social media.

Into this divide stepped a most unlikely presidential candidate, Barack Hussein Obama. The son of a Kenyan graduate student and a Kansas mother, Obama was a bi-racial child born at a time when several U.S. states would not recognize the marriage of his parents. Unfortunately, the union did not last. Ann Dunham, Obama's mother, married and divorced again to become a single mother raising two children. This is hardly the sort of privileged life that traditionally fosters great political ambition. Obama benefitted from the opportunities of an excellent education with financial assistance from scholarships and loans. He graduated from Columbia University and earned a law degree at Harvard Law School, where he was the first African-American president of the Harvard Law Review. Rather than practice or teach the law, Obama became a community organizer in Chicago, Illinois. He ran for the City Council and lost. He was elected to the Illinois State Senate in 1996. In 2004, an opportunity arose to run for the United States Senate. To advance his campaign, Obama was chosen to deliver a keynote address at the 2004 Democratic Convention. The nominating speech for John Kerry was a tremendous success and Obama was thrust into the national limelight. He won his Senate seat and in just two years declared his intention to run for the Office of the Presidency. Few political observers gave the first term Senator much of a chance against the heavily favored Senator Hillary Clinton. Yet Obama won that primary, the presidential election of 2008 against Senator John McCain, and was re-elected in 2012 against former governor Mitt Romney ("Obama Biography").

Barack Obama became the first African-American president of a country that once considered his ancestors to be three-fifths of a person. He ran on the themes of "Hope and Change" forever immortalized in the colorful posters of Shepard Fairey. It was a historic moment in America, a time of great optimism and anticipation. In the story of the X-Men, hope came in the form of a little, red headed girl and the flaming figure of a mythic bird.

The story of the rise of Hope Summers was a major Marvel event detailed over several series ("Messiah Complex" MC, "Second Coming" SC) and culminated in the "Avengers vs. X-Men" (AvX) finale. One day, after no new mutants had appeared for some time, without warning or fanfare, Charles Xavier registered a new mutant manifestation. It was a force so powerful that it knocked out the mutant search engine, Cerebra, and pained Xavier. The mentor of the mutant team declared, "That ... may just have been the rebirth of *Hope*" (MC 1, 14). The new mutant was discovered in Cooperstown, Alaska, and the X-Men quickly rushed to the scene to investigate. They found the town in ruins. A team of X-Men jumped in to action, helping the survivors while trying to discern what just happened. The X-Men discovered dead Purifiers (anti mutant Zealots) and Marauders (a rival group of mutants lead by the evil Mr. Sinister) victims of a violent confrontation (MC 1, page 18). The mutant psychic, Emma Frost, suddenly realized that while the X-Men saved several adults from the destruction of the city, she could not hear the thoughts of any living children in the town (MC 1, 19). The X-Men then discovered that this was not a teenage mutant manifestation but, rather, the rare mutant birth. Religious metaphors were invoked when it was revealed that the Purifiers employed a Passover-like strategy slaughtering every child in the town (MC 1, 24–25). Evidence led the X-Men to conclude that new mutant was still alive, likely in the hands of Sinister (MC 1, 27). A massive search was begun to find Sinister and the mutant infant before it was too late.

Readers quickly learned that the Purifiers did not have the child in their custody but were likewise hunting for the infant believing her to be the Mutant Antichrist (MC 4, 10). In an effort to understand the meaning of this first mutant birth, Cyclops sent two X-Men to a very dark future where mutants were imprisoned in camps (MC 4, 22). It was said to be one of the possible futures that resulted because of the birth of the powerful new mutant. The X-Men discovered that the camps were a response to a six-minute war enacted by the Mutant Messiah that killed six million humans. Homo sapiens responded by killing or capturing all remaining mutants and placing them in camps (MC 9, 3). In the present timeline, it was revealed that Sinister and his team did not have the child, but that Cable, former X-Men and son of the mutant leader Cyclops, took the child from Cooperstown (MC 5, 42). Cyclops formed a team called X-Force to be led by Wolverine. The mutant leader crossed a dangerous line when he instructed Wolverine to bring Cable in and get the child back "by any means necessary" (MC 6, 40). Sinister and his team captured the child forcing Cable, now secretly teamed with Xavier, and the X-Men to mount an attack on the base of the Marauders (MC 10). They saved the child, but in the process, Xavier was shot and killed by the traitor Bishop. Cable, with Cyclops's blessing, escaped with the child to the future. The hope was that this would allow the child a chance to grow up and choose a path that would not lead to war between humans and mutants. The final scene of *The Messiah Complex* was that of Cable and Hope facing the dawn. "Sun's coming up kid." Cable said. "We made it. Now comes the hard part" (MC 13, 31).

A year passed; the world of the X-Men was a very different place. The mutant team had moved west of San Francisco, on the island of "Utopia," which was once the floating fortress known as Asteroid M. Utopia was not only a base for the X-Men but became an extended sanctuary available to all surviving mutants. With the destruction of the former Xavier Institute in Westchester, New York and the loss of their headquarters in San Francisco proper, the X-Men were literally pushed to the edge. Utopia was declared a sovereign nation, a mutant safe haven, but these dreams were far from realized as mutants continued to be killed by external enemies.

Cable returned from the future accompanied by the grown mutant messiah, a young girl aptly named Hope. The two materialized in the ruins of the

X-Men's former mansion and were immediately attacked by human supremacists. Across the country in Utopia, Cyclops and the X-Men were alerted to
Cable's presence and quickly assembled a team to bring Cable and Hope safely
to Utopia. They were met with opposition every step of the way. Bastion, a
Sentinel from the future lead some of the X-Men's greatest foes in an attempt
to kill Hope before she could reach the island. The cross-country journey
became a deadly and dangerous trek for the X-Men: Magik was trapped in
Limbo, Ariel was killed, and Karma lost a leg. In a final valiant act, Nightcrawler leapt between an attacking Sentinel and the young girl. Nightcrawler
teleported Hope to Utopia and with his dying breath said: "I believe in you"
(SC 5, 26).

The remnants of the team made it to Utopia only to be trapped on the
island by an impenetrable energy sphere. The mutants were trapped in their
sovereign space. Bastion then created a time bubble allowing him to send waves
of futuristic Nimrod Sentinels back in time to attack the X-Men. The only
hope for the trapped mutants was to attack the enemy at its source. Cable led
a team of X-Men into the future to disable the Sentinels. To return to the present, he sacrificed himself to save the lives of the team. The death of her father
figure left Hope distraught and angry. In this moment of crisis, Hope drew
upon all the abilities of the mutants around her to manifest her powers. She
destroyed Bastion with an overwhelming force and the sphere surrounding
the island dissipated. The Mutant Messiah had saved her people. Within a
few days, Cerebra registered the presence of five new mutants. The rebirth of
the mutant population had begun.

In 2007, when Obama announced his run for the presidency he did so
in front of the Old State Capitol Building in Springfield Illinois, the same
spot where Lincoln delivered his "House Divided" speech nearly one hundred
and fifty years earlier. Obama said, "...I know that you didn't come here for
me, you came here because you believe in what this country can be" ("Presidential Announcement"). When Hope Summers returned from the future,
she materialized at the birthplace of the mutant movement, the Xavier Institute. Cyclops and the Beast, two of the original X-Men met to discuss a plan
for the future. Cyclops stated, "I believe that Hope is the key to preserving
the *Mutant Race.*" "That's the problem with faith," the Beast responded. "The
stronger it gets the more people tend to die" (SC 7, 11). The worlds of Obama
and the X-Men were in crisis. Lives had been lost in war and the future was
at risk. The resolution of each crisis called out for new hope, new direction,
and new leadership. At first, change seemed impossible. Obama was a young
African-American, first term senator and Hope was just a teenage girl. Time
passed and they were tested again and again and rose to the occasion. Obama
won the election and Hope saved her people. When Hope used her power for

the first time to destroy Bastion, she drew upon the collected powers of the seemingly defeated X-Men to create an unstoppable attack. The sphere separating the mutants from humanity shattered and suddenly the X-Men were once again connected with the world. Obama also shattered barriers bringing in young voters, minorities, and the politically disenfranchised. On August 28, 2008, the forty-fifth anniversary of Dr. Martin Luther King, Jr.'s "I Have a Dream" speech, Barack Obama accepted the nomination of the Democratic Party to run for the Presidency of the United States. Obama told his audience: "For eighteen months, you have stood up, one by one, and said enough of the politics of the past. ... You have shown what history teaches us—that at defining moments like this one, the change doesn't come from Washington. Change comes to Washington. Change happens because the American people demand it—because they rise up and insist on new ideas and new leadership, a new politics for a new time" ("The American Promise"). A month earlier in Germany, Obama addressed an international crowd with a similar message. "I know that I don't look like the Americans who've previously spoken in this great city." He said, "Tonight, I speak to you not as a candidate for President, but as a citizen—a proud citizen of the United States, and a fellow citizen of the world" ("A World That Stands Alone"). The sphere of separation caused by the war in Iraq was coming down. In his first term as President, Barack Obama would be (unexpectedly and somewhat controversially) recognized with the Nobel Peace Prize for his "extraordinary efforts to strengthen international diplomacy and cooperation between peoples" ("The Nobel"). The United States was still waging war on two fronts but the hope of a new era of global cooperation was at hand.

Obama's first term as president saw many accomplishments: The Affordable Health Care Act, the repeal of "Don't Ask Don't Tell" to afford gays/lesbians equal opportunity in the military, the Lily Ledbetter Equal Pay for Woman Act, a Stimulus Plan for economy recovery, and the death of Osama bin Laden.

Yet conservatives made gains in the midterm elections, challenges to President's birth certificate persisted, and the political divide in Washington, D.C. grew deeper. Hope's triumph over Bastion led to the emergence of new mutants, but things were not resolved in Utopia. As great as it was that new mutants were manifesting their abilities, their powers seemed to be broken. Hope had to personally stabilize each new mutant. There were losses. One new mutant killed himself in a panic over what he was becoming. Another youth destroyed a city before Hope brought his powers under control. Both Hope and Obama were trying to bring change, but each step forward seemed to bring more opposition and steps backward.

As the president's reelection campaign against Mitt Romney entered full swing in the summer of 2012, in the Marvel Universe, the Phoenix force was returning to Earth. News of the Phoenix spread quickly. Cyclops asserted: "There has to be a reason the Phoenix keeps coming back to us." Magneto reminded him: "It brings with it death and destruction." "**And** rebirth," Cyclops added. "**Always** rebirth" (AvX, 27). Captain America flew to Utopia to take Hope into the protective custody of the Avengers. The X-Men refused and thus "Avengers vs. X-Men" series was born.

In the first confrontation with the energy force, Tony Stark split the Phoenix Force into five pieces, which came to reside in Cyclops, Emma Frost, Namor, Colossus, and Magik. These hosts used the power of the Phoenix to remake the world, creating a Utopia for all, mutant and human. But absolute power corrupted absolutely, one by one the power became too much for each host to handle. In each instance, the remaining hosts assumed a larger measure of the power of Phoenix. When confronted by the Avengers, disenfranchised X-Men, and Charles Xavier, Cyclops took the last full measure of power from Emma Frost to enable himself for the final battle. Cyclops killed his mentor, Charles Xavier, and quickly became the Dark Phoenix. Finally, Hope joined forces with The Scarlet Witch to defeat Cyclops. The Phoenix force finally claimed Hope but then the Scarlet Witch explained: "This is your destiny. You're right. You were **born** to be the Phoenix. But not so you could wield this power. It's because you're the only one with the strength to let it go" (AvX 12, 34). The Alpha and the Omega then joined. The Scarlet Witch and Hope clasped hands and proclaimed: "**No More Phoenix**" (AvX 12, 35). The curse of M-Day was lifted; Cerebra soon indicated that the energy force had dispersed all over the Earth and that mutants were returning to the planet. Cyclops prophecy was correct: The Phoenix always brings destruction and rebirth.

Conclusion

At the dawn of the twentieth century, Hugo de Vries extended the theory of evolution with the publication of his text, *The Mutation Theory*. De Vries studied primroses and asserted that new forms of the plant did not necessarily evolve over time but could result from an abrupt event to create a new, stable form of the plant (McCarthy). One doubts that Stan Lee considered the research of this famous scientist when he conceived of the "the superheroes with the X gene" but their conclusions were similar: mutations occur naturally and sometimes in response to events. The difference between the norm and its mutated counterpart can be the source of an enduring narrative: Mutant as "The Other." As Michael Mallory wrote in *X-Men: The Characters and*

Their Universe, "The on going conflict between homo sapiens and homo superiors is one of the key factors that have allowed *X-Men* and its various spin-offs to become the most successful comic book franchise in history." For more than half a century, minorities in America, Jews, Asian Americans, African-Americans, LGBTQ citizens, and young people have been invited to identify with the story of superhero as outsider embodied in the narrative of the X-Men. These collected minorities elected Barack Obama as the President of the United States.

The demographics of the political victory in 2012 were stark and revealing. Mitt Romney won the majority of white voters (59%), male voters (52%), and those over the age of forty-five (53.5%). The candidate who represented the changing face of America, Barack Obama, won the new majority. Obama won 93% of all black votes, 73% of the Asian vote, and 71% of the Hispanic vote. At a time when Asian and Hispanic voters are increasing by percentage points every four years, these are powerful new voices beginning to speak up in the American electorate. Obama also won 56% of young voters and 76% of gay, lesbian, and bisexual voters ("Election Results"). In comic book terms, Romney won the "Captain America vote," Obama won with the new "X-Men majority."

It has been said that the only constant in the world is change, be it in science, politics, or comic book narratives. From the time of de Vries, to the birth of the X-Men in the Silver Age of Comics, to today, the United States has undergone some remarkable changes. The country has survived World Wars, endured the Great Depression, unleashed the threat/promise of nuclear energy, and recognized the civil rights of women and African-Americans. In the mythic tale of Pandora's box, the young girl is overcome with curiosity and opens the gift from Zeus. The curses of humanity are released: fear, disease, envy, crime and hate. Change might be listed among those curses, for it certainly evokes fear, envy, and sometimes hate among those who are unprepared for it. In dark times we must always remember that one thing remained in Pandora's box: Hope. Change can bring about crisis, the threat of losing the traditions of the world we knew versus the opportunity of an even better tomorrow. Change is inevitable and unrelenting, still many fear its coming. Readers may disagree on the comparison of the rise of the Mutant Messiah, Hope Summers, and the political assent of Barack Obama but both stories are certainly historic reflections of the dramatic divisions and the hope for change in 21st century America.

In 2012, the 1,000 Genomes Project analyzed the DNA of 179 people from around the globe. In an article to be presented in *The American Journal of Human Genetics,* the research team reported that: "the average person has around 400 defects in his or her genes" (Stein). Fortunately, it seems that other genes may be compensating for seeming deficiencies in their genetic counterparts. These findings were reported on National Public Radio under the banner headline: "Everybody Has Flawed Genes" (Stein). We prefer the succinct appraisal of James Evans of the University of North Carolina: "We are all mutants" (Stein). To face the inevitable changes and challenges of the future, let us band together in hope and accept our common mutant make-up.

WORKS CITED

Aaron, Jason (w) and Adam Kubert (a). "Avengers vs. X-Men Round 12" (Dec. 2012). NY: Marvel Comics.

"The American Promise, August 28, 2008." *obamaspeeches.com*. ObamaSpeeches. Web. <www.obamaspeeches.com>

Bendis, Brian Michael (w) and John Romita, Jr. (a). "Avenger vs. X-Men Round 1" (June 2012). NY: Marvel Comics.

Bostdorff, Denise M., *The Presidency and the Rhetoric of Foreign Crisis*. Columbia: University of South Carolina Press, 1993.

Brubaker, Ed (w) and Marc Silvestri (a). "X-Men: Messiah Complex Chapter One," (December, 2007). NY: Marvel Comics.

Brubaker, Ed (w) and Billy Tan (a). "Messiah Complex Chapter Six." *Uncanny X-Men* #493 (Feb. 2008). NY: Marvel Comics.

_____ and _____. "Messiah Complex Chapter Ten" *Uncanny X-Men* #494 (Mar. 2008). NY: Marvel Comics.

Carey, Mike (w) and Chris Bachallo (a). "Messiah Complex Chapter Five" *X-Men* #205 (Jan. 2008). NY: Marvel Comics.

_____ and _____. "Messiah Complex Chapter Nine," *X-Men Issue* #207 (Feb. 2008). NY: Marvel Comics.

_____ and _____. "Messiah Complex Chapter Thirteen," *X-Men* #207 (Mar. 2008). NY: Marvel Comics.

"Election Results." *nytimes.com*. New York Times. Web.

Kyle, Craig and Chris Yost (w) and Humberto Ramos (a). "Messiah Complex Chapter Four." *New X-Men* #44 (Jan. 2008)

Kyle, Craig and Chris Yost (w), David Finch (a). *X-Men Second Coming Chapter One* (July, 2010). NY: Marvel Comics.

Kyle, Craig and Chris Yost (w), Mike Choi (a). "Second Coming Chapter Five, *X-Force* #26 (Jul. 2010). NY: Marvel Comics.

Mallory, Michael, *X-Men: The Characters and Their Universe*. New York: Universe Publishing, 2011.

McCarthy, Eugene M. "Hugo de Vries." *macroevolution.net*. Retrieved December 27, 2012 <www.macroevolution.net/hugo-de-vries.html#.UNONy/UqmRA>

"The Nobel Peace Prize 2009". *Nobelprize.org*. Nobel Media AB 2013. Web. 26 Nov 2013. <http://www.nobelprize.org/nobel_prizes/peace/laureates/2009/>

"Obama biography." *Whitehouse.gov*. The White House, President Barack Obama. Web. <www.whitehouse.gov/administration/president-obama>

"Presidential Announcement, February 10, 2007." *obamaspeeches.com*. ObamaSpeeches. Web. <www.obamaspeeches.com>

Stein, Rob, "Perfection Is Skin Deep: Everyone Has Flawed Genes," All Things Considered, NPR, December 6, 2012. Web.<www.npr.org/blogs/health/2012/12/06/1666 4818>

Wells, Zeb (w) and Ibraim Roberson with Lan Medina (a). "Second Coming Chapter Seven," *New Mutants* #13 (May 2010). NY: Marvel Comics.

"A World That Stands Alone, July 28, 2008." *obamaspeeches.com*. ObamaSpeeches. Web. <www.obamaspeeches.com>

About the Contributors

Adam **Capitanio**, an independent scholar in New York City, holds a Ph.D. in American studies from Michigan State University.

John **Darowski** is a Ph.D. student at the University of Louisville. His essays have been published in *The Ages of Superman: Essays on the Man of Steel in Changing Times* and *The Ages of Wonder Woman: Essays on the Amazon Princess in Changing Times* (both McFarland).

Joseph J. **Darowski** teaches English at Brigham Young University–Idaho and is a member of the editorial review board of *The Journal of Popular Culture*. He is the author of *X-Men and the Mutant Metaphor* (2014), and editor of *The Ages of Superman* (2012), *The Ages of Wonder Woman* (2014), and forthcoming volumes on superheroes, including the Avengers and Iron Man. He has also published on television shows such as *The Office, Chuck, Downton Abbey*, and *Batman: The Animated Series*.

David Allan **Duncan** is a professor in the Sequential Art Department at the Savannah College of Art and Design, where he is pursuing a graduate degree in art history. He also presents comics workshops around the United States.

Timothy **Elliott** is a Ph.D. student in technical communication and rhetoric at Texas Tech University, where he is a graduate part-time instructor. His interests include visual rhetoric, comic as a communicative medium, comic history, visual culture and urban spaces.

Maura **Foley** is a data analyst in Chicago. She holds a bachelor of science in biology and sociology from the University of Wisconsin–Madison and is pursuing a master of science in analytics from the University of Chicago.

Margaret **Galvan** is a Ph.D. candidate in English at the Graduate Center, City University of New York. She teaches writing and research seminars in the Gallatin School of Individualized Study at New York University and is an instructional technology fellow at Brooklyn College. Her dissertation is "Archiving the '80s: Feminism, Queer Theory, & Visual Culture."

Eric **Garneau** is a writer and editor working in the fields of education and pop culture. He manages the comic book operations of Pastimes in Niles, Illinois, one of the Midwest's largest hobby shops, and writes and produces for the Chicago sketch comedy group the Nerdologues.

Jeff **Geers** is a Ph.D. candidate in the American culture studies program at Bowling Green State University where he is studying "noncontinuity" stories in superhero comic books and the development of fan communities. He teaches communication and media courses at Sinclair Community College and the University of Dayton.

Nicolas **Labarre** is an associate professor (*maître de conférences*) at the University Bordeaux Montaigne in France. His research focuses on issues of cultural legitimacy, on genre and on the adaptation process in comics. He also writes and draws comics as well as children's books.

Todd Kimball **Mack** specializes in the literatures and cultures of the Iberian Peninsula, specifically the modern Spanish and Catalan traditions. He teaches at Southern Utah University in Cedar City.

Gerri **Mahn** lives in Philadelphia and has spent the past ten years working in academics and health care. Her writing and research focus on art history, pop culture, literature and gender studies.

Christian **Norman** is a doctoral student and graduate instructor at Georgia State University's communication department. He specializes in rhetoric and cultural studies with a concentration on identity issues regarding race, gender, sexuality and national identity formation.

Daniel J. **O'Rourke** is an associate professor of communication studies at Ashland University. He has co-written essays on Spider-Man, Superman and Silver Scorpion and is co-editor (with Robert S. Brown) of *Case Studies in Sport Communication*.

Morgan B. **O'Rourke** is an undergraduate at Ohio Wesleyan University in Delaware, Ohio. He first assisted his father, Daniel J. O'Rourke, conducting research on Captain America in World War II at the Library of Congress. He co-authored an essay in *The Ages of Superman* (McFarland).

Nicholaus **Pumphrey** is a Hebrew Bible Ph.D. candidate at Claremont Graduate University. He studies how literature, ancient and modern, influences and is influenced by the Bible and has presented papers on comics and religion.

Jacob **Rennaker** is a Ph.D. candidate in Hebrew Bible study at Claremont Graduate University. His research deals with religious imagery and worldviews from a variety of times. Other research includes how to use popular culture to teach religion in classroom settings.

Brad J. **Ricca** is a SAGES Fellow at Case Western Reserve University. He is the author of *Super Boys: The Amazing Adventures of Jerry Siegel & Joe Shuster—The Creators of Superman*.

Rich **Shivener** is assistant director of the Office of First-Year Programs at Northern Kentucky University. He helped develop teaching strategies, assignments and an event about David Mack's graphic novel *Kabuki: The Alchemy*, assigned as a reading program for first-year students.

Clancy **Smith** teaches philosophy at Belmont University in Nashville and has published in journals and edited volumes on critical theory, race theory, philosophy and popular culture and American pragmatism.

Robert Dennis **Watkins** is a Ph.D. candidate in rhetoric and professional communication at Iowa State University. He is focusing on teaching students visual literacy by designing comics digitally or by hand through multimodal processes.

Jean-Philippe **Zanco** teaches economics and social sciences in a high school and at the Institut d'Etudes Politiques of Toulouse, France. He is author of *La Société des Super-Héros: Economie, Sociologie, Politique* and lives in Auch, France.

Index